TRAUMA, STIGMA, AND AUTISM

TRAUMA, STIGMA, AND AUTISM

Developing Resilience and Loosening the Grip of Shame

Gordon Gates

Jessica Kingsley *Publishers*
London and Philadelphia

The quote on page 52 from Merleau-Ponty 1964 is reproduced
with kind permission from Northwestern University Press.

First published in 2019
by Jessica Kingsley Publishers
73 Collier Street
London N1 9BE, UK
and
400 Market Street, Suite 400
Philadelphia, PA 19106, USA

www.jkp.com

Library of Congress Cataloging in Publication Data
A CIP catalog record for this book is available from the Library of Congress

British Library Cataloguing in Publication Data
A CIP catalogue record for this book is available from the British Library

ISBN 978 1 78592 203 9
eISBN 978 1 78450 477 9

Printed and bound by CPI Group (UK) Ltd, Croydon, CR0 4YY

Dedication

I would like to dedicate this project to my wife, whose support has gotten me through one mess after another. If it weren't for her attentive perseverance I might never have come to acknowledge my Autistic identity, which made it possible to counter feelings of unworthiness with a therapeutic framework of human difference. Her insightful passion for understanding human behavior contributed immensely to this book. I would also like to thank the participants in my research on Autistic stigma as well as the many clients I've seen over the years who've shared moving stories about the impact of stigma and trauma in their lives. These pages are animated by their courage to work through the patterns of anxiety, sadness, self-judgment, and emotional escalation planted in us when our humanity is chronically invalidated.

What the hell was the matter with us? Why did we not join the rest of creation, and all have a great time on this glorious jewel of a planet together? No, nothing like it. Why not? In God's name, why not?

R.D. Laing

Contents

Part D: Critical Autism: Destigmatizing Autistic Experience

Acknowledgments

I remember having coffee with Granny at her kitchen table. I told her I wanted to write a book someday. I didn't know what it was going to be about, but I felt my life was leading up to it. She would encourage me in that warm, supportive way of hers. If it weren't for the kindness and support of my family and too many others to mention, these pages never would have happened.

Amy Sequenzia and Andrew Bloomfield, Autistics needing high levels of support who communicate primarily with typing and advocate tirelessly for this population, generously provided feedback to help make sure the writing was not offensive. Andrew's friends and fellow members at Bridges-Over-Barriers, Kevin Vasey and Ken Moon, generously allowed their words to be used so the book could be graced with heartfelt voices. Ido Kedar allowed many of his previously published words to be cited, and Autonomous Press kindly allowed the quotation of further vulnerable voices. Many researchers and writers helped inspire this work, including trauma research pioneer Bessell van der Kolk who said he would be honored to have his words cited in the book. Without the enthusiastic support of the incredible team at Jessica Kingsley Publishers this book would not have hit the shelves. Any blunders in the text that create further stigma are my own responsibility.

In the brief time I worked with him, Dr. Phil Walsh introduced me to what was to become a lifelong anxiety, stigma activation, and trauma self-recovery practice. Phil, as he preferred to be called, traveled to indigenous communities in northern Canada regularly to share his techniques with First Nation peoples. Trauma and anxiety are a huge problem there and resources are scarce. I was honored to be a patient of Phil's. He died in 2015 about a year after our brief sessions together.

Finally, I would also like to give a shout-out to everyone who makes an effort to treat other people, especially those they don't understand, with a spirit of flexible generosity. People may not realize what a difference it makes to connect with others with a spirit of uncondescending receptivity, particularly when trauma and stigma have forged a defensiveness that makes relationship especially challenging.

––––––––––

To make comments, ask questions, or read about/post issues related to trauma, stigma, and autisticy go to www.sociophenomenal.com.

Part A

STIGMA, AUTISM, AND INVALIDATION

Chapter 1

TRAUMA AND AUTISTICY

Stigma is a form of trauma. It targets people on the basis of beliefs about them that have nothing to do with who they are. It undermines a person's humanity and overshadows the fullness of their identity by placing assumptions about negatively perceived qualities over openness to their actual personhood. This book is an examination of stigma and the lasting impact it can have. Although trauma is often framed in terms of a terrorizing event, it is the perceived physical and/ or psychological threat to our personhood and residual self-protection that underlies much of the suffering involved. Having our humanity threatened, undermined, and devalued is fundamentally traumatic. It can shift us into a hyper-aroused state of defensive safety seeking or guarded withdrawal and self-isolation. This kind of trauma is experienced as shame. Theologian, philosopher, and counsellor John Bradshaw (1988/2005) explored shame thoroughly. He distinguished "innate" shame related to healthy humility and "toxic" shame acquired through experiences of abandonment, rejection, blame, and abuse that oppress us into believing our fundamental humanity or true self is "defective and flawed" (p.xvii). The repeated messages and cues of stigma have the same demeaning effect. Stigma provides a vantage point to assess the damage of shame and this perspective can help us find ways to manage the associated emotional pain.

Chronic invalidation can lead to an over-sensitive danger alarm in the body–mind waiting to be activated by the smallest trigger. We have much to learn from autism in this regard, because the humanly erosive process of chronic invalidation is constantly at work through stigma and stigmatizing micro-events that can make us feel like "crawling under a rock" (Robison 2007, p.5) or even "aliens on this planet" (Dubin 2009, p.12). Feeling judged and dismissed amplifies existing emotional regulation issues providing a model that illustrates the cycle. In this book we will work towards a better understanding of stigma for those who experience it as well as those wanting to better manage the ways they unintentionally stigmatize others. We will find ways to diminish mental health stigma by going beyond diagnosis to better appreciate how people share much in common regarding the fundamental challenges of what I call *autisticy* (the term will be defined in the "Understanding Autism" section later in this chapter). As the book goes on, we will learn more about these common struggles and how trauma in various forms can make whatever challenges we already face harder. A better understanding of stigma and autism not only provides a unique perspective on the widespread problem of invalidated humanity but also gives us helpful traction to work with this poignant difficulty. Loosening the grip of shame is possible one step at a time by managing the defensive reactions associated with invalidation trauma. Finding ways to counter everyday stigmatizing processes and reimagine stigmatizing beliefs and assumptions helps create an environment of validating acceptance that nourishes shame resilience. This book looks at the issue from both perspectives.

Stigma can be based on visibly apparent things such as skin color, gender, and overt behaviors. It can also come from concealable things like certain forms of physical and mental health, diagnostic labels, sexual preference, socio-economic status, and religion. Sometimes the most challenging forms of invalidation come from intangible things that are hard to pinpoint but can still be used to determine a person is *not one of us*. The stigma of autism comes from all three sources and often involves oppressive coercion to conform, as one autistic woman puts it, "as if I am only worthy if I behave in a certain way that neurotypicals find acceptable" (Autistic Self Advocacy Network 2012, p.350). We will look at the stigma of being different and not fitting in. We will see how certain core challenges we all experience can lead to stigma when our difficulties stand out more than "normal." The book is written primarily from an Autistic perspective not only because of my own Autisticy, but because the history of autism is so intertwined with this complex form of oppression. Anyone whose life is touched by autism or who is interested in this form of personhood should appreciate the exploration this book undertakes. We can learn much about the mechanisms of stigma from autism and acquire helpful cautionary tales. Anyone whose life has been made difficult by the effects of chronic invalidation will better understand what they are dealing with. The techniques of stigma resilience and practices of self-intervention discussed can be used by anyone even though the framework was developed for people who have experienced wounding invalidation.

Different Traumas

Trauma happens when people are overwhelmed by bad things. We may not remember specific incidents, but the body remembers. When past trauma is activated, the familiar routines of life may no longer work. Usual coping mechanisms may become ineffective. Anxiety can become intense. It may no longer be possible to take simple things for granted. The degree of trauma experienced after emotionally damaging events and the corresponding challenge of recovery is associated with many factors related to vulnerability and personal resilience. These factors may include formative experiences, exposure to multiple traumas, the safety of one's current environment, sense of belonging, physical and mental health, self-care strategies, available supports, the strength of one's values and the flexibility to reassess them, ability to connect with emotional and spiritual intelligence, mindfulness, self-esteem, self-confidence, and many others. Trauma can also take many forms. The most recognizable variation of trauma is caused by overt catastrophic events such as war, assault, hostage-taking, natural disaster, terrorism, injury, near-death experiences, serious accidents or near accidents, and witnessing tragic events. This is the kind of trauma associated with PTSD (post-traumatic stress disorder) in the *Diagnostic and Statistical Manual of Mental Disorders* (DSM).

Trauma is not always so extreme and is not necessarily related to single catastrophic events. It can also be associated with poverty, harassment, bullying, loss and chronic invalidation. Trauma can be perpetuated by self-beratement and complicated when it involves repeated exposure over time, such as ongoing abuse, disregard, neglect, and being forced or choosing to endure a toxic or oppressive environment. Such trauma is often referred to as complex trauma. Judith Herman is often credited with first articulating this in her seminal book *Trauma and Recovery* (1992/2015). She specifically mentions "prolonged terrors" such as captivity, child abuse, and spousal abuse as sources of this kind of trauma and talks about a new diagnosis called "complex PTSD." This formulation has not been officially adopted in the DSM, although a condition called DESNOS (disorders of extreme stress not otherwise specified) was proposed and rejected for the fourth edition in 1994. A more refined and specific diagnosis called "developmental trauma disorder" was proposed with support from the National Association of State Mental Health Directors and rejected for the more recent DSM-5 (American Psychiatric Association 2013). Bessel van der Kolk (founder of one of the first trauma centers in North America) was instrumental in both these proposals and continues to work towards greater recognition of this form of socio-erosive trauma. His ground-breaking book *The Body Keeps the Score* (2014) is a comprehensive and engaging account of both the psycho-physiological effects of relationship-based trauma and the growing body of eye-opening research on the impact of impoverished relationship. Meanwhile, practitioners are starting to ask themselves if they can "continue to work within the bounds of the constraints of the traditional approach" by not taking such trauma more fully into account in their work with patients (Rahim 2014, p.557).

Writers such as Levine (1997) distinguish between *shock* trauma, such as a car accident or assault, and *developmental* trauma involving disturbances of emotional attachment growing up such as abuse, neglect, and failure to provide for social and emotional needs. *Invalidation* can be seen at the heart of such trauma. Much of the emotional pain in such cases is related to assaults on a beleaguered self. In shock trauma these assaults are primarily physical. Developmental trauma can involve physical assault, but often more damaging are perceived attacks on our personhood and the resulting invalidation. These may be overt or subtle, and such invalidation does not necessarily involve blatant violence. There may be unaddressed patterns of behavior in which the child feels overwhelmed or uncomfortable with some aspect of a caregiver's manner towards them. A child's behavior may not be a sufficient warning signal of potential problems. They may be well behaved and high achieving, but their efforts may be strategies of gaining acceptance or compensating to meet their unique needs. This core of invalidation often stays with a person right into adulthood and creates internalized shame-related problems.

Autistic individuals often experience the chronic assault of invalidation trauma in the form of stigma, as do many others who don't fit dominant expectations of what people are "supposed" to be like. I have seen many clients experiencing long-term effects from such invalidation. One woman minimized her trauma by saying she never experienced abuse or neglect: "just never knew how to make friends and was always the last one picked for teams and stuff like that." As an adult she had a long history of depression. Her relationship suffered because she required high levels of affirmation and became anxious and escalated if she did not get it. This would often cascade into an episode of depression. Medication did not seem to help. This woman and many like her describe having supportive, loving parents. Although Gabor Maté (1999) argues that repeated humiliation such as "memories of having failed at many tasks" can only activate existing developmental trauma and not create its own shame (p.136), he may under-estimate the full power of ongoing stigma and invalidation.

I think of a young male client who had no stories of overt abuse but could not make appropriate eye contact, always felt different from others, and eloquently described the pain of not being accepted by peers or family. This became trauma in the fiber of his being. It manifested itself in the form of dissociation, an inability to be present in the moment when stigma became activated, hyper-vigilance to rejection, and high levels of physiological arousal triggered by per-ceived deficits of acceptance. Another client experienced a painful injury when he was young. It wasn't the injury in itself that left an easily activated shadow of trauma. It was feelings of isolation and abandonment during his long recovery. The quality of an individual's life can be significantly impacted by accumulated feelings of perceived exclusion, abandonment, and disrespect.

When we experience repeated stigma, judgment, rejection, and/ or prejudice because of qualities inherent to our personhood, qualities we may not be able to change or may not have chosen, we may end up experiencing *identity fatigue*, a form of complex trauma involving chronic assaults on the fullness of our humanity. Chronic invalidation builds up traces of shame ready to activate when over-sensitive safety scanning puts us on physiological high alert to threats that may not logically seem to justify our response. We may wonder what's wrong with us. We may wonder too much what others think of us. We may be on the lookout for potential sources of further invalidation and defensively protect ourselves with outbursts that make it difficult to function. We may experience sadness and unworthiness that lead to isolating protective measures. We may automatically lash out and wonder why, but pride does not allow us to back down because it feels like further invalidation. All this is normal when our humanity is devalued over time and part of a natural defense mechanism.

Hugh Butts, a Black forensic psychiatrist, published a paper arguing that the DSM definition of PTSD was overly narrow and that the effects of racial prejudice should be included among the recognized causes of PTSD (2002). He described the "annihilative" impact of racial discrimination and noted mental health impacts in three categories: reliving the events in memory and dreams, avoiding situations where trauma has happened, and easily triggered physiological arousal. He did not mention Herman's work or how the trauma caused by racial discrimination might fit with her proposed diagnosis of complex PTSD. Racism is based on a highly visible difference from the dominant mainstream and comes with a more explicitly violent and dramatically abusive history of oppression than autism. Invalidation trauma plays an important role in this dynamic of marginalization but is often overshadowed by overt acts of brutality and discrimination. The more subtle dynamics of shame involved are often overlooked.

In her John Bowlby Memorial Lecture of 2007, years after her seminal book, Herman discussed the "state of chronic humiliation" of feeling unaccepted, how shame can be a "physiologically stressful experience," and the "role of shame in the development of traumatic disorders" (p.5). Repeated experiences of stigma related to various forms of invalidation can become emotionally damaging events and a source of distressing complex trauma. Stigma is not just an unpleasant social problem but a source of personal suffering with life-altering consequences. Awareness of this aspect of stigma should be considered part of the growing sensibility in our culture about the impact of trauma in society.

As an example of this growing awareness there is an emerging program in Toronto aimed at curbing the incidence of HIV that takes trauma, a seemingly unrelated problem, into better account. The project is run by the ASD & HIV Needs Assessment Advisory committee and the organizer, himself Autistic, knows of no other programs taking this approach. Trauma-related factors may include the risk-seeking behaviors traumatized individuals often feel drawn to, having to compensate for an impaired ability to discern risk and heed the physical alerts of the intuitive self because of trauma residue, and frequent emotional escalation related to trauma activation that causes the frontal lobes to go offline, resulting in poor self-care decision-making. The program also seeks to address additional risks involved when autism and/or intellectual impairment are part of the picture, for example trusting too quickly, not wanting to look "stupid" or being further stigmatized by asking questions, and unconventional eye contact that broadcasts an individual's vulnerability and/or leads to demeaning assumptions. This team of social advocates and community researchers works on a model that maintains that safe sex education is not sufficient to address the problem. It integrates the impact of developmental trauma and does not make judgments or cast blame on people whose challenges make them difficult to reach with conventional approaches. This out-of-box thinking can transform the way client services are delivered and address hidden issues that orthodox frameworks sweep under the rug.

Ghost Town

The idea of finding ourselves in a ghost town may be familiar to many of us. We find ourselves there when we are lost emotionally, when we disconnect from the flow of life due to sadness, fear, threat, rejection, or difficult circumstances. We may notice ourselves sliding into Ghost Town and recover quickly or find ourselves there in the doldrums of a bad day. We may feel anxious trepidation at the edge of Ghost Town or be lost in full emotional exile at the heart of that isolated place. Sometimes it can be challenging to find our way out. A supportive guide or cheerleader can be very helpful. Sometimes it seems like we'll be trapped there forever and lapse into weary hopelessness. We look for quick fixes, emergency rescues, and magic solutions when nurturing ourselves firmly but gently is often the best prescription for recovery.

Remembering to practice self-care strategies is crucial. The more quickly we notice we are sliding into Ghost Town the more quickly we can take appropriate care of ourselves so we don't get entrenched there. We don't need to have a ticket in order to make a special trip. More often Ghost Town creeps up on us when we're not paying attention. Sometimes we can change something in our environment to blow the dust of Ghost Town away. Other times we can change our perspective to get back on track by assessing the moment and reimagining our response to it.

Finding subtle shifts in the way we approach a troublesome issue is almost always more helpful than waiting for some dramatic change to happen. Sometimes we can only take care of ourselves the best we can while the forces that thrust Ghost Town upon us recede on their own. Acceptance is paramount at such times in order to avoid panic and escalating deeper into pain, almost the way we sink proverbially deeper in quicksand the more we struggle against it. This doesn't mean we don't use all the resources at our disposal to make whatever sensible efforts we can to take effective care of ourselves. Actively accepting rather than panicking or lapsing into dull resignation always puts us in a better position to recover. Panic worsens our predicament and may result in self-destructive desperation. We must be especially careful not to feed negativity and worry. These only lead us deeper into Ghost Town.

There are as many connections to that unpleasant place as there are individuals who experience it, and it serves us well to be familiar with the topography of our own personal Ghost Town. If we are aware of the triggers and conditions that lead us there, we can design our day to account for these. Sometimes addiction is part of the picture. Attempting to avoid Ghost Town by fueling ourselves with substances, things, or certain people only plunges us deeper into the places we most want to get away from. This book revolves around the Ghost Town of invalidation trauma. It can evolve when something about us leads to the experience of stigma and exclusion from those around us, especially when we don't know what that "something" is. It happens when we are abused and neglected, especially as children when our neurological wiring is still being developed. We may experience a pattern of explosive relationships, lost jobs, never feeling comfortable with ourselves, not good enough, or just drained from keeping up appearances. Sometimes we go from doctor to doctor trying to discover the source of this emotional misery. We may be labeled in various ways and prescribed medication, but still nothing seems to address the deep roots of the issue. Accumulated experiences of invalidation may be a big unacknowledged part of the picture.

Stigma in the Mirror

When it comes to stigma, there may be images of unwanted individuals ostracized and left to languish in isolated places. In the not-too-distant past, autistic people were routinely institutionalized and shut away from the rest of society. It is not hard to find extreme cases of stigma. Forced sterilization and eugenics, which has led to some of the worst atrocities of the twentieth century, come to mind. Yet it is not necessary to go into the past or far from home to find examples of stigma. Marginalization and oppression based on markers of difference can take place at any moment right before our eyes. If we are honest, we will be able to identify ourselves as participants in the stigmatization of others who, due to various conditions and differences, feel rejected by others, put in a judgmental spotlight, and marginalized by society. There are bullies who parley their privilege in terms of health, strength, intellect, and power into deliberately hurtful acts of terrorism against those who find it difficult to defend themselves. More commonly, vulnerable individuals are excluded, degraded, denied access, and/or negatively labeled by otherwise well-meaning individuals who don't know how to interact with differently equipped others.

Unfortunately, this often includes the unknowing actions of the very advocates and professionals who could be providing helpful support. Attitudes about autism have changed from a time when it was "isolating and almost wholly misunderstood to today, when stars flock to a Broadway theater to talk about and raise millions for the cause" (Donvan and Zucker 2016, p.xii). Stigma, however, continues to play a role in the experience of those whose lives are characterized by autisticy to any perceivable degree. This remains a grim social problem causing unethical levels of avoidable pain.

I was diagnosed with Asperger's Syndrome at the age of 44 and have dealt with the challenges of exclusion and judgment based on misunderstanding my whole life. My own Autisticy exposes me to the confusion and rejection that can result when the often-unconscious expectations of mainstream others are not fulfilled. This refers not only to specific social, communicative, and behavioral standards that are unnatural for Autistic people to meet, but also to those awkward moments when social encounter breaks down and people get hurt and offended. Rather than turning away with uneasiness, we will try to learn from what happens when entrenched comfort levels are thrown off by individuals who do not conform to habitual formulas of what a person is "supposed" to be.

Stigma is the real source of pain for autistic and Autistic individuals, especially those of us whose autistic qualities are not pervasive, perhaps barely visible, and not associated with language difficulties, intellectual impairment, or painful physical challenges. This kind of Autistic personhood is often called Asperger's Syndrome, although diagnostic restructuring in the DSM-5 homogenized autistic condition into a comprehensive condition called "autism spectrum disorder." The term "Asperger's" no longer officially applies. This kind of Autistic agency has also been referred to as "high functioning," but this term was never officially adopted and many Autistic individuals find it judgmental and demeaning. Who's to say what it means to be "high functioning"? If this refers to conventional standards, hardly anything is conventional when it comes to Autistic lives. No matter what it looks like to others who don't understand or appreciate our experience, we may be extremely high functioning given the challenges we are facing. It is best not to relegate others to a category of "low functioning" by creating a tier for the "high functioning." As one of my social work professors used to say, we always have to consider who's being thrown under the bus by our use of language, assumptions, and conventions. We have to continually challenge and evaluate the way we think in order to promote fairness and avoid unintentionally hurting others. This effort takes courage and honest, undefensive, and almost scientific rigor in assessing the impact of our thoughts, beliefs, and actions.

Many people seem to believe Autistic inner worlds are flat, desolate, and isolated by their very nature. The most important reimagining here is to see that Ghost Town is not connected inherently to autistic existence but emerges from the stigma and marginalization society imposes on Autistic difference. Douglas Biklen was trying to get at this with the title of his pioneering study about the experience of autistic people who type to speak: *Autism and the Myth of the Person Alone* (2005). The inner world of Autistic people may be contoured differently and involve unconventional priorities, but qualitative studies tell us that autistic inner experience is lively and more complex than it may seem.

Autistic people have the same fundamental need for belonging and connection as socioconventional people. It doesn't require a scientific study to reveal this. Simple curiosity and special efforts of compassionate communication allow us to see it for ourselves. The fear stigma creates can flatten curiosity, which might otherwise allow unique and different others to disavow us of the stereotypes and assumptions that get in the way of enriching human encounter.

In my original research on stigma and autism at the University of Victoria, conducted in 2013 and involving in-depth interviews with six individuals diagnosed with Asperger's, participants gave poignant descriptions of bodily felt shame and rejection resulting from the stigma associated with their Autistic personhood. The names of the participants were kept confidential, although many of them said they felt their commitment to advocacy and education far outweighed the emphasis on anonymity laid out in my research methodology. One participant said he heard himself being called "retard" throughout his life. Another graduated from college on the dean's list with excellent marks but never got a call back from a job interview. Another said he responded to more than 200 profiles on a dating website, yet only went on three dates. Participants reported extreme difficulty making friends, not being heard, and not being included. "Most people just don't bother talking to me," said one participant. Another complained he got "the cold shoulder" from people regularly and voiced a common theme when he said, "I just don't seem to fit in." Another said, "People don't want to include me; they make false and misleading assumptions about me." Yet another said, "People show utter contempt towards me for no reason." One participant was worried about his long-term health because of all the rejection he had experienced.

Around the time the research was conducted a petition circulated to have autistic people recognized as an official minority by the United Nations. Autistic adults have been referred to as a "new minority" that can no longer be ignored or rejected by any society that claims to hold fairness and compassion in high regard (Mandell 2013, p.751). The chronic trauma experienced by this population because of stigma needs to be acknowledged and addressed.

Understanding Autism

Thankfully we are far beyond the "refrigerator mother" days of autism. Kanner is credited with introducing this theory in 1948 as an early explanation for the condition (Donvan and Zucker 2016, p.554). It implicated emotionally unavailable parents as the cause of autism. Because of stigma as the "weaker" sex who stayed home to raise children, women bore the brunt of this notion. The mothers of Autistic children were terribly stigmatized and a lot of blaming took place. For example, in his influential book *The Empty Fortress* (1967), while Bettelheim recognized the importance of secure, consistent, and supportive caregiver support in the development of healthy children and adults, he went on to claim that autism develops in children "as a consequence of feeling persecuted by the mother at a critical moment" (p.70). He described "autistic withdrawal" as a "spontaneous defense" against "the destructive intents of the mothering person" (p.71). Drawing on similarities between the behavior of traumatized concentration camp victims and some of the symptoms of autism (such as averted eye contact), Bettelheim drew the best conclusions he felt he could but did not pay sufficient attention to the stigmatizing toxin carried by the conventional theory he built on. If he had more carefully considered his position in this light he might not only have come up with a more socially just theory but also have made a more enduring contribution to science.

Although it alleviated a source of stigma and paved the way for current physio-neurological models of autism, debunking the "refrigerator mother" theory may have thrown the proverbial baby out with the bathwater. Although Autistic people have painful invalidating experiences related to their condition and are more likely to experience various forms of trauma (Brown-Lavoie, Viecili, and Weiss 2014), the "refrigerator mother" period may have resulted in the role of trauma being minimized as a factor in the trajectory of autism and the suffering of Autistic individuals. Aside from overt bullying, the relationship of autism and trauma is not well understood; indeed, trauma is hardly mentioned as a factor in autism (Hoover 2015; Kerns, Newschaffer, and Berkowitz 2015).

Acknowledging the impact of developmental trauma in childhood is not to lay blame. Detached, unsupportive, and emotionally unavailable parenting is often part of a longstanding cycle that, like addiction, takes persistent effort to heal over generations. Blame is not helpful here. Acknowledging the importance of secure attachment, safety, and emotional validation in childhood need not be taken defensively. To be useful information it only needs to increase our motivation and provide the germ of an emotional framework to be better caregivers. We learn best from the past when we do so without shaming.

The fate of Dr. Kanner's theory provides a lesson about how framing potentially fruitful insights about autism as singular causes can lead to the loss of therapeutic insight. Trauma may not *cause* autism, but it is certainly a factor in Autistic lives. When it comes to further understanding the many dimensions of autism, we cannot afford to discard any possible fragments of a comprehensive picture. Especially because trauma is such a universal problem, the more perspectives we see it from the better it can be acknowledged in all its forms.

So-called "classic" autism often involves physical disability, profound challenges with communication, and debatable rates of intellectual impairment. Hans Asperger identified an apparently less pervasive syndrome of autistic characteristics around the same time, but partly because "Asperger's" is no longer officially recognized I refer to myself as ASHFA (Asperger's syndrome/"high functioning" autism). This term gives a nod to the medical condition to which it is often associated but does not necessarily point to pathology because diagnosis is optional. It refers, rather, to a kind of person. I am ASHFA because I identify with various unconventional personal characteristics, feel different because of them, and must endure certain kinds of stigma. Many individuals like me maintain they are not impaired or disabled but merely *different*. Maybe the difference between "classic" autism and ASHFA is one of severity, but more needs to be heard from both groups to understand what exactly they experience relative to each other.

Right from the start, it was hotly disputed whether the two conditions were distinct. Despite people diagnosed with classic autism wondering "why on earth do we have the same diagnosis?" (Kedar 2016), this debate has been put to rest at least temporarily as both are currently considered more or less severe cases of autism spectrum disorder (ASD). Many, including Luke Tsai in the Department of Psychiatry at the University of Maryland (2013), believe Asperger's or something like it will be back as a distinct diagnosis. The question is far from settled. Nothing about autism is settled. "Experts" whose beliefs about autism are based on scientific convention and current thinking may find themselves on precarious ground. Rather than distinguishing these two groups based on current diagnostic standards, assuming ASHFA is "mild" and the other "severe," for the rest of this project I will refer to CLAWHS ("classic autistics" who need high levels of support). This acknowledges the medical condition historically associated with the challenges but refers to the population on their own terms without taking anything for granted. We will discuss the stigma experienced by many in this group in the last chapter and refer to them throughout the book. My own lived experience and research is with ASHFA.

Many controversies have raged around autism over the years, such as the role of vaccination. Vast amounts of enthusiastic energy have been spent promoting this putative answer to the "autism problem," mostly before science and journalism revealed questionable research and conflict of interest behind the passion. There is no shortage of books reporting miraculous recoveries following different regimes. Parents of autistic children have been encouraged to try a multitude of treatments, administer large amounts of this or that, avoid various things, go on special diets, and purchase a wide range of products. Despite health problems and even death, some parents resort to desperate "cures" such as making their children drink bleach to rid the body of autism (Porter 2018). Optimism about a "cure" often leads to collateral damage and shattered hopes. Following a multi-dimensional plan of optimal health to build strength and nourish the self may be a better approach, especially basic things like good nutrition and consistent exercise. This promotes maximum wellness rather than betting on risky singular approaches hoping for dramatic change (Herbert and Weintraub 2012).

Speculative contention has a long history in autism research and has been influential in the creation of stigma and misleading stereotypes. Unifying theories attempting to understand autism in terms of fundamental mechanisms of impairment create deficit expectations that impair openness to unique strengths and abilities. Impaired theory of mind, for example, results in an autism stereotype of people who are incapable of social insight and empathy. This image became so ingrained that the first books written by individuals diagnosed with autism were discredited and challenged as a farce, almost as if being an autistic author was an impossible contradiction (Sacks 1995; Hacking 2009a; Tammet 2017). The classic big three proposed underlying mechanisms of impairment in autism, specifically theory of mind, central coherence, and executive functioning, are perhaps not best seen as "impaired mechanisms" that specifically disable autistic people but areas of functioning that present typically human challenges. Theory of mind, or mentalization, involves the ability and *making the effort* to read what others are thinking and take other perspectives into account. Central coherence involves the ability to step back, organize details into meaningful wholes, and see the bigger picture. The problematic opposing tendency is to become self-absorbed and over-invested in the particulars of self-interest and self-gratification. Executive functioning involves, among other things, prioritizing, setting goals, keeping things straight, and following directions. These three areas of difficulty, as well as more recent proposals identifying emotional dysregulation at the heart of autism, will be referred to in this book as *autisticy*. The challenges of autisticy will be considered from a lived perspective with the intention of building bridges between people rather than creating stereotypes. Different mental health and neurodevelopmental conditions are associated with characteristic profiles of autisticy as well as different flavors of stigma. Trauma and invalidation will be seen to further provoke these difficulties in all of us.

Complexity of Stigma

Stigma is defined in the dictionary as the possession of a "mark of disgrace" (Oxford Dictionaries 2018). Erving Goffman, the Canadian social scientist who pioneered the study of stigma, defined it as the possession of an "attribute that is deeply discrediting" (1963, p.3). Although his work stands as an insightful and comprehensive exploration of stigma, it can seem dated. He often uses sexist language that would be unacceptable today. Like those who take their lead from his seminal work, he puts disgrace at the heart of stigma rather than the socially divisive process of putting our interpretation of certain qualities before receptivity to the humanity and uniqueness of the person. Perhaps most importantly, his words tend to reinforce the separation of "we normals" and "discounted" others. Yet when he talks about "spoiled" and "tainted" people, he does not mean to imply something is wrong with stigmatized individuals. He refers to the way their humanity has been devalued by stigma. Words are important, and the use of stigmatizing language in the study of stigma is a paradoxical hazard.

Stigma cannot be captured in a tidy definition and has much less to do with qualities that are possessed than our own fear of not being perfect and the typically human aversion to the unfamiliar. There are several types of stigma, including *overt stigma*, which may be related to labels or visible differences, and *concealable stigma* related to conditions that can be hidden. The pain of concealable stigma is often related to the anticipation of stigma that would be experienced if the condition was discovered. There is also pain related to devaluing one's own person by having to hide parts of the self, as well as the oppressive social injustice that creates pressure to hide. When it comes to ASHFA, it is *conduct stigma* that plays the greatest role in a person's pain. Consistent with the results of earlier research (Butler and Gillis 2011), participants in the study underlying this book reported that the stigma they experienced was not due primarily to the label of autism itself but to the unconventional social behavior associated with their autisticy. Whatever other challenges they reported, they felt it was their different social orientation that made it most difficult for them to fit in and led to repeated experiences of rejection.

A still more elusive source of social marginalization for ASHFA are *stigmas of presence*, which are based on sensed rather than concrete differences that may be difficult to pinpoint or articulate. The participant in my study who walked into his first bar and was immediately belittled and asked to leave may have been describing an example of this. He didn't announce to the room that he was autistic. He wasn't aware of doing anything to cause this reaction. People just sensed his difference. I experience this when people treat me with condescending dismissal just from the impression they get on our first encounter. Maybe you've had the experience of feeling uncomfortable around someone you don't know because of something you can't put your finger on. You try to be polite, but it leaks out when you try to hide it. Those of us with Autistic natures feel the brunt of this on a chronic basis. We also participate in the kind of stigmatizing that results when such discomfort is felt with different unfamiliar others. I have found it possible to defuse this sort of discomfort with curiosity. Not unkind curiosity as in "What's wrong with you?" or morbid curiosity as in "What does someone like you eat for breakfast?" but willing-to-learn curiosity such as "Why don't you look at me?" or "Why don't you ask what I think?" or "Why do you cover your face in public?" Such simple non-judgmental efforts to better understand can provide a safe space for stigma-defusing communication.

Stigma and Vicarious Invalidation

Stigma is a complex phenomenon that involves many processes such as stereotyping, ignorance, disregard, cruelty, avoidance, rejection, discrimination, judgment, assumption, and prejudice. For those who experience it, stigma involves emotional pain and dehumanizing invalidation that can undermine their quality of life.

Repeated experiences of stigma result in trauma, and trauma can make people armored and defensive. We may become hyper-vigilant to whatever reminds us of the source of our trauma and easily triggered by events remotely resembling what traumatized us. Something we went through long ago may have planted seeds of trauma and internalized shame, like fat cells ready to balloon if we don't watch our eating. Such trauma conditioning can cause confusing distress, and sometimes the most innocent-seeming conditions can trigger uncomfortable high-alert arousal and defensiveness for no apparent reason. For example, if I do not understand what you are asking it might seem simple to ask for clarification. However, all the times I was called slow, stupid, and retarded may come back to me. The trauma of past stigma becomes activated, and I escalate, becoming defensive for no apparent reason. This is due physiologically to a primitive sub-organ in the brain called the amygdala. It is part of the limbic system and one of its main functions is scanning for safety. In concert with other parts of the brain it heats up the inner furnace of our metabolism in alarmed preparation when it recognizes danger. Accumulated experiences of invalidation trauma provide a set of templates that act like virus definitions for threat recognition. When these are activated by experiences that trigger the pain of past invalidation it can lead to tortuous and crazy-making physio-emotional escalation. Kedar describes it as "triggered turmoil" that makes him feel "trapped and miserable" (2012, p.118). Autistic children who have been exposed to traumatic experiences demonstrate higher levels of disruptive behavior (Mehtar and Mukaddes 2011). In my case the resulting disruptive behavior carried right into adulthood, although the effects may be subtle and difficult to capture with standard assessment tools.

More research is called for if we want to obtain more insight into this. I believe autism has deepened and amplified the effects of trauma in my life just as trauma has aggravated the challenges of my autisticy. I have seen clients in my practice with all kinds of conditions and no diagnosis at all whose emotional reactivity and hyper-vigilance associated with developmental, invalidation, and other trauma is significantly pervasive and troublesome. Any avenue we take to better understand this phenomenon is important, and autism can provide valuable insight.

Prior to any medical diagnosis, it was the pain of stigma, isolation, rejection, and confusion about not being accepted that fueled my own personal need to understand what was happening to me when I was growing up. The participants in my research who were diagnosed later in life said the same thing. For me, identifying with this Autistic community began with relating to patterns of stigma described in online forums where people understood each other's experiences. Such forums are not exclusive clubs in which membership can only be obtained with a medical diagnosis. They are accessible and relevant to anyone who experiences the characteristic stigma associated with Autistic presence. What often draws people to these communities, more than any list of "symptoms," is shared identity fatigue.

Identity fatigue can be vicarious. It can be experienced just by associating with a primary target of stigma. Sometimes intimate others take it upon themselves to identify their loved one as autistic, not because they are medical experts, but because it gives them a way to understand the ways we frustrate them, make them feel lonely in relationship, seem uninterested or unable to provide emotional validation, meet their needs, or engage in what a relationship is conventionally supposed to be. These are common sentiments of spouses not only of those with a diagnosis but also of those whose partners live with often unacknowledged challenges of autisticy (Bellamy 2013). My wife says she feels like the one who lives with autism, a comment that made me confused and resentful until I realized she was referring to how oblivious I can be to the emotional pain my lack of attentive support and self-absorbed interaction put her through.

The partner of a person with characteristics of autisticy may need a way to understand why their relationship does not present to the world the way a typical couple is supposed to. They may fear or feel the brunt of judgment. They may not feel supported by their partner the way they feel they should be. Their partner may or may not have a diagnosis, but identity fatigue is experienced just as strongly in the relationship. In fact, the autistically stigmatized person's partner may be more acutely aware of identity fatigue, because they shield the Autistic person from stigma by giving them a safe place to be themselves. They may give each other a welcome zone of safety in various ways, but the autistically stigmatized person's partner not only shares the characteristic stigma of unconventionality in their marriage, they must learn to adjust their expectations to accommodate the behavior of their partner. They may strive to be as accepting as possible but have to manage frustration, disappointment, and frequent confusion. In addition to this, the partner may encounter the frequent activation of invalidation trauma in their loved one, which can range from hyper-defensiveness on the one hand to emotional shut-down on the other. This in itself can exaggerate the challenges that set them apart from the mainstream and lead to even further stigma.

The diagnosis of autism in the DSM-5 only involves two core diagnostic criteria, which are difficulty with relationships and social communication along with repetitive stereotyped movements such as rocking and hand-flapping. Being Autistic is so much more. No diagnosis even scratches the surface of our humanity. It is not just a matter of specifying the nature of relationship difficulty or what these repetitive movements look like. Various characteristic challenges of autisticy also come into play. Identification with Autistic personhood may also involve anxiety, obsessive-compulsive tendencies, apparently bizarre behaviors and eccentric collections, sensory over- and/ or under-sensitivity, need for sameness, difficulty with change, and trouble applying language in the flow of lived interaction. There may be various degrees of fine motor control ranging from awkward clumsiness to an inability to talk or point. Stigma is experienced by people who experience such challenges, and the activation of accumulated stigma is often exaggerated by associated problems with emotional regulation. Autism provides a good vantage point from which to explore all this because the associated stigma is chronic and often intense.

When invalidation trauma is activated, we have to practice steps of self-recovery. We must make an effort to step back from these shattering inner disruptions and shift the trajectory of ourselves in the moment to preserve peace and maintain the flow of relationship. In order to take care of ourselves appropriately, reassure ourselves of safety, and regulate our emotions we can practice techniques that reorient us to the present moment. Regulated breathing is crucial not only to de-escalate associated physiological arousal but also to reconnect us with the present moment. People who have been in abusive relationships or experienced other forms of trauma may be defensive and mean towards their currently supportive loved ones and not understand why. They may become agitated and emotionally escalated not only by things that remind them of abusive situations but also by the smallest things that trigger their experiences of invalidation. Grounding ourselves in the present moment rather than the activation of past invalidation is a powerful practice.

Invigorating Notions of Autisticy

Stigma associates autism with loss and diminishment. Yet there is a higher truth; Autistic lives are pregnant with possibility. Possibilities of all kinds overflow the stereotypes associated with this human condition. Possibilities also overflow the way autism is understood. Autism has been called "one of the most frequently studied conditions in the field of mental health" (Matson and Kozlowski 2011, p.418), yet its mysteries far outweigh the claims of current understanding. The very categorization on which the above quote is based can be questioned. Is it a mental health issue to be autistic? Is it a disorder or disability? Should it be seen as an illness or affliction? In many cases, the physical and mental challenges associated with being autistic are not necessarily or directly related to autism. Intellectual impairment is a separate diagnosis. Seizures are an indication of epilepsy, the inability to use speech may be diagnosed as verbal ataxia, and the movement difficulties thought to be behind many of the challenges of pervasive autism may represent underlying but separate neurological issues. Some researchers are convinced movement difficulties are not part of autism at all, despite first-hand reports, because this is "unfounded" in the context of current scientific thinking.

Autism has many meanings to different people. People who take it to mean primarily a medical diagnosis think of *having* autism. People with the autism label who frame their condition this way insist autism does not define them. Others see autism as a way for a person to *be*. Such folks are more likely to say they are *Autistic*. Those identifying as such are more likely to acknowledge Autisticy as deeply and inherently part of who they are. This is like the distinction between "deaf" (a medical diagnosis and raw physiological condition) and "Deaf" (the community of non-hearing people and their way of being human). Along with the participants in my study, I see myself as Autistic. It is part of my heritage as a person, not something wrong with me or some kind of mechanical flaw. When autism is seen purely as a kind of medical pathology, it becomes something to be resisted and pushed away like some kind of undesirable attribute. The diversity movement, which advocates for autism to be seen as a form of difference rather than impairment, challenges the medical model's pathology-based conception of autism. Since we will not be concerned primarily with autism as a medical condition, the term will often be used in the same sense as racism, ageism, and sexism to indicate the stigma, judgment, and prejudice experienced because of one's autistic identity. When I use the term "autism" (with a small "a"), it refers either to an impairment-based medical label or the stigma attached to autism and being Autistic. Capitalized, Autistic refers to a being a kind of person. As Ian Hacking (2006) points out, being this kind of person is not a static unchanging category but a living dynamic way of being whose evolution depends at least partly on how we come to understand this form of personhood.

Diagnosis, Identity, and Politics

Personal identity is a messy, complex matter that relates not only to how we see ourselves but also to our unique tolerances and abilities, how we relate to the conventions of the social environment, and the way we want others to see us. It is never a simple matter of biology. A person with two X chromosomes usually refers to themselves as a woman, but this is not straightforward. Many individuals see their gender identity in a non-binary way not directly connected to biological properties. If gender identity can be a socially constructed concept that goes beyond biology, so can Autistic identity. Not that there aren't biological correlates to be explored as part of our knowledge of the phenomenon, but these don't have to be considered defining or absolute. The medical model, in its quest to identify pathology, sees only that people *have* autism, as if it were simply a troublesome biological abnormality in a human container falling short of its normal healthy condition. Homosexuality used to be seen as pathology in this way. Sexual and gender disorders are now seen in terms of the dysphoria or the suffering people experience around these issues, which is mostly caused by stigma and unmet social expectations. In much the same way, an untold degree of the suffering associated with Autistic personhood is related to stigma and not meeting dominant expectations.

If the medical establishment has not been involved and there has been no diagnosis, a young adult with characteristics of autisticy may have escalating confusion about why they experience stigma and lack of belonging. This can result in distressing levels of trauma, anxiety, hyper-vigilance to rejection, and defensiveness. Diagnosis, especially when young, can be crucial to sort out different conditions and possible treatments if appropriate and desired. Alternative conceptualizations to the impairment-based model of diagnosis can provide more personally congruent frameworks of identity formation for people who intuitively or rebelliously reject the medical model and choose not to think something is "wrong" with them.

Families that struggle to support autistic children may have difficulty understanding how autism can be seen as anything but a disability (Berg-Dallara 2014). The parents of those with autistic characteristics know something is different about their children and this difference can be more or less disruptive for the family. If the child keeps to themselves and does not participate in relationships like a child is "supposed" to, there may be some concern. If the family has difficulty functioning socially or as a unit, concern escalates. If the child has additional challenges such as pain, lack of muscle control, difficulty communicating, seizures, or intellectual impairment, these may be attributed to their autisticy. Depending on the degree to which parents are called upon to provide unusually demanding care, they may appeal to the medical profession to provide answers. Diagnosis can provide a way of understanding what is going on and alert the family to helpful strategies of special care and accommodation. As the child grows into adulthood, the identity they assume around their autistic characteristics may evolve. They may come to see them as an inherent part of their personhood, which may differ from the mindset their parents adopted in an attempt to cope. In the young person's efforts to manage stigma and develop confidence in their uniqueness, changing values and perspectives of self-identity may supersede the family's frame of reference.

Parents are wise to avoid getting too attached to the pathology model so they don't become a barrier to their children's search for a positive identity. An adversarial relationship can develop between Autistic adults and parents in this regard. Sensitivity to issues of stigma and the resulting trauma can bridge differences. This does not only apply to families, but also to autism organizations such as Autism Speaks that at times find themselves at odds with the individuals they are supposed to be serving (TheCaffeinatedAutistic 2013; Sequenzia 2014; Schultz 2017).

Leaving the extensive psychological analysis of stigma to others (e.g. Jones *et al.* 1984), this book explores stigma as a bodily felt source of humanly damaging trauma. Readers are invited to embark on a process of discovery, whether their life is touched by autism or not, in order to learn how we can decrease our footprint in the world of stigma, see what a deeper understanding of this issue can do, and begin to recover from this violence of shame and shaming. The self-feeding cycle of stigma and traumatization can become difficult to manage. I see the pattern again and again in my practice, and this alerted me to the process in my own life. It also allowed me to see it, after the fact, in the participant reports disclosed in my study. I did not explicitly discuss trauma then, but subsequent counseling experience and further reflection led me to the connection. The insights emerging from carefully designed qualitative research continue to grow long after initial results are reported.

Chapter 2

RESEARCH AND THE OTHERNESS OF ASHFA

When one of the participants in my study was given an opportunity to give feedback on the final results, he said it was the first time he had ever seen the actual mechanisms of autistic stigma articulated. Although he had been managing stigma and feeling the pain of not fitting in his whole life, the results of the study helped him put his finger on what was actually going on. Getting a diagnosis that provides medical validation for difference is one thing. Understanding the dynamics of stigma that lead to rejection in everyday life is another.

Basic ethical guidelines did not provide a sufficient framework to ensure I engaged participants in a responsive manner that did not cause unintentional harm. My Asperger's diagnosis could be seen to impact my ability to conduct social research because of associated "difficulties with empathy and social skills" (Attwood 2007, p.22). It might have caused me to overlook or misread important information and make the participants feel unheard or misinterpreted. I appealed to the ethics of encounter rigorously articulated by Emmanuel Levinas (1961/1969) to compensate for this possibility. This aspect of his work may only be a fraction of what Derrida calls the "historical shockwave" of his thought (1999, p.12), but he maintained that lived encounter with another person must "overflow" our beliefs and assumptions about them. In this ethical framework we must make a conscious effort to be receptive to how people present themselves and let their impact on us come from who they are rather than what we believe, assume, or make up about them. Levinas insisted the people we encounter must not be reduced to our ideas about them. This would result in their "neutralization" and render them into mere objects (p.43). From his perspective as a Jew in Nazi Germany, this would be "murderous of the other" (p.47). The receptive, validating attitude towards others this framework represents is a powerful remedy for stigma and was particularly important for me to keep in mind as a researcher with a tendency to intellectualize encounter. It is beyond the scope of this chapter to fully explore the development of this ethical framework, but Levinas builds his case powerfully with sustained argument. It provides a model of non-stigmatizing relationship.

This ethical orientation reflects and painstakingly articulates the wisdom of spiritual masters through the ages, for example:

> You look at your neighbour, at your wife, at your husband or your boyfriend or girlfriend, whoever it be, but can you look without the imagery of thought, without the previous memory? For when you look with an image there is no relationship. (Krisnamurti 1972, p.7)

The ethics of encounter is a poignant ethical orientation to be mindful of at all times, not only from my point of view as ASHFA doing research but for all of us to deepen our interaction and honor others more fully. In particular, it can help us relate to vulnerable marginalized people and minimize the stigma that so often throws a shadow over relationships. The ethics of encounter provided me with a solid framework of interaction to lean on in the study. Social workers adopt this framework to help them provide the most client-centered and responsive service to clients (Rossiter 2011). More importantly, it can help all of us deepen our encounters and guard against stigma.

Detailed descriptions of the methodology, methods, and data analysis used in the study are provided in the original thesis (Gates 2014). A more detailed investigation of the results can also be found there. In this chapter we will only touch on the basic sources of stigma ASHFA experience as a lead-in to the rest of the book where the roles of trauma and the basic challenges of autisticy are explored from various perspectives.

Measuring Behavior

All the participants in the study spoke about how they often find themselves at a loss in social situations. One participant said she often felt "stupid" and found herself "in tears a lot of the time trying to understand what I was supposed to do" in social situations. Another participant talked about the challenge of trying to logically construct how he was supposed to act. "I just find myself telling myself in my head things like 'OK, now listen for a bit, add something now, don't rebuttal here,'" he said. This experience of deliberately constituting social behavior was most apparent in the complex area of dating. One participant described how "there are a lot of non-verbal cues and expectations going into dating. Do we kiss? Do we hold hands? I never quite know what to do." ASHFA seem to experience a kind of social blindness regarding conventions others take for granted and have come to expect. This has been articulated as difficulty "in the spontaneous processing of social information" (Channon et al. 2014, p.161).

Again, dating provides a poignant example. One participant described being in an intimate situation with a member of the opposite sex. He said he was just starting to like her but got confused at one point because she was standing before him with her eyes closed as if expecting a surprise. He had no idea what was happening, but closed his eyes to play along. The moment passed, and he could not figure out why she never acted the same towards him. It wasn't until years later he realized he had rejected a woman expecting to be kissed.

Another participant told how he once bought tickets to a special event long in advance hoping to get paired up for a high school dance. Strategically, he asked one of the plainest girls he could think of, hoping she, at least, would go out with him. He did not know how to talk to girls and had not interacted with her at all in the past. Understandably she refused him. His approach towards her was stigmatizing and based on qualities rather than getting to know her. The participant said he was sad when he went to his next class, where one of the most popular girls in the school sat next to him. He asked her if she would like to go to the upcoming dance and remembers how she said, "yes" enthusiastically. Did he smile happily? Did he feel lucky? No, he handed her his tickets and told her to have fun. The participant said he thought about this incident for years and could never understand why the girl seemed to want nothing to do with him after that. He did not realize until years later that he had unwittingly asked her on a date only to reject her. After "getting it," he said he mourned the lost opportunity and felt colossally stupid, although he never mentioned being sorry for hurting her.

Dating complexities notwithstanding, such misunderstandings were a commonly reported theme with participants. A relationship seems to be going reasonably well until something happens and from that point on others are not the same. At such times interaction assumes an air of "wrongness" and befuddlement. Discomfort floods the space. A transgression of socioconventional expectation and break in the flow of social relationship has occurred. The degree of awareness that such a disruption has taken place, however, varies.

Hapless Violations

Autistic individuals receive feedback about transgressions of conventional social expectation in various ways. The other person may become hurt and angry or feel they've been treated badly. They may read deliberately offensive intentions into acts. Seeking confirmation is always a good idea to avoid such misunderstandings, even if it seems obvious that "everyone knows it's unacceptable." Other people may simply begin to regard the offending person as odd or strange and distance themselves. Reserving judgment is a difficult but useful skill for autistic and socioconventional alike. Feedback can be immediate or delayed, and it may be years later if at all that ASHFA begin to appreciate the implications of an episode. Unless they receive explicit feedback regarding the impact of their offending statement, action, or lack of action, they may not know why the social climate seems to be turning against them. Regardless of the other person's reaction, ASHFA are largely unaware of *hapless* social code violations. Not only is the nature of such disruptions elusive, but sometimes the fact that there has been a transgression at all passes unnoticed.

ASHFA experience this frequently, sometimes due to lack of insight about the expectations being breached and sometimes due to lack of reflection. Once I had a neighbor who I spoke with from time to time when we met in the driveway. I often feel proud of myself for engaging in small talk, as if it were some kind of small victory because it is so uncomfortable for me. I thought I had a decent relationship with this neighbor until my wife asked me one day why I was being so mean to him. I was shocked. I asked her to explain what she meant. She said I didn't ask him how he was, didn't seem interested in what was going on in his life, and was always abrupt. I had no idea. She had spoken to the neighbor that day, and he told her about a time he offered to have a beer with me. He said I just bade him goodnight and went into the house. He said he was hurt and offended. I remembered that time. He hadn't come right out and said, "Do you want a beer?" In hindsight,

I could see how he had alluded to having a beer with me, because he was already having one and mentioned he had more inside. I had not broken a rule of social conduct intentionally, but had affronted someone by ignoring their invitation when I didn't recognize it. I had not been on the lookout for his invitation. It was not even on my radar of encounter. This is ironic given all the times I was dying to get an invitation and felt passed over.

The next time I saw the neighbor I apologized profusely. I told him about my Asperger's. He understood, and we had a laugh. This could be termed a late catch discovered through third-party intervention, and it makes me wonder how often this kind of thing must go by without my knowledge. Evidence of hapless violations include people who don't seem to like me, avoid me, or as one participant put it, act as if I'm "not worth bothering with at all." I wish people would just tell me when I'm making a social blunder, but that would not only take more energy than they might think it's worth but might also make them vulnerable to further abuse. There's always the possibility they are actually dealing with someone who *is* deliberately trying to send them a message. The social world can be incredibly complex.

Channon *et al.* (2014) cite multiple studies demonstrating that individuals diagnosed with Asperger's score consistently lower on tests eliciting an explanation of what makes certain social situations awkward, identifying inappropriate social conduct, and working out the significance of human behavior. The authors point out that these findings may be associated with "inappropriate responses in everyday social situations, but little experimental work has explored this directly" (p.152). My research, let alone my life, tends to confirm this. Difficulty processing complex linguistic constructions such as double entendres, irony, and sarcasm in real time are characteristic, but the difficulty extends beyond the use of language and causes frequent misadventure in lived social situations of all kinds. Not all social blunders leading to stigma, however, are totally hapless on the part of individuals diagnosed with autism, identifying as ASHFA, or struggling with challenges of autisticy.

Willful Violations

There are also *willful* violations of social conduct. Whereas hapless violations usually take place in the minefield of subtleties involved with social interaction, willful violations are often clearly identifiable. One participant said he refuses to participate in conventions such as greetings and celebrating birthdays. He says he has taken flack for this but resigned himself to the situation. "I'm now at the point where I can say, 'That's a neurotypical ritual and I'm not participating in that.'" These may be termed blunt violations. He gives the example of sorry rituals and greeting rituals. Another participant asked, "Why would you ask how I am when you don't care, and why would I ask when it makes no difference to me?" Sometimes this involves the avoidance of uncomfortable situations. For example, I may not give someone a present or procrastinate until it's too late because I can never seem to get a good one and experience so much stress trying to come up with one. Leaving obvious clues or referring the person to someone in a position to help, like a friend of the family, can make a positive difference. The Autistic person may need to be reminded (or remind themselves) that it is not always their own feelings that are at stake but those of someone who is important to them. Sometimes, like with birthdays and anniversaries, it is hard to remember events that are important to others, and we don't bother making the effort. Just saying hello when we come into a room can be like this. It may not seem necessary because it's obvious I'm back, and we may as well get right down to it, but socioconventional people seem to require it.

At other times, willfully violating social rules is due to a genuine feeling that the social conduct in question is "illogical." At such times we may need to be reminded it is not logic that is important if we want relationships to go smoothly but the gesture of addressing often illogical needs and expectations. At still other times, willful violation is to make a point or address an overlooked item of concern. One participant said he often "sticks my neck out to challenge stigma" by calling attention to questions no one seems to be addressing, identifying populations that are being neglected, or pointing out patterns no one seems to want to acknowledge. In this participant's volunteer work with the HIV community he has come to believe there are "unwritten rules against asking big questions." Bravely, though, he continues to ask them. He says he chooses to ignore the advice he was given when he graduated college to "keep my mouth shut:"

> There are countless studies that I think are all connected together, but they can't see the connections, and they choose to ignore

> it. I have to ask why, and this gives me my reputation as "the social critic"...there are a whole set of false rules, social rules, and social paradigms we have to live under. It's very easy to say I don't subscribe to those paradigms, but then I leave myself open to stigma and discrimination.

The client's lack of concern for socioconventional routines and expectations helps him in this case, because it leaves him free to notice and address gaps in the established system others don't seem to see or give importance to. Such systematically willful disruptions can be beneficial, although they take courage because of the additional stigma they cause. Rather than being seen as helpful, they are often put down as part of ASHFA's "difficult" and "contrary" behavior. Stigma can keep people from contributing the unique skills and perspectives that make them different but allow them to fill in the blanks left by others.

Precarious Violations

A third category of social code transgression might be termed *precarious* violations. These are closely related to willful violations but their intentionality differs. Willful violations involve an element of conscious defiance. Precarious violations occur when ASHFA blurt, rant, tattle, or pontificate about issues that seem perfectly logical to them but violate codes of polite restraint or expected conduct. One participant talked about how careful he has to be to "think about what I'm going to say before I just blurt out an inappropriate statement or something." This does not refer to the kind of unconscious blurting that happens in Tourette's syndrome, with which one of the participants was diagnosed in addition to Asperger's. This participant talked about his frustration when socially frowned-upon terms and statements "slip out like a sneaky fart." These involuntary social violations seem independent of the complexity of social interaction and happen randomly. Whereas willful violations reflect the desire to make a statement, precarious violations involve semi-deliberate blurting often in the service of boosting the ego to compensate for the invalidation of stigma. Because there is not an important message at stake, the social disruption involved is often better avoided. This demands a kind of restraint not particular to ASHFA. As is often the case, however, autism provides an extreme example of the familiar. Rather than occasional blunders associated with carelessness, personal agendas, misunderstanding, or isolated lapses of impulse control, ASHFA regularly get themselves in trouble with their habitual incapacity, or seeming incapacity, to recognize what is supposed to be socially appropriate. One participant talked about how he would always get himself into conflict with teachers, for example:

> Sometimes you can listen to people and they'll say things that are wrong or incorrect or just kind of dumb. Some people can sit there and kind of politely nod. I just have to go out and call them on it.

Sometimes this kind of violation involves throwing caution to the wind in order to make a point. In such cases they become willful, and sometimes the line between these and precarious violations is a fine one. Reflection on the consequences of previous experiences with this kind of blurting can prevent social incidents. They are precarious because the individual, if they reflect on it, can see the potential social damage that may be done if they continue with the behavior. At times I hear a quiet voice in my head saying, "This could be trouble." Still, I may feel it is only logical to provide the correct information or offer a better way. I also know, after many bitter lessons, that logic is not the only yardstick of what is appropriate. Struggling with this was a common theme with the participants. Sometimes I have to restrain my habitual dependence on inexorable logic (which is often in defense of ill-considered impulses). At such times I give myself a gentle nudge and shift gears to make avoiding potential consequences a priority. I must focus, I tell myself, on caution. "Sorry" means nothing unless we remember how sorry we are going to be and use this self-notification to choose a course of action that will work out better for us. This might seem like a simple matter of letting common sense prevail. I prefer to see it as choosing to stand down after giving weight to the quiet inner voice warning me I'm going to get in trouble, hurt someone, violate a boundary, or make a mess of things again.

This kind of standing down from impulse and logic is an all too familiar challenge for many of us and is often at the threshold where things either continue to run smoothly or start falling apart. What do we defer to at such times? It is a quiet, easily ignored knowing within that can be easily trampled by impulse, logic, and self-gratification. This inner intuition often becomes stronger but remains delicate as we grow in age and experience. I think characterizing it as an ethical conflict that demands ongoing mindful resolution better captures the spirit of effort it calls for rather than "self-control."

Precarious violations often involve an impulsive carelessness in favor of making things more logical, orderly, and correct in the individual's eyes. These violations can involve a certain pomposity or self-righteousness that immediately brings on a kind of stigma characteristic of ASHFA (which I describe as *frustigma*). I suspect I was guilty of such a violation on one of my first days of class in postgraduate social work. The professor had just explained a categorization of social frameworks. I thought about it and came up with what I thought was a much better way of doing it. I went up to her after class and critiqued her system as if I were an expert. I thought this would improve her system and show her I was listening. Instead, I felt this professor never regarded me in quite the same way again. I could not put my finger on it exactly, and I'm not sure she was aware of it, but I felt somehow disliked by her after that incident. It is not that being liked by her was particularly important to me, but years of stigma have sensitized me to the feeling of being disliked, regarded negatively, or disregarded entirely.

Another variation of precarious social code violation occurs when ASHFA discover a fact or statistic they find intriguing. They may blurt it out inappropriately when an unsuspecting readily available person is busy doing something else or when a conversation is totally unrelated. When this happens, a sense of confusion and sometimes demeaning judgment emanates from other people. I completely identify with the participant who said he restrains himself with internal narratives such as "Don't say anything, don't say anything, don't come off like a smart ass again." We may also gush personal information inappropriately or talk about other people's business when it isn't our place. Any of us can make precarious social blunders, especially when our self-esteem is threatened. ASHFA may work especially hard at seeking social assurance to compensate for stigma, but it often seems like a losing battle based on faulty intelligence gathering.

Telegraphic Sense

Many stigma events involve being flustered due to a sense that something incongruent has happened, although ASHFA can't say exactly what. It involves a telegraphic sense that something is wrong, that "I've screwed up again." ASHFA can tell they've made some comment, not responded when they should have, interrupted the flow of interaction, made a gesture that didn't go over well, or somehow breached social expectations and caused a disturbance. Sometimes they haven't said anything, sometimes they just came in, and sometimes they're just standing there. Their very presence may have triggered a disruption of some kind with socioconventional others. They feel "threatened" and sometimes "overwhelmed" with a feeling of being "put in the spotlight" for their difference. Their inability to fit in, or the incomprehensible barrier to fitting in before them, is accentuated and dramatized. They may feel like "disappearing into the floor." It is not necessarily any overt violation of social conduct that is distressing; it is the feeling of being exposed for not fitting in and "not getting it." In this case ignorance would be bliss. Hapless violations are much less painful. One participant describes telegraphic violations in existential terms that evoke a feeling of crisis:

> Although we don't have the ability to know what someone is thinking, we are acutely aware when people are waiting and judging. Their being can actually put us into a meltdown.

Sometimes this has an identifiable source, such as the use of language:

> There's a disconnect between what's being said and what we're sensing, although we can't articulate it. If somebody is saying something that has a double meaning, for example, and I'm taking it in the literal form while they're meaning it in a non-literal form, I'm going to sense they're intending something else than what I'm hearing. I'm not able to clue into the intended or implied version, so that will send me into meltdown because I know I'm not getting it because their being is telling me I'm not getting it. It's an emotional reaction that I sense in other people. I just know something's not right and I get overwhelmed.

Philosopher Michel Foucault talks about the "all powerful glance... from behind each eye [that] can be said to eat away at the flesh" (1963/1998, p.81). This is commonly known as a "withering look." It conveys invalidation. Sometimes it's not even a look but an invisible form of dismissive regard experienced the way we sometimes know someone is looking at us from behind. It is an inarticulate feeling pressing down on us without a word having to be spoken. Sometimes we feel we won't hurt others if we don't say or do anything mean. More than controlling overt unkind words and behaviors, to avoid stigmatizing we have to manage our very orientation. Our demeanor, through looks, subtle facial expressions, and other little cues, somehow conveys our true feelings. If we allow our stance towards someone to come from a judgmental place, it devalues their humanity and feels to them like "what a stupid person" or "what a poor person" or "you must be less of a person." Some may not notice this, but those chronically oppressed by stigmatizing attitudes respond to it physically. When we focus on qualities rather than openness to who a person is, basing our response to them on a combination of assumptions and unmet social expectations, the person picks up stigma telegraphically. This is true for anyone who does not conform with the sameness of dominant culture. The invalidation and shame of being humanly downgraded by encounter filtered through a reaction to attributes rather than openness to unique personhood is traumatizing no matter what qualities such demeaning regard is based upon.

Looking with fresh eyes, the oppressive forces of social exclusion impact marginalized identities with a bewildering array of stigmatizing messages. ASFHA tirelessly have to examine the cues and social information they inadvertently convey to avoid as much relationship disruption as possible, especially with those socioconventionals we function alongside and care about. This monitoring of social intelligence also characterizes the struggle to resist and minimize stigma. To a certain extent it is a private struggle to avoid pain. As an effort of general reform to make the world a better place by not stigmatizing others, we all have a part to play.

The telegraphic transmission of stigma is difficult to prove. The more "solid" the evidence being sought the more quickly the phenomenon disappears like tears that dry up when we get self-conscious about crying or a sneeze when we think too much about it. The event can be clearly felt but does not easily survive objectification. It can be studied, but the research must begin with lived experience. Most important, whether we understand it or not, when we pay lip service to stigma rather than making genuine efforts to counter the conventions and deeply rooted automatic responses that perpetuate it, the superficial nature of the resulting orientation can be felt and leads to "celebrations of inclusion and diversity that don't ring true or effect change" (Dolmage 2017).

Flustered and Falling Short

Goffman's insightful descriptions of experience are as powerful now as when they were written. His discussion of embarrassment and social flustering is not directed specifically towards ASHFA, because he does not consider autism in his writing. He does say an embarrassed person, after drawing attention to themselves with some kind of socially awkward behavior, will "sense what sort of conduct *ought* to be maintained as the appropriate thing" (1967, p.105). Imagine how much worse the experience must be for someone who is foreign to socioconventional behavior and has no sense of what is supposed to be appropriate. The "disqualifying attribute" of differently constituted social apprehension was not considered by Goffman, although it sounds like he might be describing the experience of ASFHA when he adds:

> The person who falls short may everywhere find himself inadvertently trapped into making implicit identity-claims which he cannot fulfill. Compromised in every encounter which he enters, he truly wears the leper's bell. (p.107)

It is an autistic Catch 22. The more invisible ASHFA is the more intensely stigma is experienced because socioconventional expectations are not diminished by the appearance of "symptoms" and "disability." This is the opposite of stigma associated with conditions, for example, like epilepsy where more intense and frequent seizures result in greater stigma (Bandstra, Camfield, and Camfield 2008). In this way the inverse rule may not apply to autistics who experience clearly visible differences from the mainstream. For ASHFA, at least up to a point, the experience of stigma goes down as the visibility of their stigmatizing differences goes up. Shtayermman (2009) found this in his research, although he tried to explain it by saying the stigma of Asperger's must come from the diagnosis itself and not the symptoms. This is not consistent with previous research, for example Butler and Gillis (2011), who found the label of Asperger's was not correlated with stigma. The participants in my research agreed with this, and the inverse rule of visibility for ASHFA may be better explained by how the unseen nature of their difference reinforces socioconventional expectations. The more hidden the differences the higher these expectations get. Countering the tendency to rely too heavily on immediate impressions and reserving judgment can address this, serving to decrease stigma where autisticy may not be readily apparent. Countering initial fear and judgment by making an effort to practice receptive openness can more than compensate for any moments of unsettled surprise when someone does not fit our expectations.

A combination of hapless, willful, precarious, and telegraphic social incidents can lead to exclusion and accumulating invalidation trauma. Willful and precarious violations can be minimized with effort. At work and places where the consequences of social blunders can be high a special effort is often made, but it is hard to sustain this consistently at home where we let our guard down (in Goffman's terms, when we are "backstage"). Hapless and telegraphic incidents seem inevitable. From a more socioconventional perspective, when such disruptions occur, we must try not to be too surprised and retain a non-judgmental stance. When we find ourselves violating conventional social expectations, we must make an effort to remain as graceful and humbly undefensive as possible to avoid making things worse. Most of us can find ourselves on either side of this unfixed social divide.

Contradiction of Diagnosis

This leads us to the highest conceptual leap of theorization based on the outcome of the research. It was rooted in a silent contradiction contained in participant reports and points to the deconstruction of diagnosis as a dominant validating framework of Autistic difference. Here I use Derrida's term "deconstruction" to refer to a process of challenging established concepts, practices, and power structures not just to be critical and destructive but to make room for productive new possibilities (1967/1997). Participants acknowledged a socially disabling aspect to their condition, but also maintained they did not feel inherently impaired. They described their condition as "part of myself I have to work with and around."

At the same time, participants diagnosed as adults expressed feeling relief when they were diagnosed. The participants confirmed previous research in this area by reporting that their diagnosis provided a validating framework that brought healing and positive change.

Self confidence grew, relationships became easier, and others became more empathetic and patient all because of the validating discourse provided by diagnosis. One Autistic individual posted online that he was not able to quit drugs until after he was diagnosed because the label deflected self-blame and gave him "the confidence to try and confront life without numbing the pain artificially" (Countryboy 2010).

Yet paradoxically, diagnosis represents a paradigm that characterizes autism as an inherent disability, a position the participants did not endorse. Murray (2012) points out that "the idea of autism as a 'problem' or 'deficit' is in fact built in during diagnostic evaluation" (p.13). In other words, when medical diagnosis provides the main validating framework for Autistic personhood, it imposes at the same time a pathologizing model that implies ASHFA are diminished, impaired, afflicted, and disabled. In accepting diagnosis as the resolution to a search for validation, ASHFA paradoxically undermine their "autistic integrity" (Barnbaum 2008, p.204). This is only logical since "to be situated in a discourse of pathology is to be delegitimized" (Tremain 2005, p.83). For ASHFA, accepting a diagnosis means accepting a socially constructed mantle of disability even if they prefer to see themselves as simply *different* and oriented towards the world through their unconventional social orientation and style of communication.

One alternate validating discourse involves the theory that ASHFA represents an exaggeration of male characteristics. Hans Asperger himself noted that typically male characteristics such as logic, abstraction, precise thinking, and explicit formulation were heightened in autistic patients. One participant who was diagnosed with Asperger's at a young age invoked a different validating framework with the concept of emotional intelligence (Goleman 1996). The participant said, "I just think that I've got more on the intellectual side and less on the social side." He noted the stigma involved when mainstream people do not respond well to communication that lacks the expected emotional content, a state of affairs both ASHFA and socioconventionals find frustrating.

Efforts to construct an alternate framework for understanding autisticy can be seen as a part of a larger attempt to "normalize autism through an association with general human variation" (Murray 2012, p.35). Such attempts include the emerging field of *diversity theory* and are an outgrowth of critical disability studies. This philosophy can decrease the stigma experienced by ASHFA because it focuses on celebrating diversity rather than pathology. Yet such frameworks have been criticized because they generalize the definition of ASHFA to the point where autism becomes "meaningless" and "much of the specificity about what the condition actually is" gets neglected (p.35).

The most widely accepted form of diversity theory is known as *neurodiversity*, a term coined in an undergraduate thesis by the mother of an undiagnosed girl with autistic characteristics (Singer 1998/2016). In the author's introduction to the reprinted thesis, she said she was motivated by "painful personal experiences of exclusion and invalidation as a person struggling in a family with a 'hidden disability' that no one, let alone us, recognized for what it was" (evolution of the idea, paragraph 9). People touched by autism who did not or still do not have a framework for understanding the stigma they experience, like me and some of the participants in my study, tend to both value the power of explanatory frameworks and not be entirely comfortable with medical diagnosis as the sole source of validation for their experience.

Although it captured the imagination of Autistic people, especially ASHFA whose suffering comes primarily from stigma rather than the condition itself, the concept of neurodiversity can be seen to be philosophically problematic in relation to the same contradiction found at the heart of my study. This idea goes far beyond the confines of the study itself, however, and will be further explored as the book progresses. Another variation of diversity theory I call *sociophenomenal diversity* will be explored in Part D as a way to embrace human diversity in a manner that accounts for the most poignant stigmatizing difference between ASFHA and sociodominant culture. This approach will be seen to complement neurodiversity and more directly address the lived experience of devalued humanity encountered by ASFHA and others who live with the challenges of autisticy. Meanwhile, now that we have explored the perspective of ASHFA and have a better understanding of the associated stigma, we will look at diagnosis from a different perspective.

Part B

DIAGNOSIS, DIVERSITY, AND AUTISTICY

There is said to be a wall between us and others, but it is a wall we build together.

Maurice Merleau-Ponty
(*Signs*, 1964, p.19)

Chapter 3

AUTISM, OTHERNESS, AND INVISIBILITY

In 2013 the DSM-IV was replaced by the DSM-5. In the DSM-IV Asperger's was seen as one of five pervasive developmental disorders that also included Rhett's disorder, childhood disintegrative disorder, autism, and pervasive developmental disorder not otherwise specified. The DSM-5 eliminated all these disorders and wrapped all but two up in a new condition called autism spectrum disorder. One of the ones left out was Rhett's disorder, which had unique diagnostic criteria among the pervasive developmental disorders. Although it involved impairments of social interaction early in its course, it also included abnormal head and brain development, worsening gait and movement problems, and loss of previously developed skills. In 1994 when the DSM-IV came out, little was known about the condition. In 2000, when the DSM-IV was revised, Ruthie Amir at Baylor University discovered Rhett's was associated with a mutation of the MECP2 gene on the X chromosome. This provided a concrete neurological correlation for the condition that further explained why it only happened to females. Rhett's came to be viewed as a neurological disorder of known physiological origin rather than a mental health condition. It was no longer included in the DSM-5.

This has interesting implications for autism. As specific neural correlates underlying autism are discovered, will it be considered a strictly medical disorder (or series of disorders) rather than a mental health issue? Will autism only remain as a catch-all for those conditions whose neurological correlates have not yet been discovered? It makes one wonder about the ephemeral nature of diagnosis and what might become of autism in the future. It is subject to ongoing revision, even though the lived experience of the world it involves is deeply rooted in the structure of a person's felt agency. One of the main criteria in the DSM common to many conditions is that there must be significant impairment in day-to-day life to necessitate diagnosis. One autistic online forum participant expressed confusion about this. He commented, "It's almost as if you can 'go in and out' of the diagnosis based upon your ability to cope at a particular moment in time" (Spacetraveller 2014). ASHFA is one variation of living with autisticy that represents more than the troublesome experience of certain challenges. It is a fundamental aspect of our personhood. We may go "in and out" of diagnosis depending on current criteria and how they are interpreted, but autisticy is intertwined inseparably with us and part of who we are. Whether socially dominant institutions such as medicine validate ASHFA with a diagnosis due to relative severity or other criteria is not as important as the way these qualities affect the way we live, interact with each other, and modulate the way we find adventure and thrive according to our own potential.

Pervasive developmental disorder not otherwise specified (PDDNOS) was also dropped. Social communication disorder became a new category in the DSM-5 that roughly corresponds with this. It covers cases involving difficulty with the pragmatic social flow of language in the absence of the restricted and/or repetitive patterns of behavior. The DSM-5 acknowledges that individuals with social communication disorder often experience "social deficits" as a result of their differences in communicative style, although not presumably to the extent of those with more pervasive forms of autism. Individuals diagnosed with social communication disorder probably experience much the same stigma as those with other forms of autisticy, and research indicates this condition may not be all that distinct from autism (Mandy, Wang, and Lee 2017). When a person is born with these different abilities and unconventional social orientations, even though different frameworks of understanding can modify the negative way they may come to see themselves because of their differences, it is changing the environment of judgment and stigma they live with that can make the biggest therapeutic differences in their life.

The elimination of Asperger's was the most controversial change made in the DSM-5 (Wylie 2014). Many of the changes were accepted as technical alterations not affecting anyone but medical practitioners. Others, such as eliminating the bereavement exclusion for depression, were seen to further pathologize the human condition (Francis 2013). Still other changes, such as eliminating the term "retardation," were seen to be much overdue (like when homosexuality was removed as a mental disorder from the DSM III in 1987). All in all, to many critics, the changes introduced in the diagnostic manual represented mostly organizational shuffling "based on expert consensus" rather than any kind of scientific progress (Paris 2013, p.187).

The proposed elimination of Asperger's caused a huge outcry from the Asperger community. Parents worried their children's eligibility for funding and services would be diminished by the change. People wondered how rates of diagnosis would be affected, possibly destabilizing mainstream validation for individuals experiencing mild symptoms and disqualifying them from service. Diagnosis, in this sense, can be seen as a fundamental strategy of "administrative autism identification" (Travers and Krezmien, in press, p.11). There was concern that women coping with Asperger's, who display symptoms differently from men and often remain undiagnosed, would be overlooked by the medical profession in even greater numbers (Laucius 2013). Giles (2014) explored the reaction of the online Asperger's community to the changes in the DSM-5 and identified responses ranging from acceptance and reassurance to rejection, fear, and suspicion. Uncertainty about losing social supports, fears about losing self-identity, and concerns about increased stigma set off a flurry of concerned discussion. All this controversy has now died down and the term "Asperger's" continues to be used unofficially to describe a "mild" range of autism that does not involve language and/or intellectual impairment or the need for substantial support.

"Asperger's" has been an increasingly popular designation for ASHFA since the term was introduced by Lorna Wing in her translation of Hans Asperger's 1944 paper "Die 'Autistischen Psychopathen' im Kindesalter," presented as "Asperger's Syndrome: A Clinical Account" (1981). Receiving the diagnosis brings automatic belonging in a strongly defined community with unique challenges. Almost from the start, the designation began to take hold. Online communities and grassroots organizations grew up around it. The sense of uniqueness and affiliation associated with being diagnosed with Asperger's can be empowering. Having this unifying descriptor taken away in the DSM-5 was experienced as a form of medical oppression by many of us. The manual says people with autistic disorder, Asperger's disorder, and pervasive developmental disorder not otherwise specified should be given a diagnosis of autism spectrum disorder.

Those who do not follow this directive are engaged in their own small resistance to current medical convention. Such resistance can be an important way of not relinquishing personal power to impersonal systems. This not only includes continuing to identify with Asperger's despite its removal from the DSM-5, but framing one's challenges in whatever way one chooses. This includes the choice not to be diagnosed at all. As for me, I felt it was important to revisit my diagnosis to make sure the validating framework provided by the medical community was still intact. I had not yet come to fully appreciate an alternative to make sense of my difference. To be honest, I also felt being diagnosed with Asperger's would give me credibility as the author of this book.

Self-Diagnosis

When I told the psychiatrist that I was there because of the diagnostic changes, he nodded knowingly and said things had changed drastically for the condition over the years. He said it used to be considered a disturbing diagnosis that was difficult to break to patients. Now, he said, "people get mad at me if I won't give them the diagnosis" (personal communication 2016). This reminded me of how Jerry Seinfeld announced in a television interview that he thought he was on the autism spectrum because social engagement had always been a struggle for him and he always felt different from other people (Howard 2014). His announcement did not seem to surprise people on the spectrum, who have been growing accustomed to celebrity autism. Darryl Hannah, Dan Aykroyd, Courtney Love, James Durbin, Susan Boyle, and Dan Harmon are just a few of the celebrities who have disclosed an autism diagnosis. David Byrne said he used to have Asperger's but grew out of it. Rumors have long been around that Steven Spielberg is on the spectrum as well as Bill Gates, Albert Einstein, and Wolfgang Amadeus Mozart.

Such theorizing about famous people who are, may be, or may have been autistic began with the intention of making people with autism feel more hopeful about themselves and less stigmatized. The phenomenon has gone far beyond that. Self-diagnosis has come to provide a growing population of individuals who feel different and unable to fit in with a sort of validation for their difference.

Some people who actually have the diagnosis are not comfortable with this. One individual posting on WrongPlanet, for example, refers to self-diagnosis as "the height of arrogance" (Takenaback 2016).

Seinfeld's announcement was found offensive by many parents of children with pervasive autism who felt this rich, successful individual's identification with autism minimized the suffering of the condition. A storm of controversy ensued, and Seinfeld quickly rescinded his statement (Iyengar 2014). Asperger's as an official diagnostic term does not currently exist, but being on the spectrum seems as fashionable as ever. Identification with the social alienation of autism has been described as the "self-diagnosis boom" (Wallace 2014) and continues to be referred to as a "growing phenomenon" (Lewis 2017, p.2410). It goes beyond the technical misstep of taking medical diagnosis into one's own hands and indicates a gray area where people who experience stigma due to their difficulty fitting in need some kind of model to validate their difference from the mainstream.

Autism has become a kind of template for human uniqueness and rallying point for socially excluded others who don't feel they fit in. They may be successful but still feel the pain of outsiderhood. A growing number of people identify themselves with the portion of the spectrum in which the primary suffering is related to stigma. It is not the suffering of more pervasive forms of autism with accompanying movement disorders or epilepsy or verbal ataxia that draws people in. Individuals who feel different from the mainstream, have a hard time relating to others or interacting socially may see themselves, like Seinfeld, on the spectrum of autisticy in some "drawn out" way in order to feel validated for their difference. Few people clamber to be on the "severe" part of the spectrum requiring high levels of support. This is another issue. It involves deeper biological issues involving overt disability that go beyond autisticy, although the humanity of the people is equally potent, full of its own potential, and precious.

Diagnosis, Autisticy, and Stigma

The elimination of the term "Asperger's" has not slowed this trend, and a growing number of people are more than willing to assume a label of autism if it brings an explanation for feeling like a social misfit. There has been more than one individual in my office desperate to find a way to understand their difference from mainstream others by questioning whether they have autism. These people may be considered autistic "cousins," the description used by Autism Network International for people who have "significant social and communication abnormalities" and are "significantly autistic-like" (Sinclair 2005). Most cousins are people with neurological conditions such as attention-deficit/ hyperactivity disorder (ADHD), learning disability, and Tourette's syndrome, although people with mental health conditions such as schizophrenia and obsessive compulsive disorder (OCD) can also join the party. It was meant to make autism forums more inclusive but the term fell out of use. Some think it was replaced by "neurodiversity," and there is debate about which conditions should be included as cousins (grassroots 2016). Others think the term "autistic cousin" unfairly makes autism "the center of the neurodiverse universe" (smoothroundstone, undated). This is not the intention and will be further discussed later.

A framework of autisticy allows many people to make sense of the challenges they have been managing all their lives. Many have these challenges minimized by medical professionals and dismissed as insufficient to label with pathology. They are often told "nothing's wrong with you," the familiar slogan of reverse stigma reported by ASHFA in my study. This may be done as a form of reassurance or a strategy to dismiss a potentially difficult client, but the person's perceived lack of ability or unworthiness to be heard is reinforced. Discussing the contribution of invalidation trauma and how this can make our challenges even more difficult can also be helpful in a great number of cases. I often discuss with my clients how accumulated experiences of invalidation related to abuse, neglect, and stigma as well as other violating assaults on our personhood can cause trauma to build up in our body. This leads to *heightened safety distress*, or defensive physiological escalation triggered by the organism's need for safety (which may or may not be conscious). When over-activated, such safety distress can trigger a cascade of difficulties, including emotional escalation and flustering that worsens whatever challenges of autisticy may already be present. Although this double framework involving invalidation trauma and autisticy has clinical utility as an explanatory scheme, it can be very uncomfortable and disruptive to experience. If we are able to step back and activate recovery practice in response to the associated emotional arousal, which I describe as *NAB it!* later in the book, we can at least partly transform potentially disruptive escalations into immediately deployable actions of self-care such as acceptance, mindfulness, and self-soothing to help us keep from making things worse when they are already difficult.

When seen as challenges added onto the personality, these different packages of difficulty can be understood as variations of autisticy. When the person sees them as part of who they are, the challenges become Autisticy, a self-identified aspect of their identity. Accounting for the role of invalidation and other forms of trauma can provide an even more complete understanding of what has been happening.

Awkwardness

Tashiro (2017) identifies another kind of autistic cousin, namely those who don't obtain test scores high enough to be stamped with a diagnosis of pathology but still experience various social challenges and difficulty fitting in. He calls such individuals "awkward," because he notes the high internet interest in awkwardness over the past few years and considers himself awkward. He feels belonging with a population that seeks understanding of their socially challenged condition but do not fit the criteria of any specific diagnosis. The term "awkward" is innocent, simple, and neutral. It's not so bad being awkward; Tashiro maintains, it can even be "awesome!" Not everyone experiences their difference from others in such a lighthearted way. Isolation, rejection, emotional pain, worsened mental health issues, and difficulty functioning sometimes turn the mild experience of being something of a misfit into a chronic emotional crisis, especially when invalidation trauma is part of the picture. Maybe I am seeing it too exclusively through the eyes of a practicing crisis worker, but even so a framework of autisticy can provide a way to more specifically understand the source of this awkwardness and better grasp the oppressive aspects of these difficulties. Tashiro describes the underlying challenges of autisticy compellingly and greatly humanizes this way of being different.

Awkward people experience many of the challenges of autisticy and much the same stigma as those with a diagnosis of autism. Tashiro does not look closely at this stigma and seems to dismiss it as an inevitable consequence of the human condition. He tells us children start to develop social expectations around the age of ten and, in what may be one of the more unfortunate developments of growing up, "start to judge other kids' social value based on their ability to meet these expectations" (p.6). Even small deviations from these more and more entrenched expectations sound a "primal alarm" that alerts us that the person does not fit our projection of what they should be and conditions a physio-emotional state of defensiveness or safety distress. Tashiro calls this automatic social judgment "an important mechanism" and describes how it is rooted in thousands of years of human evolution. He traces it back to when there were tribes competing for survival. Sensing someone was different set off an alarm and served as a warning they should not be brought into the tribe in the interests of self-preservation.

Sometimes psychologists take statistical trends in behavior, rationalize them, and report them uncritically just because they are "normal." If Tashiro's evolutionary theory is accurate, such social judgment is like a coping mechanism adopted by a three-year-old to survive in a chaotic household that no longer works when they get older. This stigmatizing practice leads to suffering, people falling through the cracks, and people being adversarial. In a world where we depend on each other through trade and connect everywhere through rapid transit and the internet, we limit each other's ability to survive with stigmatizing separation. As a survival mechanism, relying on expectations of sameness is hopelessly outdated. Tashiro goes on to imply that this process of hasty judgment still helps keep us safe by providing a quick way to "evaluate the trustworthiness of people" in populous modern societies (p. 11). Rather than keeping us safe, however, profiling on the basis of such expectations discriminates on the basis of qualities such as social orientation and leads to stigma. Stigma is the social malaise that causes the primary suffering associated with awkwardness and autisticy. Stigma is one of those counterproductive behaviors we can notice ourselves sliding into and make an effort to shift. It is one of many behaviors we can target as an automatic response, re-evaluate, and counter in order to do things differently in the interests of promoting growth, wellness, and relationship.

The personal damage done by stigma is related to processes like stereotyping, exclusion, shunning, intolerance, pointed incivility, and dismissive indifference. It can also be transmitted through more subtle means, such as the arrogant smugness of certain individuals who emanate superiority when people are not inclined towards witty banter or are slow to respond because of executive functioning difficulties. Some people are stigmatized because they are not as "mature" as they are "supposed" to be because of emotional regulation issues, or because they're too absorbed in their own world to notice social dynamics going on around them. Many subtle differences related to autisticy lead to stigma, not just the four core challenges (executive functioning, emotional regulation, self-absorbed local focus, and difficulty accounting for the perspective of others). Other personal qualities can be experienced, for example difficulty with change, an overly literal use of language, inattention to details others think important, unusual sensory issues, and clumsiness. Recognizing these qualities in ourselves and each other can normalize autisticy and reduce stigma. Additional "symptoms" can represent treatable challenges and underlying conditions but do not affect the core human potential we must strive to see in each other. More insidious is stigma whose source is largely invisible. Stigma transactions often take place so subtly they escape identification even as they send a clear stabbing message that *you're not one of us.*

Physiology, Safety Seeking, and Polyvagal Theory

If there is a psycho-neurological framework accounting for the biological correlates of such stigma, it is the polyvagal theory of Stephen Porges (2011). Grounded on a career of research and innumerable publications, polyvagal theory describes the way humans have evolved intricate neural connections that promote self-protection as well as complex social interaction. One of these networks involves several cranial nerves (the vagal system) and forms an integral aspect of the human organism's autonomic safety management system. Complex neurological linkages make the face a central locus for messages of safety and danger, allowing powerful stabilizing cues of de-escalation to be conveyed through tone of voice and expression. As a crisis worker I am only too familiar with the importance of these mechanisms. They are how we help co-regulate each other in times of stress. Caution is necessary though, because messages of damaging invalidation can also be transmitted by the face. Destructive barbs of cruel abuse can be transmitted without a word being spoken.

In everyday social interaction a lack of expected facial cues through expression, eye movement, looks, and even slight muscle movements can trigger safety distress and defensive escalation/withdrawal by activating different branches of the autonomic nervous system via the sensitive neural pathways of the ventral vagal network. Threat and emotional injury can be transmitted intentionally through the face, as in rolling eyes, but subtle safety distress can also be triggered when facial patterns do not align with expected fundamental templates of familiarity. This may be partly why people who are different from the socioconventional majority, like Autistics, experience so much silent stigma.

This part of polyvagal theory provides validation for the emphasis put on the face both in the work of Wolfgang Köhler, the pioneer of social intuition, and Emmanuel Levinas, who developed the ethics of encounter so central in this book. The two would agree that the face, although on one level a "thing among things," also "speaks to me and thereby invites me to a relation" (Levinas 1961/1969, p.198). This does not refer to the face as a collection of physical characteristics but the felt locus of an "epiphany," inviting us into the unique world "opened by the face of the Other" (p.225) and "welcoming" us to an experience of encounter (p.214). According to the ethics of encounter, our "responsibility before a face" as the presence of another being is to be receptive and curious, and allow ourselves to be altered by the impact the other person has on us with their personhood (rather than defining them according to our own concepts, assumptions, conventions, and expectations). All this does not refer to the face as a "mosaic of coloured spots" but as an outpouring of humanity, for example as a shining forth of "friendliness" (Köhler 1947, p.131). All this may sound very mysterious, but polyvagal theory provides a physiological framework to explain how a face can be all this. The deep and far-reaching neural connections of the polyvagal network make the face a beacon of intentionality, a projector of our deepest self, and the most powerful herald of our humanity.

The polyvagal network involves physical, emotional, and communicative centers that come into play before thought and speech intervene, which helps explain why stigma often seems telegraphically sensed and conveyed yet so powerfully associated with physiological escalation, flustering, and confusion. The deep-reaching vagal network connects these cues with breathing and heartrate controls, auditory filters that discern the human voice from background noise, pupil dilation, digestive function, salivation, muscle tone, hormone release, and even immune system functioning as well as additional autonomic mechanisms of biological regulation through the silent primeval intelligence of the brainstem and the intricate connectivity between various neural networks. People can unconsciously learn to read the vulnerability of others based on facial cues connected with their deepest selves, which may explain the mysterious radar that leads some people into relationship after relationship with abusive others despite their best intentions. In alignment with polyvagal theory, this may not be a sign of weakness but a combination of the effectiveness of this biological messaging system, deeply etched scars of trauma and invalidation, and our tendency to misread familiarity for safety.

We have seen how stigma, especially what I have termed telegraphic stigmas of presence, may be enacted in relation to qualities and characteristics not consciously selected or readily identifiable. This is related to what Porges calls *neuroception*. Developed to its current complex form through evolution, this process involves automatic physiological scanning for harm prevention. Polyvagal theory describes in a neurologically detailed way how socially oriented safety cues involving the voice and face, cues that do not depend on conscious volition and are part of what he calls the neurological "social engagement system," constantly register and feed off each other. Familiarity with autism and other forms of autisticy can make us realize how differently these cues can function in diverse types of people at different times. When hard-wired templates of safety are not recognized in the social data provided by these cues, the body mobilizes defensively. Withdrawal, escalation, pre-emptive distancing from the non-conforming party, and stigma result. Bullies and terrorists base aggressive violent behavior on an intentional focus to do harm. Most people have good intentions and can be seen to enact stigma unconsciously in automatic response to these silent precognitive mechanisms of self-protection.

Polyvagal theory is a truly biosocial and socio-organic perspective that deepens and transforms our understanding of social differences and challenges. It leads us not only to a new appreciation for the importance of safety but also to the wisdom of engaging biological systems to promote healing. More and more research has shown that things such as yoga, play, dancing, drumming, and drama can activate healing that medication and psychotherapy cannot access (Porges and Dana 2018). Eye movement desensitization (EMDS), a trauma treatment that engages biological systems through eye movement, has been shown to be more effective than fluoxetine, a popular medication used to help manage the emotional distress associated with PTSD (van der Kolk *et al.* 2007). Direct neurological interventions such as transcranial magnetic stimulation show promise and more established techniques such as neurofeedback (biofeedback based on brain waves) are accumulating more and more evidence of effectiveness. Researcher and trauma ambassador Bessell van der Kolk calls neurofeedback "a new frontier" as a treatment for people "who up until now have been condemned to just make the best of feeling chronically fearful, unfocused, and disengaged" (2018, p.xvii). All this opens up new options for people whose deep-set trauma causes escalation, withdrawal, and distress that conventional practitioners often have trouble addressing. These treatments can also be used to improve outcomes in cases involving conditions such as autism and ADHD, preferably as part of a balanced approach to greater wellbeing.

The vagal network with its deep-reaching tentacles of neural sensitivity provides a path from the depths of our physiology to conscious awareness. Signals from the neural network within is how messages of intention and threat can be read on the face. It may also be the raw physiological source of that quiet little voice of intuition which we are all in various stages of learning to work with, listen to, and evaluate. This gives us raw inner material to respond to as we teach ourselves to listen to the signals and escalations triggered within and learn to consciously respond in ways that do not promote stigma and calm the inner storm safety distress can arouse. Fortunate especially for those of us who love to think, the vagal network also incorporates a feedback loop from conscious awareness back to the physiological roots of the organism. Porges might describe the framework of self-recovery discussed in Chapters 8–10 as a system of "top down" mechanisms under the volitional control of regulation pathways accessible to conscious awareness through the vagal network. The bodily felt impact emerging from the socially informed neurological patterns of escalation described by Porges are the very physical sensations we practice being mindful of alerting us to the need for self-intervention. Responding consciously to these signals is how we can start to manage the escalation of trauma activation as well as counter the safety distress that often leads to stigma. Physiological escalation becomes an alert to activate our toolbox of trauma and safety distress strategies. This helps us de-escalate ourselves not only to prevent further alienating others with our emotional outbursts but also to allow us to step back and counter the defensive activation that often triggers us to stigmatize others. Life is a constant dance to navigate the differences between us as we manage the reactions arising within us.

Chapter 4

INTERSECTING TRAUMAS OF DIFFERENCE

The stigma being explored in this book cuts across cultures, racial diversity, appearance, gender, sexual preference, spiritual orientation, physical disability, socio-economic barriers, and mental health issues. My own stigma as ASHFA falls into this category, and for most of my life was not associated with any diagnosis. I did not understand it at all. Many people feel this kind of undefined and confusing stigma in their lives. Others are able to associate the stigma they experience with a specific diagnosis. Many conditions involve exaggerated combinations of autisticy as well as unique symptoms. These are subject to ongoing organization and categorization in psychiatric manuals such as the DSM, although it is important to note these categories do not represent specifically identified physiological illnesses but clusters of characteristic mental health challenges that sometimes get out of control. One of the few specifically identified causative factors known to be associated with such conditions is trauma. What this book refers to as invalidation trauma can be associated with what John Bowlby articulated as the disorganization of emotional attachment (Reisz, Duschinsky, and Siegel, 2018). Such threats to the safety and security of growing children due to a lack of consistently supportive caregiver attention have been shown to better predict extreme symptoms of emotional dysregulation and mental health distress in adults than the severity of various other forms of abuse (van der Kolk, Perry, and Herman, 1991). This speaks volumes about the importance of respect, non-judgment, and nourishing interaction when it comes to human wellbeing.

Many people who experience the lasting impact of invalidation trauma may have no "measurable pathology" to conventionally categorize. They may refuse to collude with the medical establishment by declining diagnosis altogether but their relationships and levels of happiness may suffer greatly. Those with autisticy, or differing combinations of challenge due to difficulties with executive functioning, emotional regulation, self-absorbed local focus, and taking account of other people's perspectives not only have their challenges provoked by invalidation trauma but tend to be further invalidated because of their challenges. The resulting unconventional social orientations and patterns of functioning can result in very troublesome social relations. Autisticy seen in this way is not a specific disorder but a social construct, a formation of self-in-society that provides a framework for better understanding the many people who deal with these challenges and how different forms of invalidating relations like stigma come into play. Autisticy has its own wide spectrum that includes patterns of alienation, social marginalization, and suffering due to social judgment.

Those of us who manage the burden of stigma related to autisticy often suffer additional invalidation because of the labelling diagnosis involves. Still, it is our behavior, communication and quality of presence that brings the most poignant stigma. In other words, it is our behavior, communication, and quality of presence that brings the most poignant stigma. We are judged, dismissed, marginalized, rejected, and stereotyped because our actions do not conform to conventional standards and our social value is diminished accordingly. Autism is but one specific diagnosis associated with autisticy and the only one I experience directly myself. As a counselor I see the same quality of stigma being experienced by people with various diagnostic labels who report some or all of the key challenges of autisticy. Just as frequently, such people have no diagnostic label at all. If the stigma cannot be explained by differences in appearance, orientation, or other identifiable factors people will start blaming themselves. These are the ones most desperate to find out why they experience stigma and who seek most diligently to better understand what makes them different.

I refer to these stigma-producing characteristics of personhood as autisticy not to put autism on a pedestal as a medical super-condition, but because much of the research done in this area has been related to efforts to explain autism, which is a highly diverse and enigmatic condition not only increasing in occurrence but resonating deeply with people. It was in the course of autism research that many of these challenges were identified and explored. It has only been relatively recently that the role of trauma has been explored as a factor in mental health. Trauma can make the challenges of autisticy worse and cause great emotional suffering, yet it may be the most neglected variable of all.

Intersecting stigmas are experienced when an individual possesses more than one set of attributes or belongs to more than one group that is stigmatized by society. A few intersecting stigmas in addition to a diagnosis of autism were represented by the participants in my study. One had Tourette's syndrome. This participant spoke of the frustration of blurting out in public, but did not speak of the stigma he experienced as coming from two sources. He did not report that Tourette's added to his load of stigma. Perhaps this is because he didn't know what it would be like not to have this condition, but his report of only a single unified experience of stigma tends to go against the "double jeopardy" model of intersecting oppression. This theory holds that individuals who experience more than one form of oppression or stigma experience it cumulatively (Purdie-Vaughns and Eibach 2008, p.378). According to this, the above participant would feel both the stigma of Asperger's and the stigma of Tourette's and hence a resulting increase in stigma. The theory could still apply; perhaps the participant does feel increased stigma but isn't aware of it. This would be difficult and of questionable utility to measure. The cumulative theory is hard to prove and may have limited application.

Gender

One participant was female. Although she did not report stigma associated with her gender, there are definitely gender-related issues involved that complicate the experience of ASHFA. Females may be targeted more profoundly than men with the stigma of autistic difference even as their condition becomes harder to recognize because male presentations of ASHFA dominate common understanding and diagnostic manuals. Asperger's is thought to occur predominantly in males, but females may be under-identified. The socially challenging aspects of ASHFA may be more pronounced in men since male stereotypes often involve detached silence (as in the much romanticized "strong, silent type"). Men can lapse more easily into this. Women have more complex social demands placed on them and are socialized almost from birth to be relationship-oriented. They are supposed to be nurturing, empathetic, and "lady-like." This brings unwelcome pressure to demonstrate female "social skills" that puts them more at odds with convention than male ASHFA. The resulting efforts to compensate for their natural orientation can create intense pressure to conform even as it camouflages their condition. Female ASHFA feel "doubly challenged" (Faherty 2016, p.10). They may be resentful of ASHFA males who can more easily get away with things like self-absorbed withdrawal, neglecting their appearance, and messy handwriting. Stigma helps shape male and female ASHFA with different profiles of expectation.

Young adults are under bewildering pressure to conform to peer pressure at school (Wiseman 2013, 2016). It is hard enough for any youth, but ASHFA hardly stand a chance to live up to the complex demands of conventional social politics. Iland (2016) describes how teenage girls size each other up at a glance to evaluate worthiness hinging on status. If we outgrew this social profiling based on dominant expectations, stigma would only be a high school problem. With less experience, maturity, and confidence, kids have few resources to put up conformity resistance. Despite rebellious behavior, youth can only benefit from a role model that values selfhood and relationship rather than valorizing social expectation. Not knowing what else to do, we try to help them "appear mainstream" by providing the latest styles and gadgets. Girls may be more susceptible to this pressure than boys, especially ASHFA desperate to escape the social circus.

The unconventional behaviors of female ASHFA may amplify the disempowering forces of male dominance towards them. They may be further marginalized because of the additional element of diversity ASHFA represents. Women are already more vulnerable than men in a male-dominated social structure and marginalizing autistic differences in their behavior can add to this vulnerability. The stigma of being regarded as an object for pleasure may lead some exploitive dominant others to read gaze avoidance, for example, as a sign of coy submissiveness no matter how unwelcome their scrutiny. Gaze avoidance is characteristic of Autisticy but also shame and at times sexual politics. Straight men are typically oblivious to all this, and it must be noted that many of these comments apply equally to LGBTQ (lesbian, gay, bisexual, transgender, queer) as well as other "non-binary" individuals not fitting within traditional male/female categories. These populations are typically marginalized and face great challenges related to stigma in society. Still, in addition to unique safety issues, this creates special unique challenges for differently gendered ASHFA that can make it especially difficult to function "in a world that can be so cruel to people who are different" (Willey, 2012, p.21). Women, for example, are "supposed" to have a better handle on their social cues and more often find themselves the reluctant focus of judgmental attention.

Approval-seeking behaviors to compensate for accumulated invalidation may lure female ASFHA dangerously close to sexual manipulators interested in furthering their own agenda rather than appreciating uniqueness. This does not make female ASHFA weak. Women in female ASHFA support groups consistently report "the desire to be respected as an individual and a woman" (p.14). The stigma they experience has a quality of its own that requires attentive understanding and special strategies to help convey the strength and value of the person often scrambling to manage the stigmatizing expectations of dominant others. Parents and teachers need to address the resulting challenges and vulnerabilities with understanding, education, and frank discussion.

Gay People and People Living with HIV

One participant was gay and diagnosed HIV positive. This participant clearly distinguished different sources of stigma. There is much more literature on stigma experienced by both these populations than autism (Herek 1996). Still, this participant stated clearly that "although living with HIV is considered a disability, I would say it's been less debilitating than autism." He went on to say that "even above HIV, I would say Asperger's makes me feel more different":

> There seems to be a hierarchy. Being gay is a little bit more acceptable than being HIV positive, and Asperger's, well autism is probably at the bottom of the pile. Being gay was no problem for me; I came out when I was 16. I told everybody and had no regrets. I knew the skinheads were going to spit at me every time I

went out but I didn't care. Becoming HIV positive, well, I've always been out about it. I've always advocated for condom use and people knowing my story. But Asperger's is really hard to explain.

The participant said autism is the most pervasive and intense source of stigma for him. He went on to say that part of the reason for this is that he finds it hard to explain this source of difference even to himself. The participant is active as an organizer in the PHA community (persons living with HIV/Aids), and says, "I feel that in the HIV community my every word is judged…they're always trying to put me in a box and figure out what's wrong with me." He says he has been referred to as "challenging," the "social critic," and the "angry PHA." He reports that "people don't answer my emails." He says, "When I want to talk about stigma and discrimination, they shut me down." Purdie-Vaughns and Eibach (2008) describe a model of intersectional invisibility in which group members belonging to other marginalized groups do not fit the "prototype" of the main group and are not fully recognized, which "relegates them into an acute position of social invisibility" (p.381). This situation would only be aggravated by the socially challenging nature of the participant's Autistic nature.

The participant's experience of stigma also seems to match the cumulative model in that his "multiple subordinate group identities" result in a reported experience of more intense stigma (p.378). Maybe this is because his sources of stigma are more distinct than the participant with Tourette's. The stigma of autism and being gay are both related intimately to personhood, but autism results in stigmatized social interactions and generates a daily treadmill of micro-stigma with socioconventional others. HIV, meanwhile, brings stigma primarily in contexts where people are aware he has this diagnostic label. Quinn and Chaudoir (2009) would count HIV as a "concealable" stigmatizing condition and note this is a "vastly understudied" area compared to stigmas based on overtly visible features of difference (p.634). The chronic stigma of presence associated with autisticy is even less understood. Their research provides quantitative confirmation that the more central a stigmatized condition is to a person's identity and the more significance a person attaches to this aspect of their personhood the greater potential stigma distress there will be. They also found, just as predictably, that negative perceptions of the stigmatized condition by society are related to high levels of stigma distress.

What these authors call *anticipated* stigma refers to how much stigma a person expects to experience if they disclose their stigmatized condition, which for autism means revealing their diagnosis. The participants in my study reported that this was only remotely relevant to the stigma they felt in their daily lives. Whatever anxiety is associated with anticipated stigma comes largely from the direct experience of being stigmatized, or being on the receiving end of enacted stigma. Anticipating stigma is not only related to potential disclosure or discovery of their diagnosis for ASHFA, it can happen just by entering an environment pressurized by socioconventional expectations.

Race

The harsh and often violent oppression experienced by people who are shades of color is recorded in history. Dominant narratives and defensive, intolerant, often hateful behaviors serve to alienate and isolate these groups intergenerationally. The humanity of many individuals, families, and communities is undermined through no fault of their own. People are regarded as inferior on the basis of not being the same and dominant White contexts of sameness are taken as license to enact cruelly damaging atrocities. More subtle but equally damaging invalidation based squarely on the basis of being different happens routinely. The intersection of autisticy and color is not well studied and is complicated because of the multiple dimensions of lived stigma involved for both. The interplay of color and autisticy share combined sources of invalidation including assumption, stereotype, and hurtful reactivity. Subtle sociophenomenal differences may reinforce the predominant stigma and add a unique dimension of shame.

All the participants in my research were White, and race was not explored as a form of intersecting oppression in the study. Turning to the internet for supplemental information, I found an interesting pair of interviews with Mike Buckholz, a Black man who is autistic and works as a musician. He founded Aid for Autistic Children, a program providing debt relief to families touched by autism with the aim of increasing quality of life. Buckholtz refers to himself as "an Invisible," by which he means adult ASHFA (2012). He also declared he was "proud to be an Autistic POC" (person of color) and felt "unique" rather than "broken" on the basis of his autisticy (2017). Identified autistic as an adult at the age of 43, Buckholtz said "that I wasn't crazy or losing my mind was an important discovery" when he was given the diagnosis. It is noteworthy that he reported how an autism diagnosis so clearly validated the autistic portion of his marginalization over and above the stigma related to color despite the latter's more visible impact. Buckholtz reported that prejudice attached to being Black is "ten times worse" than autism, and counted it lucky there is so little media coverage of Black autistics, so they don't have to deal with this stigma on top of their already heavy load. He said lack of attention to this issue creates a perception that "the majority of Black people must be…'normal'," which he said helps them "go about their business."

Media play a role maintaining the invalidation of racism. I was watching the news with my morning coffee one day when there was a story about a young woman being stabbed. Despite the fact that my autism is supposed to make me unable to appreciate social cues, the way the reporter described the suspect disturbed me. They did not simply convey objective information as in "a Black male was sought in the crime." People will draw their own conclusions based on the most objective information, but the way she said it struck me as inflammatory. It wasn't that she used words that could get her fired for blatant racism. Yet the way she said, "a *Black man* did it," pointed blame in a shaming manner and seemed to emphasize that Black men were dangerous. I could clearly distinguish an undermining generalization in her message and sense the propaganda leaking into culture. Even if not grounded in a conscious intent to do harm but emerging from fear and/or stereotyped assumption, it is possible to catch a glimmer of the invalidating impact of such marginalizing cues.

Unless it is blatantly oppressive, the problem is sometimes putting a finger on stigmatizing invalidation. I can only speak for myself as ASHFA, but dominant mainstream others often seem to want proof it is even happening. Not everything can be reduced to concrete terms. Requiring proof can make invalidation doubly oppressive in an attempt to discuss stigma. When skeptics need to be convinced, they demand clear evidence of things that may be difficult to articulate, especially during heated moments. Recognizing the telegraphic aspect of stigma may curtail deniability in the renegotiation of social exclusion. Being receptive to the experience of others and open to exploring their lived reality is infinitely more effective than adversarial disavowal requiring "proof." It is the kind of humility demanded by an ethics of encounter in which we make ourselves deliberately receptive to the experience of others and practice respect by listening curiously. This helps us take ownership of the stigmatizing invalidation we may unintentionally convey to different and unfamiliar people.

A *Huffington Post* blog co-authored by a doctor (Martin and Vahabzadeh 2014) says limited research has shown Black children tend to be diagnosed later than those in the dominant White population and pointed specifically to a "void in the scientific literature" in this area. A survey paper on the intersection of autism and First Nations (Lindblom 2014) also talks about lack of resources and paucity of research, maintaining that Aboriginal children are under-diagnosed only partly because of poor access to healthcare resources. The author also cites statistics indicating Aboriginal children are more likely to be misdiagnosed with conditions such as fetal alcohol syndrome disorders (FASD) and intellectual disability due to a combination of narrow stereotypes and culturally inappropriate diagnostic tools. The author argues that this lack of access is strongly related to the impact of colonization and historical oppression (a case more extensively made elsewhere, e.g. Smith 2005; Talaga 2017). To illustrate this resource allocation problem for autistics who also belong to racially stigmatized groups, a paper written from an Australian Indigenous perspective describes how autism was misdiagnosed as schizophrenia in 13 out of 14 re-evaluated cases (Roy and Balaratnasingam 2010). Travers and Krezmien (in press) point to extensive literature showing that Autistics are under-identified in terms of formal diagnosis among racially diverse groups. Their own research in this area demonstrates this and leads them to caution decision-makers not to worsen the problem with definitions, policies, and reporting strategies that lead to further social injustice in this area.

In Canada, one family had to move from their home to a big city further south in order to access resources for their autistic daughter. The father initiated a petition asking the government to better address autisticy in Aboriginal communities (Robertson 2017). The petition got the required number of signatures to be formally addressed by Parliament. The government's response acknowledged the problem and discussed Jordan's Principle: Child First Initiative passed in 2016 (an act expediting medical expenses through the federal government after the unfortunate death of an Aboriginal child due to jurisdictional squabbling). They said access to medical resources should be largely improved by this legislation. They also said the government is working to create a National Autism Spectrum Disorder Surveillance System (NASS) to collect statistics, facilitate research, and promote informed policy in this area. These measures should help to relieve the burden of oppression felt by Aboriginal people in Canada, although more rigorous initiatives to deal with stigma and better mechanisms of accountability are called for around the world. When Autistic personhood and other forms of racially and historically charged stigmatized presence are combined, invalidation assumes new dimensions, calling for further research to explore and address this.

Stigma and Trauma

Invalidating events are threats to our humanity and the associated trauma is stored as easily triggered templates of peril in the body. When activated, this accumulated trauma can itself be a source of stigma. For example, when an autistic person's trauma is activated their "autistic behaviors" may increase, leading to more concentrated stigma. If I tend to rock under stress and an adverse event triggers accumulated invalidation, I may begin rocking furiously for no apparent reason. I may experience emotional arousal, find it unusually hard to step outside self-absorption, and find it doubly challenging to interact with others. This goes for anyone with the general challenges of autisticy. When a person with ADHD, for example, experiences stigma activation, their already precarious executive functioning may become even more scattered. The stigma they experience increases because they are less able to do things like take direction, stay focused, and organize themselves to complete tasks.

People who have experienced developmental trauma often experience this kind of activation. There may be no visible or medically diagnosable reason for their frequent mood swings and emotional escalations, which can lead them to be stigmatized as weak, unstable, troublesome, or "less-than." This stigmatization adds to the trauma of invalidation accumulating in the body, making escalations worse and adding still more to their difficulties. A way to begin breaking this cycle is to take the trauma at the root of these escalations seriously in order to acknowledge the depth of a person's suffering. This can help them better understand their predicament, feel much needed validation at the level of their trauma, and begin to heal.

Although my study focused on Autistic participants including myself, stigma and trauma go far beyond the specific diagnosis of autism and reach into the wider spectrum of autisticy itself and the often complex dynamics of various mental health conditions. Many of these conditions may take root through invalidation trauma, so much so that one trauma practitioner was overheard saying that the number of conditions in the DSM would shrink exponentially if the full role of trauma was acknowledged (Walker 2013). So much of what is currently identified in terms of discrete "disorders" involves the intertwining of trauma and invalidation, it would be useful for clinicians and helpful for people to better understand their suffering if a condition called something like complex trauma syndrome was included in the diagnostic manual.

Anxiety

Anxiety is not just a *co-occurring* mental health issue or intersecting source of stigma. It is part of the inherently complex nature of autisticy itself. One CLAWHS writer describes the depth of his anxiety and proposes that it "may be a key to solving the riddle of autism" (Kedar 2012, p.60). This inherent anxiety could be due to stigma, lack of belonging, social confusion, or a fragile sensitivity in the person's constitution that makes them vulnerable. In any case, autisticy and anxiety go hand in hand. I experienced lots of dissociation, awkwardness, and uncertainty as a child and young man that I blamed on autisticy when I found out I had Asperger's. Now I wonder how much of it was due to anxiety and the impact of stigma. I was totally anxious all the time as a youth. Now I'm only partly anxious half the time. Is this because an "anxiety disorder" is in remission, or am I less anxious now because I'm better able to manage my Autistic self? Disentangling these sources of stigma and distress may be hopeless because they are thoroughly intertwined.

A recent study (Johnston and Iarocci 2017) was designed to find out whether anxiety and depression were related to social competence for adolescent ASHFA. As expected, they found that high levels of anxiety and depression were related to diminished social functioning. They also found anxiety and depression to be positively correlated with the intensity of autistic symptoms (higher levels of one were related to higher levels of the other). In a convenience sample made up of volunteers from the organization's various programs, 22 percent were diagnosed with co-occurring ADHD, 1 percent with OCD, 9 percent with anxiety, and 3 percent with mood disorder. When tests were administered to measure anxiety and depression, much higher rates of co-occurrence were found. Thirty-four percent had diagnosable levels of anxiety, and 48 percent had significant depression. These higher numbers may indicate a lack of rigor identifying co-occurring conditions. There may be a tendency to let autism be an explanation for everything. The study reinforces the vicious cycle that happens when various challenges make social interaction difficult, stigma leads to further isolation, and isolation deepens our challenges which leads to worsening symptoms and even greater stigma.

The female participant in my study reported that the stigma of her autism was eclipsed by the stigma she attributed to anxiety. The participant was formally diagnosed with general and social anxiety three years before the research but reported suffering from anxiety her whole life. She had also been subject to stigma associated with autism, but insisted "the problem is more my anxiety...I don't mind having Asperger's, it's the anxiety that's bad. That's the only thing I would get rid of." She acknowledged her Asperger's and said, "I don't function as well as people think and that's why I experience such high anxiety." When uncomfortable in social situations it is the anxiety she tries to cover up, anxiety where she feels the weight of stigma. "I hide my anxiety," she says, "when I don't understand something." As with the other participants, it is behaviors that don't conform to socioconventional expectations she associates with stigma rather than diagnostic labels. However, for her, the stigma associated with Asperger's is minimal compared to the symptoms of anxiety. "I get judged because of my anxiety," she says, "I don't think it's the Asperger's." She acknowledges that "Asperger's does cause some of the anxiety with the communication problems and stuff like that, but it's the anxiety that's the main problem." Anxiety for this participant is the primary source of stigma she experiences because it is most associated with her discomfort and the behavioral awkwardness she is so conscious of. Again, she does not feel stigma from two qualitatively distinct sources. Rather, she only reports experiencing stigma from a single source, the overpowering source of intertwined sources, and for her this is anxiety. The stigma of anxiety and the stigma of autisticy merge into each other and can be hard to distinguish. Both can be related to social flustering, awkwardness, averted gaze, and social avoidance. The relationship between them is complex and perhaps not as separable as this client feels.

One study (Capriola, Maddox, and White 2017) sought to explore whether the fear of being judged was different for autistic and socioconventional people (who they called *typically developing* or TD). Fear of evaluation is a cornerstone of social anxiety, and many of the participants had various levels of reported social anxiety although none were actually seeking treatment for this. The study employed self-report tests measuring different aspects of social functioning as well as fear of negative evaluation. Understandably, scores indicated greater difficulty with social communication and social motivation for autistics than socioconventionals across adolescent and adult participants. Answers on the fear of negative evaluation test were roughly the same for all and test responses did not differ significantly in this area. Eleven of the 12 questions were answered similarly by both groups, including "I am afraid others will not approve of me." Insecurity in this fundamental regard seems to have been evenly distributed between all participants. Only one question got statistically significant different results between the autistic and socioconventional groups. Seventy-three percent of autistics responded "yes" to the question "I often worry that I will do or say the wrong thing" compared to 52 percent of typically developing peers. This is understandable given the stigma autistic individuals experience for doing things in unconventional ways that dominant culture deems wrong or gets frustrated by. This chronic aversive response to our behavior causes reasonable social anxiety in autistics rather than necessarily reflecting higher rates of anxiety "disorder." It also conditions worry about how our behavior will be received by dominant socioconventional others.

Interestingly, the only other question that approached a statistically significant different response between the two groups was "I am afraid people will find fault with me." Forty-one percent of autistics endorsed this question while 59 percent of socioconventional people reported that such thinking was characteristic of them. More socioconventionals had worried thoughts, not about doing the wrong thing but about being found at fault for things. Does this mean autistics may be slightly more confident in themselves? After all, they deal with the challenges of being a minority every day and it makes sense that they may develop higher levels of resilience to personal insecurity. Maybe having to cope with stigma provides a protective inoculation against routine threats to self-esteem.

Anxiety is very treatable. Useful interventions not only address the uncomfortable escalation of nervousness but help reconnect us with the calm non-judgmental stillness underlying our best responses to life. We all experience rationalizations motivated by anxious safety distress, risk avoidance, and often unconscious, sometimes desperate, comfort seeking. When we give these power, which is easy to do when we are escalated by the distress of anxiety, we can undermine ourselves by not taking care of ourselves in the moment. We don't do what we know is in our best interests because we see nothing but potential problems. We block actions that would be in line with what we know would best nourish us or help us move forward because we listen to the anxious chatter of racing thoughts rather than our higher wisdom. If interventions are conducted with sensitivity to the whole person and what they are coping with, rather than imposing strategies designed primarily for statistically average socioconventional people, we can learn anxiety management strategies which, if we remember to put them into practice, can make life more livable.

Debilitating anxiety may seem to sneak up on us, coming on suddenly with paralyzing results. Mindful awareness may alert us that anxiety is coming so we can perform self-intervention before we get lost in panic. Tell-tale signs of escalation include tightness in our muscles and increasingly loud, rapid heartbeat. Breathing becomes faster and shallower. Our face may turn red, fingers and toes may tingle. We may start sweating and feel hot, cold, or shaky. Thinking can become rigid; our ability to flow in the moment is increasingly impaired. Our sense of time becomes distorted and we may feel our suffering will never end. Self-recovery is much more effective when we respond to these signals than lingering in denial as panic sets in. Being able to locate where we feel the associated discomfort in our bodies is a crucial skill. Finding a way to work towards calmness is paramount so our frontal lobes stay online and we retain some sense of control. For many of us who live with the challenges of autisticy and related stigma, anxiety management becomes a familiar way of life to remain functional and preserve wellbeing.

OCD

OCD is another mental health condition that is often diagnosed concurrently in autistic people. OCD used to be categorized in the DSM as anxiety but now appears in a new section just for obsessive compulsive disorders. Like anxiety, the challenges of OCD can be an intertwined part of autisticy (Ruzzano, Borsboom, and Geurts 2015). OCD tendencies can be a dimension of challenge for any of us, especially those who identify with the challenges of autisticy. According to the DSM-5 (American Psychiatric Association 2013), obsessive compulsive *disorder* is distressing for the person and diagnosed when someone spends at least an hour a day on obsessions and compulsions. These compulsions may involve repetitive behaviors (like hand-washing or double-checking), mental acts such as praying, counting, and word repetition, or finding comfort in furious redundant activity. Almost any behavior can become the focus of obsessive attention, from making sure there are no changes in the smoothness of our skin to finding the perfect position to sleep in. We may need to be excessively early for appointments or always have to buy the same brand of products in order to relax. We may also have intrusive thoughts about potentially unpleasant possibilities that can lead us to become more and more escalated. We may fight ourselves to prevent acting out our thoughts or make desperate efforts to neutralize them. At such times being able to notice such thoughts simply *as* thoughts, rather than attending to them as disturbing realities, can be empowering and get us back on track. Noticing is the crucial first step of the self-recovery.

Compulsive acts are often thought to be a self-defense mechanism that helps anxious people maintain a sense of control over their environment. Obsessive thoughts may be due to an exaggerated focus on inner processes that become escalated by the attention we put on them. Underlying both is often a safety-seeking motive. Hand-washing and double-checking may begin as efforts to avoid disease or make sure our dwelling remains inviolate. Hoarding, a related obsessive compulsive condition, begins with efforts to ensure an amply supplied future. Unreasonable jealousy can be rooted in attempts to maintain safety and is often aggravated by a history of invalidation trauma. All these efforts can get out of control and become entrenched as ingrained neurological habits that undermine the very safety these mechanisms were originated to protect. Hand-washing may become so prevalent it removes the protective layer of our skin and creates vulnerability to infection. Hoarding may result in a cluttered fire hazard. Obsessive behavior can take so much of our attention it distracts us from life and quality interaction with others. Obsessive fidelity scanning can end relationships or keep them from deepening into the kind of togetherness we seek. Obsessive thoughts about how to best keep a job or create a good impression may result in alienating others and getting us fired or rendering us unable to work with people at all. Such patterns insert themselves below the level of rational volition and become a neurological reflex originating in safety distress. Addressing this original safety impulse in healthy ways that promote forward-moving growth is critical. We may not see the need for such safety seeking, but it is the person's perspective that informs and gives us access to their vulnerability.

Curious exploration and attention can pre-empt troublesome patterns from emerging. Once ingrained, it takes great effort to break the habit. Medication may be required to function and be able to do the necessary work. At the same time, we can all find ourselves becoming attached to safety behaviors that aren't helping. Noticing when we begin to focus on racing thoughts and desperate attempts to control is key. Only when we notice it happening can we implement strategies of self-recovery. Then we can make an effort to shift into a space where we allow experience to unfold rather than over-controlling and missing things. We can't function at our best or be responsive when we are indulging in a narrow focus on selected details.

Obsessive compulsive *personality disorder* involves a preoccupation with order, perfection, and control at the expense of flexible responsiveness, social flow, and open-minded interaction. It includes a preoccupation with details, lists, rules, order, and schedules to the point where the meaningful sense of activities is lost in details. Who hasn't had this experience or known someone who becomes like this on occasion? As a personality disorder, these tendencies become tightly interwoven with the person's personality and may be perceived as part of who they are. Such patterns can originate in response to safety distress as ways of maintaining a protective environment. Their entrenchment goes even deeper than those of obsessive compulsive disorder, becoming lodged often from an early age as indistinguishable from a person's personality. Such patterns become unassailable aspects of the person's way of being and managing them is very challenging.

Yet noticing these tendencies in ourselves can help us function more smoothly with others.

People with OCD can be "mercilessly self-critical" (American Psychiatric Association 2013, p.679). This is not just because they can be hard on themselves, but because of their tendency to escalate thoughts to catastrophic proportions with intense and obsessive focus. Anyone can find themselves feeding obsessive compulsive patterns. Is anyone immune from being too hard on themselves? Who hasn't known someone who could turn play into a structured production with excessive pressure to perform, inflexibly appealing to rules or making them up as they go to promote winning at all costs? This is a description of typically OCD behavior. Have you ever been frustrated with someone for spoiling a perfectly good adventure by insisting on predictability and stubbornly resisting any change to their expectations? This is another OCD characteristic. We must all at times exercise mindful attention to the emerging inflexibility and habit-forming impulses of OCD. People with autism almost always deal with particularly strong OCD impulses. When they become impediments to functioning in their own right, OCD may be given as an additional diagnosis. The origins of these impulses are often rooted in safety distress. Sometimes, particularly in relation to autisticy, they can also result from the relief-seeking pursuit of comfort, like pulling a blanket over our heads for at least an illusion of protection. Immersion on the computer or other hyper-focused isolated activity can be like this, as is trichotillomania (hair-pulling) and excoriation (skin-picking).

One paper (Wakabayashi, Baron-Cohen, and Ashwin 2012) notes how the traits of OCD, autism, and schizophrenia are often connected. They cite past studies and discuss some of the shared challenges involved. Their own study further investigates these using tests measuring the degree to which certain challenges of autisticy are shared by these conditions. They found some weakly correlated challenges including executive functioning impairment, anxiety around social interaction, and social isolation, but conclude the percentage of people with autism who show traits of OCD and schizophrenia "at a diagnostic level is very small" (p.724). Notwithstanding complicated problems with differential diagnosis, this finding could be used as evidence that the relation between the conditions is not significant. However, the study demonstrates a weakness shared by many research projects. First, it depends exclusively on statistical analysis to draw its conclusions, already removing it from human significance. Further isolating it from the complex dynamics faced by those who live with these challenges is the sample used to obtain the data. It does not represent a diversity of people who identify with these difficulties but university students taking introductory psychology who were administered the tests in class. In this particular study, researchers were investigating character traits with tests designed to identify specific types, which they differentiated successfully in a student population rather than uncovering how these characteristic challenges relate to and bleed into each other. Again, qualitative research exploring the experience of people actually living with the challenges being studied can only be neglected at the peril of our understanding.

To be considered pathology of diagnosable interest, these characteristics must cause significant impairment in functioning. To be considered challenges needing to be addressed, managed, and compensated for, we only need to recognize them in ourselves. In the language of the self-recovery framework discussed in Part C, we can *NAB* such tendencies when we see them and exercise appropriate efforts to bring ourselves into line with who we want to be and/or what orientation would help us function better or lead to more fulfilling relationships. Those of us with autisticy are no different, although our OCD characteristics and other challenges may be greater. Some of us may need extra help developing insight to motivate these efforts.

Depression

One mental health condition that is more like an external issue than an inherent element of autisticy is depression. It's not that depression is less common as a co-occurring issue with autism than anxiety or OCD. Depression is reported by up to 70 percent of Autistic individuals, while OCD has been estimated to co-occur as a distinct diagnosis in 17 percent of autistics (Sizoo and Kuiper 2017). The co-occurrence of diagnosed anxiety disorder has been estimated to be 40 percent (Van Steensel, Bogels, and Perrin 2011). These numbers may not represent the full extent and complexity of the inter-relationships. Anxiety and OCD are more difficult to disentangle from autism than depression. Sadness and low motivation are easier to make out as distinct issues in an Autistic character than the anxious fretting and obsessive self-absorption so often an intrinsic part of autisticy. This makes anxiety and

OCD harder to diagnose as distinct conditions. Their presence must be more intense in an autistic person than a socioconventional one to make separate diagnosis clear. Depression stands out distinctly when it is a problem for both kinds of people. Again, at least as important as diagnosis is recognizing patterns of challenge in ourselves and responding with compassionately appropriate, firm but gentle self-care and recovery strategies.

Depression and autisticy can be intertwined in various ways. The stigma, lack of belonging, isolation, and failure to thrive often associated with autisticy can lead to depression, while the lack of motivation depression brings can exacerbate the challenges of autisticy. Self-absorption increases as our emotional pain overwhelms us. Difficulty stepping back and seeing the bigger picture, including the potentially refreshing perspective of other minds, diminishes with drained vitality. It may feel like we can't spare any energy for emotional regulation. The ability of rational evaluation that allows us to set potentially therapeutic priorities becomes impaired with the diversion of energy from executive functioning to barely managing the demands of physical coping. It all becomes a difficult cycle to break out of.

The stigma attached to depression is often like the stigma attached to illness, which a person contracts as a temporary affliction rather than a familiar element of their being. At the same time, some people experience depression as part of who they are. They may not remember the last time they were happy. The stigma of depression perpetuated by those who don't understand the depths of blackness it can cause or the darkness of soul it can lead to can be painful. The person may be seen as weak. Some might think they should be able to "just snap out of it." It's not so easy, as anyone who has experienced it can attest. We are very vulnerable in this state, and the more esteem we have for the people who stigmatize us the more their stigma can hurt us.

One client said depression was like seeing the world through "shit colored glasses" in which everything looks negative and hopeless. Vitality is sapped. Energy is diminished. We may lapse into a lethargic void that takes super-human effort to start coming out of, like rising out of bed when we haven't slept for a week and can't imagine exerting one more ounce of energy. Some kinds of fatigue are the result of depletion and require rest, but the fatigue associated with depression can be more like a loss of connection with vital energy that needs renewal. Sometimes this can only be generated with effort, not unlike cranking an old car engine. It isn't easy when every cell of your body is weary with despair. We're not talking about some lazy mental attitude that needs adjustment, but a deeply rooted physical experience that requires compassionate support and appropriate treatment.

People experiencing this challenge need fortifying validation, not platitudes and judgment. At the same time, excessive encouragement of the perky variety can trigger greater depression when the person feels pressure to act happy and respond. Sensitivity to the nature of a person's unique needs, asking them what they need and the kind of help they would appreciate is preferable to imposing judgments and expected standards. Complicating the situation, the depressed person may tell us to go away, illustrating that the easiest way to cope at such times is to hide away and not have to face or do anything. At such times gentle persistence may be called for, offering to do things with them they might possibly be able to handle or used to enjoy when they were more of themselves. Offering to make them soup which they can take or leave may also help. We tend to under-nourish ourselves at such times, but this only makes us further vulnerable to the ravages of emotional emptiness.

Sometimes a person may feel such gloom the only option feels like suicide. It does not cause harm to talk about this even though it can be difficult. Be genuinely curious and don't let fear stop you from asking if they are having such thoughts. Research shows that 50 percent of ASHFA have tried to commit suicide as opposed to 4.6 percent of the general population, making supportive discussion of this issue especially important (Bennet 2016). Sometimes a tiny shift that allows us to pull back from our self-absorption can bring other options into view. For a person also managing autisticy, people walking away can trigger the stigma of rejection and further depression. Doing nothing may be easier but only leads to a deepening cycle of depression for anyone experiencing this desolate strain of Ghost Town. Negotiation and compromise, calmly encouraging any movement towards life and engagement, is a productive attitude for the person and their supporters. Social interaction can feed the vitality that needs nourishing when we're depressed. For someone struggling with challenges of autisticy, lapsing into inaction may seem especially tempting due to the additional burden of stigma. Social interaction may seem even more like a task we're not up to. Self-care at such times, as is so often the case, involves efforts in precisely the opposite direction than our natural responses would dictate. It can be extraordinarily difficult, and any small steps are a triumph.

ADHD and Learning Disability

ADHD and learning disability, like autism spectrum disorder, are categorized in the DSM-5 as neurodevelopmental disorders that represent challenges a person is born with. Often referred to simply as attention deficit disorder, ADHD may or may not include the "hyperactivity" part (ADD is no longer a separate diagnosis but ADHD can be specified as involving primarily inattention, hyperactivity, or both). Learning disabilities refer primarily to specific challenges in the areas of reading, writing, and mathematics, although many people with learning disability experience at least some of the challenges of autisticy more acutely than mainstream others. ADHD, on the other hand, is a more global pattern of executive functioning difficulty that can be complicated by challenges with emotional regulation, self-absorption, and taking other people's perspectives into account. Sometimes the challenges are not obvious to parents until social and academic demands increase with age, bringing their challenges into greater relief. The person's friends, however, may sense something different about them. Those with ADHD and learning disabilities often experience stigma from a young age. When we think of people with these conditions, we typically think of children in the classroom with behavioral issues who struggle academically. Presenting a challenge to teachers who may be used to regimented standards, these children are often "subjected to overt disapproval and public shaming in the classroom" (Maté 1999, p.14). One mother of a child with ADHD reported that her son was accused by a teacher in front of the class of being lazy and not trying. At a time when he was not yet diagnosed, she said to him, "Do you have ADHD or something?" This underscored the hurtful stigma of not being like everyone else. The trials and tribulations of the classroom, however, are just the beginning. When such kids grow up they continue to struggle with their challenges and face stigma, which as with autism and other conditions involving autisticy is not primarily due to a diagnostic label but to behaviors that do not match dominant mainstream expectations.

It is not just academic and job performance that suffers. Difficulty focusing, frequently drifting attention, and disorganization lead to all sorts of social blunders. Alan Alda, not only beloved as Hawkeye on the classic TV series MASH but founder and teacher at the Center for Communicating Science at Stony Brook University, says, "If I'm trying to explain something and you don't follow me, it's not simply your job to catch up. It's my job to slow down" (2017, p.30). However, such patience is not common and people demand fast attention at work and in conversation. Social expectations are not met when a person is slower processing information. The person's social value may be judged harshly. They may feel dismissed, demeaned, or unworthy. This can lead them to develop low self-esteem and anxiety. Repeated experiences of this lead to stigma accumulating in the body as trauma that can become easily activated and further escalates what can become a cycle of alienation and avoidance. It can be a real challenge to complete projects and the person often has difficulty taking in directions as well as planning and executing complex tasks. Reading, writing, or math difficulties may make work difficult. Disorganization complicated by anxiety may make it difficult to sustain energy on projects or interact with others effectively. Sometimes even making phone calls presents an anxious challenge. The person may constantly seek novelty to engage their easily restless nature, which can make it difficult to focus on any one task for any length of time unless it is a source of intense interest.

Some people with ADHD learn to accept themselves and compensate for their challenges, often achieving more than they thought possible. Those who don't receive appropriate intervention, don't understand what is happening to them, haven't learned or developed helpful ways to compensate, or haven't been lucky enough to find a suitable niche can end up in undemanding jobs that feel safe because they don't activate their challenges. In such cases trouble may come if they get promoted or decide to take the plunge into higher-paid areas that may provide more fulfillment but highlight their challenges. If they aren't sufficiently supported, they may feel overwhelmed, experiencing a crisis of uncertainty as they scramble to meet demands, unsure how to last in their new position. One woman with ADHD switched from stocking shelves to working in a bank, which triggered panic attacks and self-doubt. Another got promoted to manager and wondered how long he could "fake it" by working extra hard to make up for the extent of his difficulties. Seeking treatment, learning self-acceptance, and practicing strategies to compensate for challenges can make all the difference. Kelly and Ramundo (1995) provide plenty of concrete strategies to help individuals with ADHD not only compensate for their disorganization but also attract less stigma to themselves. For example, they tell us:

> Be cautious when you find yourself discussing one of your favorite subjects or pet peeves. If you find the other person mentally or physically backing off, lighten up! Tell a joke, ask a question, or change the subject. (p.172)

The problem with this advice is that a person living with autisticy may not notice a person losing interest. Difficulty taking other people's perspective into account may be one of their core challenges. Luckily, this is not an impairment in itself, as if the autistic person had some absolute internal mechanism broken and could not possibly sense or appreciate another person's discomfort. It depends on the setting, the level of familiarity, and other factors that may be differently activated in such a person. It does not come naturally to them. For example, their self-absorption may make it challenging to detect such messages. It takes a deliberate effort of will to activate such attunement. A person with ADHD and other forms of autisticy can often concentrate intensely, even become hyper-focused on things that interest them. Other people's body language and the signals they may be sending consciously or unconsciously about their internal states of mind and comfort levels may not be a captivating area of interest. Still, most of us are keen to decrease the stigma we experience and want to avoid being further marginalized (especially in situations like dating or work). We can motivate ourselves to counter the predisposition to alienate others by ignoring their signals, as well as other automatic tendencies such as blurting things out impulsively, leaving trails of disorganized clutter wherever we go, and allowing anxiety and emotional escalation to fluster us into meltdowns, by more closely noticing how we're doing and making efforts to step back and practice self-recovery strategies. These will be further explored in Part C, where a practical framework of self-intervention is discussed at length.

The everyday executive functioning challenges of ADHD are much like those of autism. Just the other day my wife asked me to pick her car up at the mechanic. I was in a hurry, so I wouldn't be late for work and called the mechanic to tell him I was driving right over to pick it up. I was going to just dash over there, but a little voice told me to call first. Good thing I listened to that little voice, because he pointed out the obvious fact that I would not be able to drive both cars back. How could I not have thought of that simple detail? He drove my wife's car over, and I drove him back to his shop, although I was a bit anxious about having to engage in small talk on the way.

When I was younger I was setting the VCR to tape an important episode of *Star Trek*. Such detailed little tasks have always been daunting for me, and I was very careful. The show was at 8pm, and I set the recorder to start ten minutes early and stop ten minutes after to provide a safe window for errors. Imagine my dismay when the show turned to static ten minutes after it started! After calming down and investigating, I found the VCR had been programmed to start taping at 7:50 and stop at 8:10. I remember calculating painstakingly: "start taping at 7:50, then it will start at 7, one hour later is 8, then ten minutes extra to be safe…" When I realized my error, I slapped myself upside the head and called myself stupid repeatedly. Making things worse, I stigmatized myself harshly even though no one saw what happened. Such lapses for those with certain combinations of autisticy are more than occasional errors. They become a way of life we get more graceful at managing.

With ADHD, executive functioning challenges are at the forefront. Other challenges of autisticy can be present in various ways that make life difficult. There may also be fine motor skill problems leading to clumsiness, although inattention can be part of being accident-prone. Restlessness and not being able to settle comfortably for long is often another characteristic challenge. The resulting hyperactivity can be confused with the manic phase of bipolar disorder. Those who experience this frenetic energy, if they can harness it to something they are interested in, can go far.

The DSM-5 lists many diagnostic categories that overlap with ADHD, not only autism because of shared social difficulties and peer rejection, but other conditions that involve co-occurring challenges. Depression, for example, involves similar difficulty concentrating. Anxiety can also lead to isolation and restlessness. Various personality disorders share features of disorganization and emotional dysregulation. It is important to distinguish these from each other to ensure appropriate treatment, but it is also important to recognize the similarities that unite us in order to normalize our challenges and not see ourselves as so very different from each other. The social impact of autisticy can range from occasional mildly troublesome episodes to pervasively chronic chaos, but almost everyone can identify to some extent with these difficulties. They are only human.

My mother grew up with undiagnosed learning disability. She had trouble with writing and spelling, but also a poor sense of direction. Executive functioning challenges affected not only her academic work but taking direction and organizing life generally. She adopted the role of class clown to offset stigma and obtain acceptance, but secretly she put everyone around her on a pedestal and thought of them as "superfolks." As she got older she was better able to manage because she developed patience with herself and did not panic when she might be drawing attention to her challenges. The world makes it hard to be different from dominant mainstream others, and many people with autisticy strive to be "normal." Others hide behind roles that provide camouflage for their eccentricities and exceptionalities. Still others just keep getting in trouble. As an elementary pupil I was a muddled wash-out until Grade 4. I got the strap twice for being lazy. My projects were always late. The rejection I experienced at school overshadowed any academic potential I might have had, and all energy was focused on what I had to do to fit in. In Grade 5 my mother moved to another school district, where she made sure I got a male teacher since I didn't have a father and she wisely felt I needed a man to look up to. Things turned around for me. My new teacher gave me positive attention for doing well, and I began to achieve mostly As. For the rest of my school career, however, I remember managing anxiety by telling myself all I had to do was get at least average marks. Average marks seemed preferable because it was scary to stand out or draw attention to myself in case my lack of "normality" would get unwelcome advertising or I invited expectations I couldn't fulfill. Others may put super-achieving anxiety on themselves to compensate for vulnerabilities they don't want anyone to see. Some people apply both strategies depending on the situation. Both can divert us from our own unrestrained natural path.

Autisticy and Relationships

I often have individuals with ADHD come into my office feeling confused about why they have so much anxiety and easily triggered escalation. This is not only part of the condition itself but aggravated by years of stigma and not fitting in. If a person with ADHD is in a marriage or common law relationship, they often complain that their spouse is angry with them all the time. The longer a socioconventional person has been married to someone living with autisticy the more likely this is to happen. If the spouse comes into the session, they may ask the client to tell them why they think they are so angry. Although the person may initially claim not to know, eventually it comes out that their constant disorganization, lack of engagement, and seeming inability to complete projects becomes intolerable. It makes the other person feel they are responsible for everything, increasing their stress and workload. The spouse may resort to nagging, which only makes things worse. It is not the spouse's responsibility to make the other person see what is disrupting the household. The sooner a person with these difficulties gets assessment and appropriate treatment the better it is for everyone. Medication can be very effective helping with these challenges. Meanwhile, once a cycle of nagging and frustration starts, things get worse because the stigma of the person with autisticy becomes activated by the anger and criticism directed at them. This awakens fears that they are inadequate. They may begin avoiding family interaction and taking even less initiative in family events and relationship-building activities. Any challenges they already have with social engagement, intimacy, and attending to the needs of others is painfully exaggerated. The cycle is best broken by outside intervention such as couples counseling that helps both parties see how they are contributing to the pattern. The partners can learn to recognize how easy it is to activate the trauma of a stigmatized person and be more careful in this regard.

It is not always possible to be calm, collected, and reasonable, any more than we Autistics can be expected to be aware so we can compensate for our challenges every time. No one is required to be "nice" and "well behaved" consistently despite difficult conditions. Healthy anger can help a person with "deaf ears" hear us and actually register what we need them to be aware of. When partners activate each other's safety distress, things can quickly get out of hand. In the face of growing escalation and emotional regulation difficulties, it can take a huge effort of self-recovery to keep the activated trauma of stigmatization from worsening a situation and driving those involved further apart. This can become an especially vicious cycle.

A person living with autisticy needs to take responsibility in order to acknowledge how their challenges affect other people. Therapy can help us move through stuck places with more awareness and less defensiveness. Partners can learn to provide the safety cues required by their spouse to thrive. This need to provide safety is true for many couples, but can be crucial in relationships where one or both partners has a history of trauma. This all best happens before alienation and resentment go too far. There may come a time when it will be too late to salvage trusting love.

The Trouble with Normal

The trouble with "normal," as Bruce Coburn tells us in his distinctively Canadian socio-political folk song, is it always gets worse. So-called "normal" people struggle to become "better than normal," and those who find themselves set apart by their uniqueness and/or challenges torture themselves because they wish they were "more normal." "Normal" is an exclusive club whose membership is based on an illusion. It is easy to pinpoint the "statistically average." Insurance adjusters do it all the time. "Normal" is everywhere and nowhere. It is normal to fall into different ranges of diversity in different areas. It is normal for some people to be outside the range of conventional social expectation and be outrageously different. No one is completely "normal." It is a target that doesn't exist, yet we hold fast to this precarious ideal and beat each other (and ourselves) up over it.

"If only I could be more normal," we say, and treat the blessings that make us who we are as if they were some kind of pestilence. Yet is it not all our fault. Mainstream society, the statistically average and dominant, hold on to social expectations and conventional standards as if they were membership requirements. When a person does not fit the image of what the majority expects everyone to be like, there is a harsh judgment of unworthiness. Membership in the clique of the "normal" is denied. A person who isn't careful can internalize this judgment and stigmatize themselves as not good enough. Stigma does untold personal and social damage.

Rather than basing trust and acceptance on meeting "normal" social expectations and conventional standards, we can ground ourselves in curiosity and allow other people's uniqueness to speak to us. It is natural to reserve trust until it is earned, but that doesn't mean we have to reject others on the basis of certain qualities. When people don't meet our expectations, it is expectation itself we need to release. Philosophers and spiritual leaders have long been telling us how expectations get us in trouble. Beating ourselves up because we don't meet "normal" expectations is a sure ticket to Ghost Town. It is normal to experience anxiety and depression. It is normal to get caught up in narrow self-absorbed prejudices, coping mechanisms, and quirky habits. It is normal to panic when we feel distress and think it will get worse. It is normal to have challenges to contend with in life. It is especially normal to not feel "normal."

It is too easy to get caught up in a losing battle to be "normal." But which "normal" do we strive for? There's "normal" with add-ons, such as a birth mark, an extra-large nose, or what I call brain cloud treadmillitis.[1] Then there's "normal" with certain parts missing, like when a gall bladder or tonsils have been taken out, an arm or leg removed, or some brain cells killed off here and there. Of course, there are the "normal" *buts*, like Frankie who's "normal" but has bad breath, or Craig who's "normal" but too nice for his own good. Let's not forget "normal" with special exceptionality, like Peggy who's "normal" and plays the scheming nurse on my favorite soap opera, or Brad who's "normal" and types to speak with a souped-up tablet. There are lots of people who do just fine and are *not* "normal" *but*, a double negative that puts them ahead of the pack. Susie, for example, is not "normal" *but OK*, because she brings cake to the baseball game. Remember Mitch? He's not normal but has a nice smile. Then there's a guy like Stephen Hawking, who was *not* "normal" with add-ons as well as "normal" *but* (his friends say he could be a big pain in the butt). In addition, he provided a great example of someone who's "normal" with special exceptionality. His gifts shone through his challenges and that's why he was such an inspiration. We can all aspire to this even if we aren't geniuses. You know, there's hardly anybody left to be just plain old not "normal." Can you think of anybody? Is it you? Let's be different proudly, keep learning who we are, and do what we have to do to take care of ourselves and each other. Let's flow with what makes us different and explore the differences between us rather than pushing each other away and not feeling good enough. What a silly bunch we are.

---

1   Brain cloud treadmillitis is a common condition in which our thoughts are shadowed by a cloud of worry and we get stuck on a hamster wheel of being hard on ourselves.

Depersonalization and Derealization

Depersonalization is a difficult-to-describe feeling of detachment, as if we weren't real, not really in our body, not connected to anything, or not part of life. I experienced this as a child frequently and called it ghost sickness. Derealization, closely connected with this, expands the feeling harshly into the world. It makes it seem as if the world isn't real, as if we were living in a movie, or nothing is really solid. We may feel life going by in a hazy fog of empty meaningless estrangement. Both sensations can be caused by trauma, and when old trauma is activated these feelings can be a tip-off about what's going on. Extreme anxiety can also cause these radically alienating experiences. When they come upon us these feelings can cause additional anxiety and panic. They can make us feel sick, unreal, detached, hazy, far away, and very separate, making our already tentative connection with others seem even more distant. When it happens, the best medicine is to remain calm, be gentle with ourselves, and try not to isolate. We don't want to subject ourselves to loud, harsh experiences if we don't have to, but we don't want to hide either. As hard as it is to appreciate at such times, the world is still the same and others are still connected with us. The feelings will pass as our bodies come back to a calmer state of ordinary presence.

Depersonalization can be triggered by drug use, especially marijuana smoking. Steve Martin eloquently describes this experience and the related distress in his book *Born Standing Up* (2011). Even more rarely, the profound alienation of depersonalization can be experienced as a more or less persistent aspect of life. This condition is called depersonalization/derealization disorder, and it can be present from youth. This condition can make it very challenging to function even though it is completely invisible to others. Such people may still find ways to function as if nothing was wrong, but they don't feel present. They don't know what it is like to be an ordinary self, so taking the perspective of others into account can be something they don't even consider. Like those with autisticy, they may have to make deliberate efforts to do this. Also like people with autisticy, they may become self-absorbed because their inner reality is so unique and confusing. They have to take it on faith that they are just like everyone else. They may give up trying to fit in. They may have feelings of hopelessness because their own lives and the world do not seem imbued with any kind of inherent meaning. Like autistics, they may reduce the operation of their lives to mechanical steps of deliberation. Still, if they give themselves to an activity, they can achieve high levels of spontaneity and seem even more engaged than others because of the special effort of abandon it calls for. Not all professionals encounter this condition and people experiencing it may not readily find someone who understands what they are going through. There are internet forums with participants who experience it, however, and these can be very helpful.

Trying too hard to comprehend these experiences can cause as much damage as the feelings themselves. The feeling has been described as "living everyday with the fear and unreality of a dream state come true" (Simeon and Abugel 2006, p.6). It is often better to practice accepting the unsettling nature of void they impose on us while not struggling to make them go away or grasping too hard for what it is like to be "normal." Not that we don't seek support and encouragement, or that we pretend we aren't uncomfortable, but we don't fight what is. This is the common challenge of acceptance many of us face. Again, the practices discussed in Part C for stigma activation recovery can be very helpful.

Borderline Personality Disorder

Borderline personality disorder (BPD) is so intertwined with a history of developmental abuse and invalidation that the Institute for Attachment and Child Development refers to it as adult trauma disorder (2017). Psychologists have long noticed this connection (van der Kolk, Herron, and Hostetler 1994), but the pervasive role of trauma is not emphasized in the DSM. Emotional dysregulation and defensive escalation characterize the condition. A history of trauma, which may be too subtle or disturbing to be readily remembered, can often be uncovered at a rate comfortable for the person to help them better understand their difficulties. Sometimes trauma is only associated with overt abuse, which overlooks other sources of sometimes equally painful invalidation that cause safety distress to become easily activated and people to be hyper-vigilantly defensive. Linehan refers to borderline personality disorder as a condition characterized by growing up in an "invalidating environment" (1993). DBT or dialectical behavior therapy, her classically eclectic treatment, is not just for those with a certain kind of personality disorder but anyone whose life is characterized by unpredictable emotional arousal and disruption including those forms associated with the challenges of autisticy and autism (Hartmann *et al.* 2012). In addition to emotional dysregulation, difficulties with mentalization (Fonagy, Luyten, and Strathearn 2011), executive functioning (Mohamed *et al.* 2016), and emotional self-absorption are core challenges of autisticy that often characterize "borderline" personalities.

Schmidt (2007) wrote his Master's thesis at the University of Victoria on stigma and borderline personality disorder. He conducted a qualitative study in which he interviewed six women with BPD about their experiences with stigma. He found such intense stigmatization and discrimination experienced by the participants, from both professionals and the general community, that he recommended the "outright elimination of this diagnostic category" (p.84). It is curious that Schmidt's thesis did not mention the behaviors of those with the condition as a source of stigma, especially since the participants in my study located their greatest source of stigma in this area. The stigma experienced by both groups can be extreme. Schmidt's participants noted "having a negative reaction when first hearing the diagnosis of BPD" (p.49), which is similar to my own negative reaction when I first thought I might have autism. Schmidt notes how borderline personality disorder is often used synonymously with the term "difficult" (p.2).

ASHFA often get the same reputation. Still, Schmidt's participants with BPD seemed to attribute the stigma they experience entirely to the label of their diagnosis. Schmidt notes the "particularly pejorative connotation" of the very term "borderline" (p.1). The participants diagnosed with autism in my study located the source of stigma, as one participant said, "not in the diagnosis but in the autism itself." What accounts for this interesting difference in findings? It could be the questions that were asked. Schmidt focused on a few questions exclusively about diagnosis, whereas my study asked a variety of questions revolving around the experience of stigma. It could also be that individuals diagnosed with borderline find their stigma increases after getting diagnosed because of stigma associated specifically with the label. When adults get a diagnosis of Asperger's, their experience of stigma may decrease because of the explanation it provides for their behavior. Could this difference be due simply to the fact that "borderline" is a more stigmatized term than "autism"? Does the term "borderline," like the tired term "retardation," have so much stigma attached to it the stigma of the behaviors is overshadowed by the stigma of the term? If so, it is time for a name change (Gunderson 2010). This may also have something to do with how BPD is seen as a treatable disorder overlaid on a person's personality, while autism is generally accepted as a lifelong neurological condition deeply integrated with an individual's personhood. The role of perception in this puzzle is complex.

In my experience as a clinician and having a family member with borderline, it is the actual behavior patterns of someone struggling with borderline (whether or not the diagnosis is known) that cause the real frustration and underlie the most poignant stigma. The diagnostic label comes to represent these patterns and the label can be abused (as in "Oh my God, another borderline client"). Persons demonstrating the patterns of behavior typical of borderline personality disorder can be challenging to interact with. These frustrating behavior patterns include intense and volatile relationships characterized by extremes of idealization and devaluation, emotional instability, intense anger often seeming out of proportion to the situation, and paranoid fear. This list can be supplemented by emotional neediness, excessive dependence on the opinion of others, easily triggered defensiveness, and frequent demands for emotional support that seem like suspicious tests. In the case of ASHFA, frustrating behaviors could include lack of interest in others, adherence to routine, rigid thinking patterns, explosive distress at small changes, and fixated interests that disrupt any situation. This list of already frustrating behaviors leads to exasperating experiences like being ignored, interrupted, resisted for no apparent reason, presented with rationalizations, and being confronted with self-absorbed ob-session (especially when empathetic validation would be a more helpful and welcome response). Those who demonstrate a combination of these behaviors find themselves, not surprisingly, facing frustration from others, not because of stigma associated with their diagnostic label but because of these very behaviors. For the autistic as well as the person labelled with borderline, whatever combination of safety distress related to trauma and neurological predisposition aggravating these behaviors, the resulting frustration may be indistinguishable from stigma and intertwined with it. In my study this emerged as a theme I called *frustigma*.

I discuss this experience of being a constant source of exasperation for others not to elicit sympathy, but because it shows how taking responsibility for these behaviors can provide a way to manage stigma. Stigmatized individuals can make an effort to identify, be mindful of, and learn strategies to address the behaviors others find frustrating to the extent consistent with their capacity for insight, ability to adapt, and readiness for change. This does not mean they have to adhere to conventional social expectations in everything. Dominant others in a position to inflict stigma must make an effort to distinguish unconventional and unexpected behavior from deliberately hurtful and selfish behavior. This can be a fine line. When I constantly say "sorry" for embarrassing, offensive, and hurtful behavior, my wife says, "If you run over someone's foot with your car, sorry doesn't take the pain away." Still, people can be mindful of the source of pain and frustration coming from traumatized and/or fundamentally different others. Efforts can be made to address it in ways that are not further stigmatizing. This calls for good will and committed effort on all sides.

Schizophrenia

The challenges of autisticy have an impact on a diversity of people with different conditions. For example, "autism-like" problems with mentalization have been noted in schizophrenia (Sasamoto *et al.* 2011). Another characteristic of autisticy, weak global coherence and over-emphasized local coherence, has been noted in both borderline and schizophrenia (Martin and McDonald 2003). Problems stepping back and integrating other people's perspectives can challenge us all and are a pronounced factor in many human conditions. Diagnosis is important to initiate appropriate treatment for these conditions, if desired by the person, yet many of the difficulties characterizing autisticy are shared more prevalently than the strict categorization of medical diagnosis would suggest. Stigma is the most poignant of these shared challenges.

Talking with individuals diagnosed with schizophrenia, it becomes clear the stigma they experience is deeply rooted. Not only do such individuals often have difficulty taking the perspective of others into account and understanding social cues, they feel so different from other people they often fall into a cycle of demeaning self-judgment that becomes pervasive and debilitating. Often unable to grasp the social knowledge that seems to come so easily to others, individuals with schizophrenia may beat themselves up constantly as being unworthy and less than others. The DSM-5 acknowledges that such social challenges may be due to lack of interest or "limited opportunities for social engagement" (2013, p.88), which seems to be to be a very under-stated way of referring to the marginalization of stigma. In my experience, people with schizophrenia have the same desire for social inclusion as others, although they may give up on the possibility or tire of the effort they must make to fit in.

One client with schizophrenia is hard on herself because she feels spiritual knowledge eludes her. She is curious and genuinely seeks to explore this area, but compares herself so severely with others that she feels everybody knows but her. She beats herself up for lacking the inner resources to obtain such knowledge and blames herself when ambiguity and uncertainty is an inherent part of spiritual seeking. Perhaps part of this is an intolerance for ambiguity, but like many of us she undermines her blessings and strengths by being overly critical of herself.

The facial expression of a person with schizophrenia may be wooden and characterized by a certain flatness. Their speech may be sparse with diminished inflection, often sounding emotionless or uninterested. He or she may also lack motivation and find it difficult to let themselves go in order to enjoy activities. These are some of the so-called "negative" symptoms of schizophrenia, which may be due to a combination of factors including neurological complications, medication, and resignation due to the lack of control they feel over their lives. Many of these symptoms resemble those of autism. Another symptom of schizophrenia is unusual motor behavior "ranging from childlike silliness to unpredictable agitation" (American Psychiatric Association 2013, p.88). This description is particularly reminiscent of autism. The two conditions seem to have a certain kinship, not only because of the challenges of autisticy they share but also because of the deeply rooted quality of stigma they experience.

People with schizophrenia experience special challenges unique to their condition. They sometimes have great difficulty separating inner and outer experience, as if the neurological filters separating their personhood from the rest of the world were compromised. The "positive" symptoms of schizophrenia include hallucinations, delusions, and disorganized thinking. It is not as simple as the presence of false images. They may hear voices coming from outside them, voices they hear as real and actual, making fun of them or telling them what to do (command hallucinations). Often these voices reflect concerns, worries, or over-critical thinking in themselves but seem to be coming from outside. They may also experience their thoughts as implanted from external sources, or when something on the television is meaningful to them they may experience this as messages being sent from outside deliberately to them.

It is not that schizophrenic individuals intellectually misinterpret the same data other people experience. Their perception comes to them in this confused form. For example, one man's love of trains manifested itself as actually hearing them go by the house even though he did not live anywhere near train tracks. Once, when he was depressed and feeling suicidal, he literally heard a passing train beckoning him to come. One woman, anxious about living alone in the country after a separation, began hearing angry voices outside her room. She developed other symptoms and was subsequently diagnosed with schizophrenia. Another man heard about a terrorist act on the radio. It had such an impact on him he developed a vivid memory of being there and was afraid he would be punished.

Delusions, or strong beliefs not changeable by outside evidence, are often related to a client's hopes and fears. One man, for example, always wanted to be in the music business and firmly came to believe he was a rock star. Schizophrenic individuals who are religious may develop delusions involving concrete personifications of good and evil or that they themselves are deities. I have seen individuals with autism have these kinds of delusions. One young man, a would-be gansta who experienced a lot of bullying, developed an unshakeable delusion that he was the leader of a street gang. A fragile neurological constitution liable to perceive inner experience as if it originated in the shared world, or to endow inner fears and beliefs with concrete reality, when combined with an over-developed sense of local focus and self-absorption, may lead to unusual and disturbing experiences. Although a person's behavior may seem bizarre and self-defeating, however, it is often a natural response to the unique experiences they are having.

Another client, when she was anxious, experienced pain in her gut experienced as an assault by evil forces. This outside source was sometimes a stereotypically beautiful and skinny woman of the kind she found intimidating in everyday life. Other times she would experience this assault coming from kids that bullied her growing up or people standing nearby she found socially threatening. In every instance she described, the situation could also be accounted for by anxiety. The source she would experience the assault coming from might depend on whether her anxiety was related to vague worry and uncertainty, her inner critic, reactivated stigma from the past, or the dread many of us identify with as social anxiety. How open the client was to discussing the possibility that the assault was actually the same kind of anxiety other people experience would depend on how she was feeling that day. At times she would be able to recognize her belief about the discomfort being imposed from the outside as part of schizophrenia. Other times, when her illness was more active, her belief would become an unshakeable conviction. When this took place, it was a cue to abandon any attempts to address the disturbing belief with reason and look at vulnerability and treatment considerations (was the client taking her medications as prescribed; when was her last blood work done; was she eating and sleeping enough; should her next psychiatry appointment be moved up, etc.).

The client's belief that her discomfort was caused by an assault from the outside rendered her a helpless victim, which reinforced the helplessness she felt as a marginalized member of society due to the stigma she experienced. Whatever mechanism of brain physiology weakened her ability to discriminate between attributions of inside and outside perception, when active it was often accompanied by disorganized thinking, decreased coherence, and lower levels of engagement in relationship. The higher levels of stigma she would experience at such times would heighten her isolation and provide emotional fuel to her confusion and alienation. This would often escalate into a cycle she would have to withdraw from society to recover from. The withdrawal might feel like a necessary break to recover, but it could also add to her isolation if she wasn't careful.

Medical treatment can alleviate the positive symptoms of schizophrenia. Anti-psychotic medication such as quetiapine, risperidone, and olanzapine are commonly used. All have potential unpleasant side effects that may increase negative symptoms such as emotional flatness and lead to stigma in their own right. Some, like clozapine, are potentially dangerous if not carefully controlled and require regular testing to ensure safe blood levels. It is often a precarious trade-off, but there are few established options to manage the disruption of florid psychosis. As with autism, many possible strategies of recovery have been proposed but the dominant evidence-based protocols of medically accepted practice remain largely undisputed.

One alternative that has fallen out of favor is the orthomolecular approach. Abram Hoffer (2004) describes this as a biochemical theory proposing that schizophrenia can be at least partly due to the brain's inability to provide, process, or eliminate the raw materials and by-products of its own biological functioning. These are the same complex physiological processes most people take for granted and often get away with abusing through poor eating habits. Most brains are able to compensate and maintain their processes relatively undisturbed. The orthomolecular approach does not have to be seen as a wholesale alternative to medication, as if the use of all drugs and other standard medical treatment should cease. Seen as a naturally corrective measure to compensate for our typical disregard for self-care, it advises heightened attention to nutrition and lifestyle to help the brain maintain its natural biochemical balance, or homeostasis. What little evidence I could find "against" the orthomolecular approach often takes a popular misnomer literally ("megavitamin therapy"), alerting us to the ineffectiveness and potential danger of trying to treat schizophrenia by throwing large amounts of random vitamins at it. This warning does not count against a careful professionally recommended orthomolecular approach to the condition. Alternatively, such falsifying research may proceed as if the orthomolecular treatment was a wholesale alternative to traditional medicine, warning us not to stop medical treatment in an attempt to cure schizophrenia with vitamins. Hoffer is clear that reducing or making traditional medication unnecessary is only a possibility to be carefully and gradually explored after practicing a long-term customized and consistent nutritional program. One randomized clinical trial falsifying the orthomolecular approach (Vaughan and McConaghy 1999) concluded that nutritional intervention had no significant therapeutic effect on schizophrenic symptoms over five months. This timeline may be appropriate for traditional medication, but is not sufficient to begin addressing the longer-term impact of a consistent nutritionally optimal diet. Another article reviewing 53 trials of therapeutic nutritional treatment of mental functioning (Kleijnen and Knipschild 1991) only found significant positive changes using this modality with an autistic population. It concluded there was not enough evidence to assess a positive impact for either schizophrenic or neurotypical people.

Hoffer's first three rules of an orthomolecular approach are first to reduce stress because the schizophrenic brain may be unable to properly eliminate the by-products of adrenaline, which is released in the "fight or flight" response. This is tantamount to encouraging us to practice mindfulness and relaxation, which is good advice for all of us. His other two rules are avoiding processed sugar as well as foods that allergy testing tells us our bodies are sensitive to. This again is not bad advice for any of us, but may be especially important for people experiencing problems of uncertain causation wanting to take all possible precautionary measures to maximize wellness.

Hoffer's book is rich with engaging descriptions of how schizophrenia affects our physical wellness, perception of the world, sense of time, mood, cognitive functioning, and above all social interaction. He addresses micro-behavioral sources of stigma when he notes how schizophrenic individuals use their eyes in ways that trigger safety distress in dominant socioconventional others. This creates "hostility or anxiety in those around them" (2004, p.52), resulting in the same kind of invisible stigmas autistic people experience addressed by polyvagal theory. In addition, he describes how people with schizophrenia often alarm those around them by describing ideas and perceptions that don't fit everyday reality and overtly behaving in sometimes bizarre unexpected ways. Although these may seem perfectly natural to the schizophrenic person as a response to the altered experience their brain presents them, people who experience the world in conventional ways do not understand and understandably react in a defensive fashion, resulting in further stigma. Hoffer tells people with schizophrenia not to "make life difficult for themselves" and advises them to "not act upon or speak about the peculiar things you may see, hear, feel, or think" (p.150). He says this not to force people with schizophrenia into hiding, unable to be themselves, but to encourage them to practice the same efforts of evaluating, countering, and disregarding natural experience we all must in our own way to function optimally with others. Hoffer uses the example of a pilot who must ignore his own senses and trust his instruments in a storm. This is advice we could all take to heart. How much damage is done by people convinced their experience of the world is the "right" one? It is important to note that people unwell with schizophrenia are no more likely to do such damage than anyone else. An article reviewing research in this area (Silverstein *et al.* 2015) concluded that "most people with schizophrenia are not violent and violence committed by people with this condition accounts for only a small percentage of overall violent crime" (p.21).

Therapeutic intervention for schizophrenia involves activating self-care and social behaviors. It also addresses the cognitive component of experience to help the individual challenge and modify any interpretations of their perception that reinforce the distortions inherent in their disorder. This can improve reality-testing as well as functioning (Naeem, Gul, and Aub 2015; Sivec *et al.* 2017). A schizophrenic person's struggle to challenge the way they understand their perception in order to stay out of hospital can inspire other people to challenge the way they perceive the world in order to build a more inclusive, less violent and socially just society. Making an effort to challenge the way things naturally seem is a common human mechanism of growth. Scott (1992) cautions us not to "appeal to experience as incontestable evidence" (p.24). Some of us have to work harder at this than others, but when we fall into the trap of getting too attached to our experience of the way things are we can justify anything from slavery and terrorism to believing we're under attack from outside forces when we're anxious. When we are too focused on our own experience and don't make an effort to allow other perspectives to inform our behavior, we autistics may not even be able to get off the computer when we're called for supper.

It is not only the alienation associated with schizophrenia that can be addressed by overcoming isolation and talking to others. Positive symptoms can also be improved with non-judgmental social interaction (Wharton, James, and Turkington 2006). Opening up to others in the community may activate intolerable safety distress because of stigma. Attending therapy groups where people understand the impact of stigma and the importance of non-judgmental interaction can fill the gap. It's not just support groups for schizophrenia that can help. Any group whose mandate includes honest communication and self-exploration can provide validation to assist an individual to normalize their humanity and lead to increased self-acceptance. Shared emotional challenges, experiences with stigma, and characteristics of autisticy provide common ground that overpowers the uniqueness of different symptomatology.

What causes schizophrenia? No one knows. Substance abuse, especially heavy marijuana use in young people, is sometimes associated with the development of schizophrenia in those thought to have some kind of neurological vulnerability. Developmental trauma can lead to psychotic symptoms (Rahim 2014) and mothers who have been exposed to shock trauma were found to be more than twice as likely to have children who subsequently develop schizophrenia (Weinstein *et al.*, in press).

Autism and Schizophrenia

In the illustrious history of autism, the orthomolecular approach was advocated by Bernard Rimland (1964/2015). An early champion of the neuro-biological approach to the condition, this orientation helped him debunk the theory that "refrigerator mothers" were the cause of autism. Schizophrenia has its own history of blaming families for the illness of their loved ones. Rejecting such judgmental approaches should not impede us from acknowledging the important role of invalidation trauma as a factor in both these conditions. Schizophrenia and autism have much in common.

The diagnostic category "autism" first emerged as a distinct type of case when Leo Kanner distinguished the condition from childhood schizophrenia in 1943. Both conditions intrigue the public imagination and the connection of the two triggers great interest. A 2017 Google search of "are autism and schizophrenia related" resulted in 16,100,000 hits. Although they are conventionally seen as totally separate illnesses, recent approaches propose that schizophrenia and autism represent a range of conditions with areas of overlapping phenomenological features and physiological associations. Quantitative research comparing the neurological characteristics of people with autism and schizophrenia is growing, leading to speculative conceptualizations such as the diametrical disorder theory (Crespi and Badcock 2008). This theory hypothesizes that autism is associated with a paternal gene bias and schizophrenia with a maternal gene bias, but this is only part of the evidence base used to support the theory that autism and schizophrenia are "two extremes on a cognitive spectrum with normality at its center" (p.241). The low co-occurrence of autism and schizophrenia seems to support the two being mutually exclusive in some way, although the two do occur together at times. The problem is not only the elusiveness of "normality" being used as a reference point but the over-simplified reduction of autism to a mechanized cognitive style and schizophrenia to a mentalistic one. Their proposal that schizophrenia involves over-ascribing intentions to others, as opposed to autism which is seen to be deficient in the area of perceiving the intentionality of others, overlooks complexities like the often context-specific nature of these difficulties. The theory also seems based mostly on paranoid schizophrenia in which threatening intentions are seen everywhere and does not account for other psychotic manifestations which may not even involve other people. Most importantly, the theory does not account for the shared difficulty both populations have experiencing social flow with dominant mainstream others.

The most striking thing about this theory in terms of stigma is that it places autism and schizophrenia as far away as possible in opposite directions from "normal." When I am talking to a person diagnosed with schizophrenia, I certainly do not perceive the two of us to be at opposite poles of some spectrum. Still, research continues and theories abound, including the presence of opposite acting "intention detector" modules (Ciaramidaro *et al.* 2015, p.178). One review paper proposes the presence of a common underlying condition called "systemic integral disorder" that results in autism if activated at a young age and schizophrenia if activated at a later age (Wang, Jeffries, and Wang 2016). One problem with this paper is that it seems to reduce psychosis to a language disorder in which hallucinations occur because the "contents of language are wrong" (p.121). Common challenges with language are used to support the theory that schizophrenia and autism share common roots, but language does not seem to provide a strong enough explanatory baseline. Language-based therapies such as cognitive behavioral therapy (CBT) can help people with schizophrenia and autism restructure their thoughts so they don't catastrophize symptoms with anxious thinking, and mindfulness-oriented therapies such as ACT (acceptance and commitment therapy) can encourage people to stop giving too much importance to thoughts generally. This can help schizophrenic individuals avoid further empowering their hallucinations by over-valuing thoughts that confirm their seeming reality. These techniques do not eliminate psychosis.

On a deeper level, it may not be language itself that provides this common mechanism but a more mysterious connection. This occurred to me the other day on my daily walk. I got lost on a network of paths and was trying to figure out the best way to go when I found myself talking out loud about the possibilities. No one was around, but I immediately shut my thoughts up in my head. It struck me that it was easy to visualize how the neuro-chemical signals going to the vocal cords could be converted into speech, but how are these signals converted into the silent expressions of language in consciousness? What background do they emerge from, what screen are they projected on, and what processes facilitate this? It is a miraculous phenomenon we take for granted, and disturbances in the currently unfathomable complexities involved may well provide a common ground underlying autism and schizophrenia as well as human challenges of many kinds.

More concrete research involves corollary (or efferent) neurological impulses. The discovery of this process can be traced as far back as von Helmholtz in 1925, but the modern concept is generally credited to Nobel prize winner Roger Sperry in 1950. Physiological studies showed that raw movement impulses are copied and sent to other areas of the brain to provide feedback enabling proprioception and better motor control. Feinberg (1978) proposed that if corollary efferent discharges were important for movement, they might also be important in cognitive processes. He proposed that they may be used to explain the positive symptoms of schizophrenia, making it difficult to discriminate between sensations originating inside and outside the body, inner and outer sources of fear and desire, and the difference between imagination and concrete independent existence. This results in psychotic experiences such as hallucinations and delusions as well as social difficulties (Ford and Mathalon 2004). Others such as Frith (2016) have suggested that collateral discharges may also play a part in autism, not only with subtle eye and body movement difficulties but also social interaction and mentalization. This is an intriguing line of investigation that may shed new light on several aspects of human behavior. Research in this area has been called "arguably the most fruitful line of perceptual research throughout the relatively short history of psychology" (Winkler and Czigler 2012).

What is really disturbing about the systemic integral disorder paper is its recommendation that a program of surveillance and eugenics be initiated with the intention of "preventing the diseases from happening" (p.128). A lot of us wouldn't be here if this kind of program was put in place and the very suggestion of anything supporting such an effort triggers apprehension of a "holocaust" (Nadesan 2013, p.125). This provides an example of how isolated academic research can result in outrageously stigmatizing positions. Qualitative research giving voice to the experience of people who live with the conditions being studied can help with this by grounding potentially valuable programs of study in human relevance, acting as a reality check to ensure social justice, and suggesting positive directions for future research.

THE IMPACT OF STIGMA AND TRAUMA RECOVERY

Chapter 5

STIGMA RESILIENCE

The participants in my research discussed various ways they build resilience to help protect them from stigma. Some involve developing behavior aligned with socioconventional expectations to make relations with others flow more smoothly. One participant said, "Over the years I have learned that people like it if you let them talk more." Another said, "I usually find another good thing is to ask people to talk about themselves." Others talked about learning to make better eye contact and not stimming (self-stimulating) in public. Learning neurodominant conventions of social interaction can be unnatural and self-defeating, not unlike forcing a left-handed person to use their right hand. The participants talked about having to "fake it" all the time, which takes a lot of energy. One lamented, "I have grown up being someone I'm not." These kinds of strategies, which might be called "performing normality" (Lester and Paulus 2012, p.267), can make life easier all around, but they can also be adopted as a protective shield against stigma that makes neurodominants feel more comfortable while it drains the energy of ASHFA. One participant made me think of a video game in which a certain number of positive rewards must be accumulated to keep the shields from dropping. Such behavioral strategies are often seen as helpful skills to improve communication, but they merge insidiously with defensive measures of forced compliance to avoid stigma from dominant others. Such strategies can become a program of assimilation. Going along with them can be seen as reasonable efforts to function in socioconventional society or attempts at self-camouflage and even auto-annihilating self-denial. The French philosopher Foucault might refer to such acts as a form of bio power, a kind of social policing "that sustains itself through its own mechanisms" (Foucault 1975/1995, p.177). The efforts to "blend in" reported by participants in this study can be associated with social pressure to conform that is disciplined by stigma.

Participants generally agreed that the use of stigma cloaking, or strategies to appear "normal" as a protective factor against stigma, become less urgent with age. One participant said, "I allow myself to do more, I guess, autistic things as I get older. I have come to know that for me it's normal, so I don't really care anymore." Another participant said, "I've just come to the understanding that I'm weird and that's OK." A third participant emphasized that "it's really important to know where your boundaries are and when, where, and how to push them." Such self-acceptance was reported by participants as building a core of fundamental stigma resilience that grows with experience and maturity. The only exception to this was one participant who reported intense anxiety that made her experience of stigma seem to worsen with age.

The importance of "getting out and talking to people, especially around events that are based on food" was discussed enthusiastically by one participant. He advised, "When you want to go and do something, just do it." This participant was very active in the community, participating in sports and other events. He also described how stigma can be encountered at any time, which means that going out sometimes takes courage. He says, "Some people don't want to talk to me and some people ignore me. I just try to talk to the people who want to talk to me, and the ones who are not willing to talk to me I just ignore." This may sound like nothing less than common sense, but for someone who deals with stigma regularly it is hard-won wisdom. I myself find social events an anxiety-provoking invitation to blunders and stigma and am with many of the participants who prefer to stay home. Developing an attitude in which you focus on positive interactions and not stigma and rejection takes practice. Another stigma resilience factor discussed by participants in this regard is spirituality. One participant attends a spiritual healing community on a monthly basis. Others attend church, and still others talked about the importance of developing a sense of purpose and meaning. For some this involved social interaction, for others it was intensely private. Every individual, and every ASHFA, is unique.

A common theme was the importance of caring, supportive adults during childhood. Parents, in particular, were described as either setting up stigma resilience or worsening stigma depending on whether they were able to foster secure attachment. Supportive parents can make a positive difference in anyone's life, but parenting a child with autism is fraught with challenges that make it difficult to be consistently available and supportive. Research has shown that parents of autistic children report higher levels of stress, more mental health issues, and lower satisfaction with work (Watt and Wagner 2013). One participant reported that the parents of many of his autistic friends separated "because they couldn't handle the stress." He added, "I'm lucky because my parents just kind of rallied around the fort." His parents were privileged and had access to resources none of the other participants in this study had access to. With all the challenges involved for autistic individuals, parents, and their families, it is interesting that research shows autistic children are as likely to develop secure attachments as socioconventional ones (Takahashi, Tamaki, and Yamawaki 2013).

Teachers were also mentioned by participants as either building stigma resilience or adding to stigma. Specifically, one participant said "everything changed" when he got a teacher who encouraged him to pursue his obsessions and directed his energy into special projects that boosted his self-esteem as well as his prestige among peers. Another participant described how the principal of his school added to his experience of stigma by unintentionally colluding with the bullies at school by not recognizing his victimization:

> I remember once being out on the playground and these kids grabbed my book and then they literally held me down and beat me up. We got sent to the principal's office and the other kids are just sitting there while I've got blood coming down my nose and the principal says, "Well, fighting is a very serious thing." So I'm thinking like, do you know what's going on at all?

Developing friendships is notoriously difficult for this population, yet one participant talked about how lucky he felt to be supported by friends throughout his life. He specified that "I've been very lucky that a lot of my friends haven't been neurotypical, so we've just been a little slow with each other." His mother used to refer to him and his friends as "the island of misfit toys." She used to joke with the participant that "you could line up a hundred people, and I would find the weirdest one in the group." Having friends who are also struggling with challenges of autisticy provided this participant with a common ground of understanding as well as a social arena without the stigma and incongruent social expectations of mainstream others. The participant described it as "a weird comrade in arms thing." Here the theme of telegraphic perception emerges again; how do individuals diagnosed with autism or struggling with the challenges of autisticy recognize each other? In the absence of consciously visible signs, how do victimizers recognize the vulnerability of such individuals? We saw earlier that polyvagal theory provides a way of seeing trauma that goes far beyond DSM diagnosis and establishes a research-based physiological framework accounting for the subtle social cues that provide information about us to each other and activate safety distress in many situations. Encountering another ASHFA, unless other factors came into play such as anger, might trigger familiar safety cues and create feelings of comfort.

I was fortunate in this study that one of the participants had a roommate who expressed an interest in being interviewed. One was diagnosed with Asperger's and one with autism. They not only agreed to be interviewed together but chose to be present during each other's interview. It was inspiring to watch them support each other, stimulate each other's ideas, and provide each other with a safe, caring environment. When one was asked about whether he felt he could contribute his strengths as a person to the community, he could not think of any strengths. His roommate immediately suggested, "You should tell him that you're a Special Olympics athlete." When one told about an experience with stigma and how upset he was that no one would tell him why they were upset with him, his roommate jumped in with "Maybe it was because they were jealous of something you had that they didn't." When one of them was being interviewed, the other picked up the recorder and held it closer to his roommate to make sure his voice would be heard.

Love relationships involving individuals with ASHFA have been explored (Aston 2003); long-term relationships with non-romantic peers have not. Klin, Volkmar, and Sparrow (2000) note that long-term relationships with peers can be a source of stigma resilience, although they acknowledge they are only drawing on anecdotal evidence. The authors suggest, "peers do not make explicit demands, but they also make few allowances" (p.397). The two roommates I interviewed seemed to make allowances for each other's uniqueness out of familiarity and mutual understanding. When asked the advantages of having a roommate with ASHFA, they both immediately agreed that "finding a roommate that won't lie, cheat, or steal from you is worth more than their weight in gold." They described instances of being taken advantage of and robbed by socioconventional roommates. I suspect an ethnographic study of roommates on the spectrum would probably be an insightful source of information about an under-documented area of stigma resilience. Both were on income assistance, and because of low assistance levels, finding a roommate in such instances can be almost as fundamental as the need to pick up groceries.

One of the participants in this study had been married to an individual of the opposite sex also diagnosed with Asperger's for ten years. Another had been with a socioconventional same-sex partner for the same length of time. Each described different challenges. Such intimacy involves complications that roommates do not have to deal with. The participant with an autistic partner reported, "We have tons of communication issues, and there are many misunderstandings. We each have problems with getting frustrated when the other interrupts what we are focused on, because we get so intense we can't switch to something else and then switch back." She was able to describe these challenges without blame or anger. The couple clearly had their challenges, but they understood each other. Their expectations of each other were in sync. The participant with a same-sex socioconventional partner enumerated several issues over which his partner gets frustrated with him. He said, "I can't validate," meaning he did not feel able to provide his partner with emotional validation. He said his partner gets angry because the participant is on the computer too much and "can't see obvious little things" such as items on the floor that need to be picked up. He also spoke about frequent conflict resulting from his routines being broken. I did not think to explore the degree to which the autistic couple met each other's needs, but if the roommates are any indication they probably found this less challenging than sociophenomenally mixed couples. Yet no matter how intense, frustrating, or challenging, no participant reported their relationship to be stigmatizing. Rather, the intimate relationships discussed in this study were reported as a source of resilience and refuge from stigma where, as one participant said, "someone can accept me no matter what." As with any relationship, there may be difficult times during which differences are ironed out and frustrations are vented, but these can lead to personal growth and deeper connection.

Resilience Research and Possibility

I'd like to share an interesting article I read the other day about autism and trauma resilience. The author (Rigles 2017) claimed it was the first research paper ever on the topic. She based it on experiences of developmental trauma codified into "adverse childhood events" and identified nine types of occurrence including financial problems, divorce, parent mental health issues, witnessing domestic abuse, and being a victim of discrimination. Her methodology depended on parents to note the incidents, making the recording process sensitive only to overt events. Incidents such as stigma and other forms of invalidation taking place silently with such things as a look or an omission were not captured despite their potentially hurtful effects and cumulative traumatic impact.

The study employed a sample of 56,746 people interviewed by telephone. Results validated previous research showing autistic children experience significantly more "adverse effects" than mainstream children, have decreased levels of physical health, and lower overall resilience. The most interesting thing is a question left hanging by the author based on a surprising result. Autistic children did not show the same tendency as mainstream children to have diminishing resilience in the face of increasing negative experiences. The more negative things that happen to socioconventional children the less ability they have to integrate and move forward. A higher occurrence of "adverse effects" reported by the parents of Autistic children was not associated with parental ratings of lower resilience. Why not? The author admitted that her study could not answer this question and noted the need for further research. She suggested that Autistic children's lower overall levels of resilience may make it more difficult for observers to discriminate negative impacts on resilience.

Some of the researcher's proposed explanations can be seen to inadvertently perpetuate negative autistic stereotypes. For example, she suggests negative experiences may "push these children further into their own world making it appear as though they were not affected" (p.199). This could be taken as an invitation to find better ways of appreciating the experience of Autistic children, so we can more fully understand and provide better support. It could also be taken to reinforce the perception that autistic people aren't reachable. Another offensive implication in the researcher's discussion involves a specific finding. Of the different sources of trauma investigated in the study, only divorce was associated with lower resilience in autistic children. She took this as a possible indication that autistic children are not impacted by emotionally traumatic and invalidating events unless their routines are broken. This feeds a negative stereotype of autistic people being devoid of human feelings and fundamentally disconnected from others. The death of a parent and incarceration of a parent were also on the list of adverse events, and these would interrupt a child's routines just as disruptively.

Rather than using it as an example that demonstrates autistic aloofness, parents divorcing can be seen as unique because it involves a greater personal crisis of invalidation. If a parent dies, this is awful but can be understood as no one's fault. If a parent is incarcerated, it can be explained as bad decisions that got them in trouble. When divorce happens, it may bring already stressful feelings of discord rushing to the surface. Children may already be traumatized by witnessing their parents not getting along. They may already be blaming themselves for the fighting because they know they cause trouble in ways they cannot understand or express. Divorce shatters the safe emotional security of a child's world as few other events can, and autistic children are no different. That divorce is the only variable associated with deceased resilience could be taken as evidence that autistic children are more emotionally present than they are often given credit for and more sensitive to invalidation than conventionally thought. This could be an importantly stigma-challenging research result, not only to break through autistic stereotypes but in our growing recognition of invalidation trauma. Maybe autisticy, as Rigles suggests, provides its own kind of protective factor against certain kinds of trauma. It is possible that autistic children, rather than being flawed in ways that make them insensitive to adverse emotional events, are more resilient and have strengths which have not been sufficiently appreciated or explored. Not just more research is called for in this area, but research informed by the unique perspective and experience of autistic people.

Chapter 6

STIGMA CLOAKING

Building stigma resilience involves self-care strategies that make us stronger and less vulnerable to being hurt, and help us recover more quickly from stigma and stigma activation. Stigma cloaking, on the other hand, refers to strategies of stigma management that deflect or avoid the impact of stigma. One maneuver participants felt targeted by but did not report engaging in themselves was offloading stigma. Goffman (1963) referred to this as "ambivalence," a process through which a stigmatized individual parries stigma by "taking up in regard to those who are more evidently stigmatized than himself the attitudes the normals take to him" (p.107). The participant identifying himself as PHA (person living with HIV/AIDs) said, "The thing that bothers me the most is when oppressed people oppress other oppressed people. I just don't get it. My mind literally shuts down." He talked about how he sees this happen "not just in the HIV community, but everywhere." People experience stigma, for example HIV, and they offload it where they can:

> They turn around and they stigmatize people who have wrongful behaviors, or that are inappropriate by normal standards. They will shut you right out, they will shut you right out. Because "You're the angry PHA and we're going to shut out the angry PHA." They make you follow these rules of engagement, and if you don't follow them they shut you out for that too.

Eliminating Asperger's as a distinct diagnosis and merging it with autistic spectrum disorder shone a spotlight on offloading stigma. I was guilty of it myself. When I was first told I showed signs of autism, even though I consider myself open-minded and non-prejudiced, I reacted horribly. I pushed the stigma of autism away from myself with every fiber of my being. It was a knee-jerk reaction, but it came down to the sorry fact I did not want to be "like them." When people diagnosed with Asperger's were confronted with being labeled with autism many had the same reaction. One participant said, "I had a friend in Australia who ended up not talking to me for a while, because I disagreed with his perspective on this. To me we're one big family." He added that "Even the low functioning Aspies don't want to be further stigmatized as autistic." None of the participants reported having this attitude, although one started the interview by saying he had been diagnosed with infantile autism as a baby and had "grown out of it." He initially distanced himself from the label by maintaining his condition had "resolved itself into a severe learning disability." It wasn't until later he acknowledged his autism.

It may be that no one acknowledged this perspective because of a desire to be socially correct (which, paradoxically, people with autism are not supposed to care much about). As one of the participants acknowledged, "People tend to hide their prejudice when they know it's socially unacceptable." This tension between acknowledging one's Autistic personality and distancing oneself from the label is an aspect of the "ambivalent ideal" of autistic openness (Rosqvist 2012, p.127).

Two participants talked about the irony of being bullied by other kids in school also diagnosed with autism. One study (Sterzing *et al.* 2012) found that 46.3 percent of autistic adolescents experienced bullying compared with 10.6 percent of mainstream others. It also found that autistic adolescents are almost as likely to become bullies themselves. The likelihood someone will pick on others is a factor of strength relative to peers as well as self-absorbed disregard of the harm caused to others as we meet our own needs. When one autistic picks on another, it can be seen as a self-defensive redirection of stigma that offloads shame onto more vulnerable individuals. The participants who were picked on by another autistic considered it an especially disturbing variation of bullying. It may be related to what Brown (2015) calls "power-over chandeliering" (p.61), which happens when people take shame-based pain out on those more vulnerably positioned in the social hierarchy. It would be interesting to design a study investigating how much bullying and sexual harassment is associated with this kind of transference.

It is arrogant to make assumptions about a stigmatized group one is not part of, but this process brings to mind "shadism," which is the term used when people of color stigmatize each other based on how dark their skin is (Adewunmi 2011). This happens across cultures largely as a result of slavery and colonialism. Stigma offloading is shame evasion behavior to be mindful of if we want to minimize our footprint of oppression in the world.

Cloak of Invisibility

Several other mechanisms of stigma cloaking were identified by participants. The most fundamental of these is the cloak of invisibility. One form of this stigma management strategy was described by Goffman as "passing" (1963, p.73), which involves what participants described as "faking it" and what Willey (1999) described as "pretending to be normal" in the title of her autobiographical book about life with ASHFA and/or Asperger's. It means attempting to pass as normal and disappearing into the dominant crowd through information control, denial, and concealment in order to avoid stigma. Such disappearing may also be accomplished by adopting what Goffman calls an "involvement shield," one aspect of which involves adopting a non-person role (1956, p.95). Goffman (1966) provides one example involving servants who are present in the room but as invisibly as possible and also speaks about sailors from faraway places who are hardly given an acknowledging glance. We must be careful here to distinguish the process of voluntarily assuming the non-person *role* as a stigma management strategy from the stigmatizing non-person *treatment* often enacted upon those perceived to be unimportant or not worth regarding respectfully (Goffman 1963, p.18). If we withdraw too readily and completely into the non-person role our stigma management strategy is in danger of becoming self-stigmatizing and lapsing into complicity with the stigmatizing practices of dominant others. Depending on the level of oppression involved, it can become "a taxing necessity and a discipline all of its own" in a desperate attempt to survive (1966, p.40).

With this cautionary balance in mind, all the participants seemed to identify with this as a strategy on some level. One participant said, "I learned when I was younger just don't say anything and you won't get in trouble." She added, "I don't want to stand out or anything." Another participant said, "When I'm overloaded I just say to myself 'that's enough, they're not interested in understanding so I'm just going to withdraw and see how things are going to play out.'" In alignment with a cloak of invisibility, ASHFA sometimes find roles they can play, not unlike the servant, allowing them to take on a function they can manage without having to engage in excessive social interaction. One participant assumed the role of group facilitator for this reason, saying he is much more comfortable doing this than being a group member. Others take on the role of note-taker, photographer, or camera man. ASHFA are often encouraged to find a way to get jobs in an area of obsession. It is also possible to turn comfortable non-person roles into careers.

The cloak of invisibility can involve what Goffman described as "covering" (1963, p.102), which is adopting socioconventional behaviors as autistic camouflage to evade stigma. It can also involve the effort to unlearn what one of the participants in the study called "spectrumy" behaviors:

> I have asked for 25 years to be measured by my own yardstick, not to be measured by everybody else's yardstick, and nobody's ever even acknowledged that statement. They ignore that statement, they don't understand that statement, they can't see how someone else could have a different yardstick, and I understand that because I don't look autistic. I can look at people in the eye. I don't have to stim. But that comes from years of abuse. Being abused not to do these things. Having your head turned—"look at me!" Not just from parents and teachers but from society as a whole.

This participant's narrative shows how sociodominants can sometimes exercise what Foucault calls a "relationship of violence" (1976/1994, p.340) over autistic people. "Look me in the eye, you wimp!" comes to mind from my school yard days. I was also admonished by authority figures for stimming and given "the strap" for not better controlling disruptive emotional escalations. Most efforts to control and autistic stigma cloaking are related to what Foucault calls the "productive aspect of power" (1982/1994, p.120), or efforts to "improve" the autistic person with seemingly positive programs of change designed to more closely approximate sociodominant expectations. Subtle pressures to go along with this like guilting, shaming, and conditional acceptance are what often lead autistic individuals to isolate, blend, and disappear. Participants often do this by "dumbing down," although one participant described how he deals with these insidious social politics by "feeling superior."

Intelligence

One participant spoke about a cloak of intelligence. Asked if he could identify behavior or characteristics sociodominants might find frustrating about him, the participant said, "that I'm more intelligent and mature than them." He added, "I was always smarter than everybody else and I wasn't modest about showing it." Another participant talked about how "everyone else was reading like the Cat in the Hat and I was miles ahead of them." It is not unusual for individuals with Asperger's to have high levels of intelligence. Even into adulthood, ASHFA can sound pedantic and pompous at times. ASHFA children often give the impression of being "little professors" (Attwood 2007, p.86). This intelligence can be seized on as a cloaking device that marginalized individuals can use to shield themselves from stigma. My uncle used to call me "Einstein." I remember how I would conceal my anxiety and social confusion with intense, intelligent expressions as if I were trying to solve a serious world problem. In a perfect example of Goffman's dramaturgy, or the use of performance to fend off stigma, as soon as I could grow a beard to scratch it, it became a permanent prop.

The issue of intelligence and ASHFA brings up another consideration. One participant remembers doing a project in public school about how gas contributes to the explosive nature of volcanoes. The teacher, probably expecting at his grade level he must mean gasoline, failed him and said gas had nothing to do with volcanoes. The participant remembers going to the school next morning with his father and "dropping about 50 pages of United States Geological Survey documents on her desk." With the support of his dad (who the family has informally diagnosed with Asperger's), the participant was able to demonstrate he actually knew what he was talking about. Without his dad, the participant may have been left feeling invalidated and ashamed. Although they may have a command of logic and facts, ASHFA may not have the presence of mind to defend themselves. I had a similar experience. My teacher in Grade 2 once asked the class what parachutes were made of. I had seen a documentary that said nylon was a good material for this purpose. I shot up my hand and proudly gave my answer. The whole class erupted in laughter, probably thinking I meant women's nylons. The teacher, rather than coming to my defense, agreed with the class and told me I was wrong. I felt embarrassed and stupid. I often wondered if it would have made a difference had the teacher known I was autistic. She might have been more prepared for answers out of her usual context of expectation. Forewarning with the language of disorder, however, may indicate an over-reliance on the discourse of diagnosis. Rather than needing medical validation to be prepared, people should be ready for diversity as a rule.

Helping

The cloak of helping can also be very effective as a stigma management strategy. One participant in particular said, "I take enormous pride in volunteering." Common wisdom says helping can take our mind off our troubles, get us engaged with the community, and help build confidence. However, sometimes ASHFA intensify things. Helping can take on a sense of urgency. The above participant said he does not understand why socioconventionals reject him, so he compensates by trying to be of service. He puts up posters offering to be of help. Yet still he runs into brick walls:

> Participant: I've tried to help people because I understand what it's like to need help. If they could understand what I intend, they would come to me and say, "I could use some help." Instead, I get the cold shoulder.
>
> Researcher: Do you think you're doing something wrong?
>
> Participant: I don't know, they don't tell me. This means I have to try multiple avenues to get the message out that I'm willing to help.
>
> Researcher: What else would you like neurotypical people to know?
>
> Participant: I just wish they would tell me what's allegedly so upsetting about what I'm doing. I feel that what I'm doing is inoffensive, yet they feel I'm bragging or whatever. I'm not. I just want to help other people. Helping people gives me an enormous sense of pride. I would love to help anyone.

> Researcher: So if people would just accept you and see you as a human being, maybe be more patient with the different way you communicate, things would be a lot better for you.
>
> Participant: They sure would! There wouldn't be such a need to put up these [*holds up a handful of his "help" posters*].

I identified with this participant. I have always been eager to be of help. It is often easy to discern when help is needed, when something "nice" will please someone. It's as if building up nice-guy credits can offset the times I frustrate people without knowing why. I never thought about it when I was younger, but for me this calculus of people-pleasing has always been a desperate strategy of impression management and stigma control. For those who adopt this strategy, the frequency and urgency of helping may be correlated with the amount of stigma they experience. It may also be negatively correlated with the degree of control they feel in their ability to manage personal relationships. More research on helping behavior could be enlightening.

For me, helping became a way to take on the cloak of invisibility. I had to be a crisis counselor from an early age because of a family member with borderline, and this generalized to my social life. I learned that a helping stance gave me a controlled, well-defined social role without having to interact spontaneously with others. Adopting this role led me as an anxious, socially awkward boy afraid to talk to anyone all the way to a career as a mental health crisis counselor. This again shows how stigma cloaking can turn into productive work. The form of stigma management adopted contributes to self-development and can lead to unpredictable avenues of insight, self-expression, and activity. You never know where what feels right will lead when you put one foot in front of the other.

Humor, Anger, and Hooliganism

ASHFA may don a cloak of humor to protect themselves from stigma. One participant said she "pretends to get jokes when someone tells one by laughing when other people laugh." Sometimes humor is unintentional but still acts as stigma protection. I don't know how many times I've made comments that made people laugh when I was being serious. The other day, for example, I was in a pizza store waiting for my take-out order. When the guy behind the counter noticed me, he asked, "What are you waiting for, sir?" With deadpan seriousness I told him, "My pizza." There have been times in my life when such literal responses and missing relevant meaning have resulted in humiliation, frustrated eye-rolling, and stigmatizing verbal assaults such as "No, stupid, I mean what is the name on the order you're waiting for?" This pizza worker, however, thought I was hilarious. He laughed out loud and exclaimed, "That's a good one." Accidental humor saved me from an experience of stigma. I experienced a flutter of stigma activation and momentarily felt a familiar rush of "stupid," but noticed it and defused the resulting flustered discomfort by gracefully laughing at myself. No one got the real joke except me, but it didn't matter. Causing others to laugh and laughing at yourself beats feeling stupid every time. Even when we don't get the joke and have no idea why people are laughing, the best thing to do at such times is laugh along.

In my study, one participant referred to himself as "goofy." One participant tended to laugh frequently during his narratives, almost like a form of punctuation that gave him a chance to assess whether he should keep talking. There are ASHFA who don't take anything seriously, as well as those who take everything too seriously. I have done both, taking a too-serious stance when I was young and finding the grace to laugh at myself when I was older.

Sometimes the cloak of humor can turn into the mask of the clown. This is when constant and overt attempts at humor give people a reason to never take you seriously and your "muff-ups" can be taken painlessly as just another joke. This strategy can help socioconventional others feel at ease and relieve social pressure, but it can also cause resentment to build and self-esteem to go down in the stigmatized person.

If humour is a response to stigma that attempts to defuse, blend, and camouflage, anger is perhaps a more congruent response to the oppression of stigma. When anger goes from being an appropriate response in specific situations to being a protective barrier, it can become a stigma cloaking strategy. The cloak of outrage was well worn by one participant in particular. He made frequent comments like "Most of the people out there are superficial, judgmental, and hypocritical." When asked what he thought of neurotypicals, he said, "You mean all the people whose only function is to breathe and expend resources? The ones who just make life harder for the rest of us? You mean the ones who are only alive because it's against the law to shoot them?" It's easy to see the source of such anger. Years of stigma, oppression, bullying, and rejection can't always be contained nicely. Sometimes anger helps protect us from more abuse.

A related stigma protection device none of the participants talked about or demonstrated but which I have observed is the cloak of the jerk. Like other stigma reduction strategies, this stance may be adopted by anyone for a number of reasons and can merge with one's personality. Whereas some individuals seem to hide their social awkwardness behind anger or humor, those adopting the cloak of the jerk adopt the stance of an uncaring, selfish curmudgeon. The reason this came to mind is I remember thinking at times growing up that this would be an easy stance to take if I didn't care so much about what people thought of me. I also remember a friend complaining once about such an individual. She said he was a "real asshole." I said enviously, "At least he's a *real* something." I meant to say I was so busy with impression management and stigma cloaking that I didn't feel like an authentic person. A variation of this theme came up in another conversation when a socioconventional spouse said they often wondered if their spouse's rude, irritating, and selfish behavior was "Asperger's or asshole."

Labels, Safety, and Extraversion

To protect against stigma, it is also possible to wear a cloak of labels. Most of the participants had engaged in some kind of self-labeling to normalize their condition. One referred to herself as "shy." Another called himself "odd." I have often thought of myself as "eccentric." Another has come to be known by his socioconventional peers as "the social critic," a label he wears proudly. Accepting a diagnosis can be seen as a medically validated form of stigma cloaking, unless the stigma associated with the label itself becomes more stigmatizing than the condition, which seems to be the case for such things as borderline personality disorder. This might also be true for the label of autism, although the term "Asperger's" has served to mediate the stigma of autism for ASHFA. Perhaps the community building and pride in diversity that has coalesced around Asperger's is being fed back into autism more generally by the elimination of this diagnostic category. If true, this change in the DSM-5 may be helping the destigmatization process generalize across the spectrum.

Labels provide an external stigma cloak. The cloak of safety provides more integrated protection and involves finding a safe environment in which one's stigmatizing condition will blend in naturally or be accepted as "normal." One participant's tendency to make friends "as goofy as me" could be seen as such a strategy. The participant described the safety and camaraderie of making friends with eccentricities like his own as a strategy of empowerment. I used this strategy when I became a hippy. It provided safety although it diverted me from larger more risky goals. Goffman calls these "back places." This refers to a place where individuals with "the same or similar stigma stand exposed and find they need not try to conceal their stigma, nor be overly concerned with cooperatively trying to disattend it" (1963, p.81). Goffman used the example of a carnival as a back place where various stigmatized individuals can find an environment safe from stigma. Some of the participants identified online chat rooms as such places. ASHFA often go to great lengths to find back places with relaxed expectations, which might be an unconventional workplace or a fringe sub-culture where deviance from conventional expectations does not draw attention to itself.

One participant had worked as a hairdresser, where the stigma associated with being gay was acceptable. He had also worked as a bar manager (in the back office with a partner who mingled with the patrons, so he didn't have to engage in too much social banter). In both these work environments, the stigma of autisticy may have been disguised by the unique social characteristics of the environment. For the participant, both had more to do with stigma cloaking related to substance abuse, which was also disguised by the environment. This self-abusive coping strategy, more a response to stigma than the inherent challenges of autisticy, will be discussed at the end of the current chapter.

This brings us to the cloak of extraversion. Although ASHFA often involves a sense of personal inadequacy and relationship failure, there is still a need for belonging. Especially with a successful cloak of safety in place, autistic people may be outgoing and even gregarious. One of the common misperceptions about ASHFA happens when people think, "He's so social he cannot have AS" (Ducharme and Gullota 2013, p.27). When I lived in my hippie back place, I become more and more extraverted. I learned to celebrate my difference because I was accepted. I helped run a coffee house, did comedy onstage, led drum circles, and ran the bar at dances. I had never been so social in my life. I even learned to flirt with women. It sure beat being afraid of them, although I didn't know how to properly manage this complex behavior. The cloak of extraversion can get out of control because ASHFA may not comprehend the intricate complications of their social behavior.

Addiction

When ASHFA want to express their sociality and can't find a way to do so successfully, they may turn to drugs for help. They may also start to abuse substances to mask the pain of stigma. One of the participants in the current study did both:

> I never fit into the community. I found I could fit in where everyone knew me at the bars growing up. I wasn't totally ousted. I had people who would look out for me, but I didn't have a lot of friends. I did a lot of drugs instead. Because of being undiagnosed through my childhood I turned to drugs for self-medication starting with pot and moving up to crystal meth.

The participant reported that drugs helped him cope at first. He described how they didn't help with his ability to make real friends or socialize effectively, but they did decrease his anxiety, boost his energy, and give him the sense that he could "be in the same headspace with other people." Then it started to become a draining routine. Towards the end, he said, substance abuse became more about managing sensory issues:

> The acceptable thing to do was to go to the bars Friday, Saturday, and Sunday nights and I wanted to do the acceptable thing. We did that doing drugs, but I did get wasted. I mean really wasted because of the flashing lights, the people touching me, and drugs would help me cope with that. I didn't like it, it was "what the hell is going on with me," but it was the only way I could get on. Towards the end it was very sensory oriented.

The participant reported that drugs were "an acceptable way of coping in the hairdressing industry" but that "towards the end I knew drugs weren't good for me." The participant says he had been active in the HIV community for years learning everything he could about the condition in an effort to prevent himself from contracting the disease when he realized drug abuse was working against this goal because of the additional risk factors it introduced. By that time, his substance abuse had progressed from a stigma cloaking strategy to a problem in its own right. He later said:

> Then I knew that drug use was a symptom of the trauma I experienced. Drugs were like a mask I was wearing. They kept my behavior in check and provided an excuse for some of my quirks. I was not aware of the additional risks drug use created, like making me more vulnerable to taking things more literally and my language skills deteriorating. Drugs seemed to help me fit it, but I more often put my foot in my mouth which made me vulnerable for retribution and being ostracized.

Research tends to confirm the participant's experience, telling us that drugs may "positively influence the subjective perception of their social skills, or cause a reduced awareness of social awkwardness, without actually improving their social functioning" (Sizoo *et al.* 2009a, p.1294). Drugs can act as illusory stigma cloaking, for example, when ASHFA is substance-impaired and not feeling as self-conscious or perhaps a bit grandiose. Clinicians acknowledge that the stress of not understanding the stigma they frequently experience can precipitate addiction, and report that they often see clients whose substance abuse is their primary presenting symptom even though they are later diagnosed with autism:

> The abuse of drugs or alcohol is sometimes a means of self-medication without proper pharmacological, behavioral, or psychotherapeutic treatment for anxiety, mood, or sleep disorders. It is probable that adults with AS are at risk of substance use because of lack of other coping mechanisms, the presence of addictions in their families (Miles, Takahashi, Haber, and Hadden 2003), their repetitive thought patterns, their difficulty with regulating mood, the effect of environmental stressors, and the absence of other socially protective influences. (Stoddart, Burke, and King 2012, p.121)

There is very little in the literature about autism and substance abuse. A quantitative study in 2010 based on a sample of 123 patients with ASD and ADHD reported that substance use disorder (SUD) is almost twice as common in ADHD than ASD and that early onset tobacco smoking is the most important risk factor in the development of substance abuse. This is followed by parental substance abuse and "adverse family history" (Sizoo *et al.* 2010, p.47). Another quantitative study based on 128 patients with ASD and ADHD (Sizoo *et al.* 2009b) found that 22 percent of participants had current substance abuse issues, 19 percent had past substance abuse issues, and 59 percent had no history of substance abuse. They also found that participants with ASD as well as ADHD got higher scores for harm avoidance than the general population, a result consistent with the comfort-seeking self-absorption explored in this book. Participants with SUD got higher novelty-seeking scores than those without SUD, and (not surprisingly) those participants with high persistence scores were more likely to overcome substance abuse issues. Interestingly, participants with past or current substance use issues got higher self-transcendence as well as higher social engagement scores. Could this be an indication that mind-altering drugs somehow tap into an enduring source of resilience? All of this is very interesting, but it begs for qualitative research to explore the experience of participants more deeply in order to give meaning to the statistical results.

Since only one of my participants reported having issues with substance abuse, I searched publicly accessible online Asperger's forums in an effort to glean more insight into this issue. I found two discussion groups in particular where ASHFA with substance abuse issues were interacting. One person posted that:

Life is hard sober. I find it a struggle. It is, however, better than life on drugs. There are many effects of drugs that can make the autistic person feel better for a time. They can help relax and increase social potential, or at least seem to...

I was diagnosed as an adult, I was almost 35yo at the time. It was then I decided to go drug free because the condition I'd been aware of having my entire life was suddenly given a name. This gave me the confidence to try and confront life without numbing the pain artificially...

> My AS has certainly caused me major problems throughout my life. The prognosis is far more positive for people with sufficient support at the right times. I drifted through early adulthood homeless, sofa-surfing and abusing any and every chemical I could get my hands on. Anything to blot out reality. However, it never worked. The drugs don't work, eventually. (Countryboy 2010)

Stoddart *et al.* (2012) point out that an important part of substance abuse treatment is building a healthy social network. This poses a particular challenge for ASHFA, who find sociality challenging. Someone posted that:

> I'm an Aspie as well. It sucks, but recovery from the substance itself (heroin) has been really easy... I can't do any of the steps, though because I'm too literal and powerless to me means powerless. I find myself insisting that I wasn't powerless or I wouldn't have been able to stop on my own before finding NA [Narcotics Anonymous]. Don't get me started on the higher power stuff...it's not always so fab being of above average intelligence (especially when you have dyslexia as well and people think you're stupid because you can't spell). Relationships are very difficult (I'm a girl Aspie so it's expected of me even more to be empathic but I don't have such noticeably odd behaviors) I found that I can't really make any decent friends in recovery because no one is on the same level as me, they all believe in some kind of higher power and I can't have those conversations.
>
> I can only talk about things I know about which are things I believe to be true. I found it much better not to waste my time with recovery "friends" go and find people that have the same special interest as you...join a club, a forum, work within the field of it—who needs the pub? (Bluesky 2010)

All of this relates to stigma not only as a predisposing factor that leads ASFHA to use drugs, but also because substance abuse adds to the burden of stigma already being experienced. Negative judgments and assumptions towards individuals caught up in addiction weigh heavily. Help seeking becomes drug seeking in the minds of weary service providers who must protect themselves from compassion fatigue and determine how to allocate precious resources. Family members who've experienced too many broken promises become pessimistic to protect their own sanity. The addict may be viewed as weak, worthless, and not worth the effort of taking seriously, attitudes further obscuring the already devalued humanity of the autistic. This is a huge additional burden to overcome, and recovering addicts must rely on the strength of their own integrity as they patiently allow the trust of others to grow based on their behavior. Having compassion for the roots of addiction in trauma and brain chemistry can be challenging in the face of the chaos and pain involved. When ASHFA get embroiled in substance abuse, the intersecting stigmas become a double blow of invalidation.

The social confusion and stigma associated with ASHFA can predispose individuals to using drugs from an early age. With pre-existing challenges to fitting in, susceptibility to peer pressure puts ASHFA in even further jeopardy. This initiates an escalating cycle of stigma and shame. Finding ways to connect Autistic young people with a self-defined sense of adventure that affirms their humanity is invaluable. Early diagnosis can provide validation for their difference, but even more fundamental is the non-judgmental exploration of stigma to better understand what they are dealing with in ways that do not involve self-deprecating feelings of unworthiness.

Chapter 7

STIGMA, AUTISM, AND PROFESSIONAL HELPERS

Service providers of all stripes are often called upon to help those trying to manage the stigma associated with autism and the challenges of autisticy. The problem is professional helpers often add to the person's invalidation with their approach. Reverse stigma happens when people are told "nothing's wrong with you" rather than being heard and helped to explore their experience. Some of the participants pointed a critical finger at social service agencies. One of the participants declined case management due to what Foucault called "hierarchized surveillance" (1975/1995, p.177), which in this case targets individuals having to claim a disability in order to access benefits:

> I tried to get a worker, but I just didn't like the whole program. They want me to do an intake interview with a bunch of questions, then you get your worker, then they want you to do another intake interview after you get into the program, then you have to meet with your worker one hour every week and then do a life planning meeting either at your house or a coffee shop. Then you have to go into the office once a year. The other thing I wasn't happy about is that they want to know that I'm going to the doctor, going to the dentist, and getting my eyes checked every year. As soon as I found out about all this, I withdrew.

Not only did the participants resent this intrusive level of monitoring, they did not appreciate the way they had been treated by many of their past workers. One participant said he did not feel listened to and often felt like a "pet project or summer job." His roommate complained that past workers would not drive him places, such as the supermarket to get groceries. He says the workers blamed this on insurance policies and organizational mandates. Both participants agreed "They have their own political agendas, these places. They're supposed to help people out, and they do everything but." One of the ways to build stigma resilience is to go out and interact, which is restricted by high bus fares. Yet their workers said they were not allowed to drive them anywhere. Participants found this ludicrous:

> If you're a worker, you should be able to drive your clients. If they need to go to the grocery store, they should be driven to the grocery store and help out with their grocery shopping, help them pick out what food they need and what food they don't need. It's all politics.

A general lack of knowledge was also mentioned by participants as a source of service resentment. One participant complained that:

> Well, here you have all these people that have university and college degrees and supposedly know their jobs, but even when I was a kid I was able to tell them stuff about my condition they didn't know. You think they know best and because they think they know best, you trust them. Then it turns out later…they were just parroting old obsolete data or whatever, either because they were naive, stupid, or just—what's the word—apathetic?

Another participant described how services are not always well integrated with the specific needs of the autistic population. When applying for a new service, the participant said she had her regular autism worker with her along with an intake worker for the program. She said the intake worker talked to her in a patronizing way, which made her feel resentful and stupid. Probably not knowing how to address the client's need for explicit, direct formulations without double meaning, the intake worker unknowingly precipitated a crisis for the participant. In a subtle invitation to autistic misunderstanding not even her regular worker noticed, when the intake worker asked if the participant needed support with self-injurious behaviors the participant became confused. This did not seem like something the organization should be supporting her to do. She did not know what to say. In a classic telegraphic episode, the participant could tell there was social incongruence making her appear out of line but could not articulate what. The stress overwhelmed her and, donning a cloak of invisibility, she engaged in a carefully disguised act of self-injurious behavior under the table right in front of the workers (which neither noticed). This does not mean only experts should work with autistic people. It demonstrates the importance of being familiar with the kinds of diversity we may encounter, whether clearly labeled or invisible and sensed marginally. Considering the growing incidence of autism, which has been called things like a public health crisis and an epidemic in the literature (Gates 2014), as well as the even greater number of people who struggle with challenges of autisticy, this is an increasingly important population to be prepared for in life as well as practice.

Accessing a counsellor is a powerful way to help work out the pain and confusion of stigma, especially when a person does not yet understand the source of what makes them feel different from others. The premature jump to problem-solving is one way these professionals can prove unhelpful. Not only does it often result in perfunctory over-simplified solutions, it neglects the most important thing. The client's perspective is not explored. They do not leave feeling understood or validated. In cases involving autisticy, the person's experience of stigma and the resulting invalidation is often a major component of why they are there. To not receive the validation of being listened to, not given the opportunity to get at the underlying perspective, the autistic person may leave feeling no further ahead. In fact, the professional they were dealing with may have added to their stigma.

As a counselor I often sense people are only telling me superficial stories rather than digging up truth. A counselor can only work with what a client has to give. If they choose to remain at a shallow level, spending their hour in denial, blaming someone else for their troubles, or trying to make themselves look good there will be little to work with in the session. They may leave feeling gratified for being the center of attention, but no further ahead for the trouble of coming. They may not be deliberately avoiding anything, not manipulating or deceiving, but if they are not ready to delve honestly into the messiness of their situation there is little a counselor can do except help them more fully uncover the motivation that brought them to the session. Therapists should not take over the client's issues by problem-solving, which robs the client of responsibility. This needs to be balanced with the risk of overwhelming clients with demanding levels of insight or asking them to take responsibility for problems they don't yet have enough trust to explore. It is also a lesson for parents, teachers, friends, and anyone invested in making an effort to communicate with different others, including autistic people.

When it comes to autism, the challenge of maintaining this balance becomes even more complex. ASHFA are often oriented to intellectual analysis and may spend a whole session rationalizing. They may be overly literal, examining the minutiae of daily activities without knowing how to look more deeply at their motivations. They may take their way of experiencing the world for granted and not see any other way of seeing things. These are only some of the reasons autism has typically been seen as not amenable to therapy. Another reason for this defeatist attitude may be that autistic individuals cannot be "cured," making some therapists think their problems cannot be "fixed" so there is no point wasting everybody's time. The point of therapy, however, is not to make problems go away or to "fix" people, but to alleviate suffering. Emotional pain does not come from autisticy itself so much as stigma, accumulated traumas and micro-traumas of not being accepted, and being different in an unforgiving world built to accommodate the conventional mainstream. Professional service providers who want to be truly helpful need to let go of the evidence-based frenzy to treat pathology or manage deviance in order to focus on the therapeutic human encounter through which the person will be able to explore, process, and make sense of their experience in a sociodominant world.

It doesn't take an expert to listen therapeutically. In fact, expertise can make listening seem unnecessary, as if our extensive knowledge has already categorized everything in terms of pre-determined categories. The business of being an "expert" can make listening seem like a time-consuming luxury. This is an unfortunate perception, because authentic, open-minded listening is the most important tool of stigma control. I once had a colleague who only listened enough to make a conclusion about what he thought his clients needed. When I confronted him with the possibility he wasn't listening enough, he said he was *listening fast*. In other words, he was listening selectively according to his model of what it was important to listen for. In order to listen therapeutically, we must take the time and make the effort to listen to the person as they describe what is important to *them*. Rather than hearing what we are prepared to hear, we listen to the narrative as presented. We prompt with simple acknowledgments that show we are trying to understand in a way that encourages further information sharing. In this way, we may discover things about a person's experience we might have glossed over. This is not so we can fix the person's problems. Help that jumps too quickly to problem-solving often leaves people in the dust and doesn't address their needs at all. We listen therapeutically to make people feel *heard*. Not only does such listening validate people and make them feel like they matter, it allows us to respond in congruence with their actual needs rather than our judgments and preconceived notions. Our filters of expertise need to be balanced with the curiosity of a beginner's mind. We need to focus on the person before us and use our skills to encourage the fullness of their perspective rather than jumping to conclusions about what they need or don't need.

Engaging autistic people with images that interest them or concepts that intrigue them depending on their unique predisposition can be an effective way to bridge barriers. Even the most evidence-based, potentially effective approach without responsive customization may fall on deaf ears or feel controlling or demeaning to the person. Others may dismiss approaches that don't interest them no matter how logical they seem to us. It can activate stigma if autistically stigmatized people feel they aren't "getting" what we say, which further internalizes damaging self-esteem. Cascades of relationship failure often take place not due to any deficiency in either person, but because one or both leans on their own conventions of knowledge or supposed expertise rather than putting curiosity first and listening to the other with an open mind.

Many professionals find themselves avoiding therapy with Autistic individuals. I have had clients bemoan the difficulty of finding service for trauma only to have their case rejected because the applicant had autism. I myself have been denied service with counselors when they discovered I had an autistic diagnosis. I have also spoken with professional peers who are reluctant to work with autistic people, sometimes blaming the client's lack of insight and sometimes their own lack of knowledge about autism. When someone comes to a therapist to address the pain of their marginalization and the stigma they experience, they may not even have a diagnosis. It is not knowledge of autism that best allows us to be helpful, but flexibly letting go of conventional expectations and curiously exploring their perceptions.

Helping others explore the sources of stigma they experience, taking direction from their expression of uniqueness rather than imposing our own assumptions, techniques, theories, or expertise upon them, is often the most help we can be. This is in alignment with the ethics of encounter.

The author of *Uniquely Human* (Prizant 2016) adopts this ethical framework when he describes how he has learned to work with autistic individuals in his 40 years of experience in the field. He says many school boards and autism workers get it "all wrong" when they apply their theories too strictly to lived situations and approach people as problems to be solved using conventional methods rather than responding in engaged, creative ways to the individual's real needs (p.16). Even those who have no voice to speak communicate their needs when we closely observe the patterns of their behavior. He cites the case of Lucy, a non-verbal student who was lunging at teachers in apparent aggression. When consulted, Prizant observed these lunges always taking place when the client's routine was altered unexpectedly. Rather than immediately deploying techniques to eliminate the behavior, he recognized it as a "plea for support at a moment of extreme confusion" (p.28). By altering the service provider's behavior so changes were introduced in a way that could be better tolerated, he found a way to manipulate Lucy's environment rather than subjecting her to "purely scientific" behavioral treatments in order to address the concerns of the teachers. Whatever our areas of experience, theoretical orientation, and training, if we do not let the person's individuality and lived experience guide us we are in grave danger of violating our professional ethical frameworks by causing harm with our lack of openness to the person's self-identified needs. Impoverished encounters that do not validate the person we are interacting with undermine them and add to their stigma. Biklen (2005) makes this the last word of his study exploring the experience of CLAWHS who type to speak. He maintained that our "obligation is thus not to assume the meaning of something another person does but rather to presume there must be a rationale and then try to discover it, *always* from the other person's perspective, listening carefully" (p.282). This goes for human interaction universally and is especially important to remember when dealing with people whose challenges we don't understand. It also applies whether we are acting as professionals or not.

ABA

Applied behavioral analysis (ABA) is a commonly used treatment modality often used to manage autism. A controversial intervention for almost as long as autism has been recognized as a disorder in the western hemisphere (Kirkham 2017), it is seen as demeaning and stigmatizing by many and has been declaimed by both previous workers in the field and autistic individuals (AnxiousAdvocate 2015; Sequenzia 2016). This technique can be effectively used to decrease harmful behaviors, such as head banging, or to increase helpful behaviors, such as increasing the variety of foods a person will eat, so they can better nourish themselves. When taken as a general approach to treatment without addressing the experience and humanity of the individuals it is supposed to be helping, it can also be perceived as an instrument of devaluation. The isolated application of purely behavioral technologies neglects the spirit of the individual, effectively adding to a vulnerable person's traumatic burden of stigma and further alienating them from mainstream society.

We only have to look to B.F. Skinner, a pioneer in developing the behavioral orientation underlying ABA, to see how fundamentally dehumanizing it can be. He calls the mind an "explanatory fiction" (p.1971, p.4) and refers to attitudes, opinions, motivations, inspiration, and other states of mind as mere "by products" (p.16). He tells us "the appeal to the mind explains nothing at all" (p.195). Shored up behind such a philosophy, what motivates a worker to consider the thoughts, feelings, and real needs of the person they are working with? The instrumental, basic repetition of mundane tasks ABA focuses on can be invalidating to an intelligent person not yet able to demonstrate their intelligence. Carly Fleischmann, for example, writes that she hated when workers would repeatedly ask her to "spell chips for a chip." She said this made her "feel like I am stupid" (Fleischmann and Fleischmann 2012, p.300). That is why we are encouraged to presume competence with CLAWHS (those diagnosed with "classic autism" who need high levels of support). The pain caused by unrestrained behaviorism not sufficiently addressing the humanity of the person is eloquently articulated by a disabled autistic man who communicates best with typing:

> They spent too much time on things I could learn eventually and that were not interesting and too little time figuring out that I had

a brain... Practice was needed for talking. Not Smarties... I think the missing link was they didn't give me a sense that they cared about me. (Bloomfield 2011, pp.25–26)

Autism creates a desperate need in a person to be validated and overcome stigma. Any treatment or relationship that adds to stigma with further invalidation, making the individual feel unheard, not good enough, or that their personhood is not being acknowledged undermines its helping potential and becomes further dehumanizing. Doing harm does not always involve negligence or overt abuse and can come in subtle forms. ABA practitioners noticing low levels of public acceptance suggest that better public relations will address the issue (Critchfield *et al.* 2017). This superficial approach neglects the ethics of encounter as an important dimension of professional self-awareness and exploration.

The therapeutic approach conditioned by behaviorism's dehumanizing philosophy is just one example of how professional expertise can become oppressive. Service providers can improve their practice with a greater awareness of stigma and by gearing their professional use of self as well as their techniques to avoid further marginalizing vulnerable populations. Balancing any approach with authentic listening and acknowledging, letting the person's uniqueness and experience inform use of self, can circumvent the risk of doing violence to their humanity. It is not just behaviorism that could benefit from further developing this practice. An unbalanced focus on evidence-based techniques and theories at the expense of genuine encounter can lead to doing harm by adding to the existing damage of stigma in vulnerable individuals. We all invite a similar potential to do harm when judgments, preconceptions, and stereotypes overly constrain our encounter with others, in particular already stigmatized individuals. We need to ask ourselves if we are allowing this interpersonal blockage to happen. This will help us take responsibility for the stigma we may be enacting on others. Shifting our focus to a more openly receptive ethics of encounter that allows us to see, hear, and accept a person on their own terms is one remedy. Building familiarity, developing awareness of our preconceptions, cultivating curiosity, and employing emotional self-recovery strategies to defuse defensiveness can help us counter the stigma we may be unintentionally inflicting on others.

Chapter 8

TRAUMA, ANXIETY, SELF-CARE, AND RECOVERY

In the next few pages a model of stigma, anxiety, and trauma self-recovery will be presented. It begins with one simple idea. If we cultivate attentiveness to what is going on inside us, we will notice the presence of anxiety, stigma activation, and the physiological arousal of trauma as it arises. When we are attentive in this way, we will be alert for such activation and when it begins we can *NAB* it (*N*otice it, *A*ccept it, remember to *B*reathe, and *B*egin to work with it). When we *NAB* it, not just wait until, as one client put it, we're "over the cliff in crazy-making land," but notice it with open eyes and ground ourselves in acceptance and non-judgment, we have already done excellent self-recovery work. *AFTER* we notice it, not just react to it unconsciously and get wrapped up in it but allow ourselves to feel it rising without judgment, we can make efforts to take care of ourselves appropriately by practicing various techniques. It is only *AFTER* we *NAB* it that we can work with it. *AFTER* stands for *A*ctivating behavior, carefully choosing what we *F*ocus on, *T*hought retooling, *E*xposure, *R*adical acceptance, and *R*eimagining. These are tools I will share in the next two chapters, so readers can have them in a handy anxiety, stigma, and trauma recovery toolbox. The process has been presented at anxiety workshops and molded into an easy-to-remember model meant to be mobilized in an ongoing way to counter the flustered escalation and dissociation associated with anxiety and the activation of invalidation trauma. The strategies can be used to help us feel better and move forward at any level of trauma and anxiety, but remember we will be talking about how to improve wellbeing with self-care practices, not starting treatment.

The support of professional service providers can be invaluable and provide an appropriate level of intervention to augment the self-help efforts discussed here. Don't fall into the trap of not accessing professional help because of stigma. Society perpetuates the idea that it is weak to seek help, which is one of those cultural stereotypes we have to be careful not to buy into. It is important to recognize silly stereotypes, like the way drinking is portrayed as harmless fun for everyone in beer commercials, or how real men must not show emotion, or women must be skinny, or it is weak to seek professional help for the damage they can cause, and not undermine our own wellbeing and self-care in the uncritical acceptance of such cultural myths. It demonstrates ingenuity when we access appropriate resources and inner strength when we know ourselves well enough to realize when support is called for.

Some helpers can worsen stigma with their approach. We may have had a negative experience with this or know someone who has. In this regard, it is also important to advocate for ourselves, not continuing to work with someone without speaking up if we find we are being invalidated or not heard. We needn't rely completely on self-care that is not proving sufficient when professional support is available, and we must never let professional support lull us into feeling we don't need to practice self-care. The intuitive wisdom of our body can be our greatest ally.

There is an alternative to feeling victimized, confused, and awful about ourselves when we get upset or disrupt relationships with anxious safety distress and trauma activation. In the *NAB* it and *AFTER* care model we focus on non-judgmental noticing and self-regulation. We cultivate an awareness of the invalidation that plants micro-trauma in our bodies and makes us susceptible to escalation that can "hijack" us (Goleman 1996). We *NAB* it by noticing it, accepting what is happening, remembering to breathe, and using the resources at our disposal to take care of ourselves appropriately. This isn't easy and may never become completely automatic. It is a practice, and like any practice gets more natural the more we do it. We may get tired of having to do it over and over, but that's better than being beaten into escalating pain, withdrawal, and isolation by activated distress that repeatedly takes us by surprise.

Micro-trauma (everyday instances of stigma), pervasive complex trauma (for example, from ongoing abuse), and full-blown PTSD (from acute traumatic experiences) toxify our emotional wellness. Each follows the same pattern in increasingly intense and invasive ways.

Negative experiences are remembered in the body and lie waiting to re-emerge when environmental, cognitive, or emotional triggers activate the body's alarm system and ramp up our level of arousal in a defense pattern designed to protect us. The residue of this arousal can leak out in nightmares, chronic anxiety, anger and irritability, avoidance, withdrawal, inability to experience enjoyment, heightened sensitivity to sensory stimulation, sometimes painful muscle tension, and high alert readiness that leads to hyper-vigilance and easily triggered startle reactions. If your experience of such trauma is chronically uncomfortable and intense, whether or not you can remember explicit instances of terrorization, attack, or shattered shame states, seeking professional help to explore this is critically important for your wellbeing. It is fruitless to go on being strong. Acknowledge your pain and find someone, preferably someone who provides trauma-informed service, to take a closer look at what can become a toxic cycle of life-sucking agony.

Ten years as a crisis counselor does not make me a trauma expert. This experience, however, along with a lifetime of invalidation related to developmental trauma and stigma related to my autisticy, put me in a position to understand patterns of arousal and emotional exile that can throw us off balance. This and still blossoming insights generated by my research help me as a counselor show others how to recognize trauma and micro-trauma and what efforts they can make to better manage it. Because stigma activation, trauma, and anxiety are so closely related, the same strategies work for all three in terms of crisis management and self-recovery. They can also provide a good self-help model for anger, depression, and almost any form of emotional issue tending to overwhelm us if we aren't careful. Whatever your personal Ghost Town may be, don't avoid accessing appropriate information and resources. Be curious and receptive.

Don't, as my wife says, come to the party with "long hands and hard ears." In her culture, you never go to a gathering with your hands empty. You bring something such as some kind of food or a gift. In the context of self-help, don't flounder with your hands empty. Learn what is known about what will promote recovery. Have techniques at your disposal and remember to use them. Those with "hard ears" don't listen and aren't receptive to what might be helpful. This is what the *NAB* it and *AFTER* care model is all about: an easy to remember framework of helpful strategies. Don't try these things only when you're desperate for immediate relief. If they don't bring instant change, don't stop because they "don't work." If you decide to lose weight you don't give up on healthier eating just because the scale doesn't register immediate results. The real value such practices offer builds up over time, developing strength and resilience that may only be noticed gradually. The nature of the practice may change over time as you make it your own, but it is consistency that wins in the end. In the rush of events happening around all of us, remembering patience and guarding against the hazards of instant gratification can make all the difference in getting ourselves out of the emotional exile of Ghost Town.

All the resources in the world will mean nothing if we have "hard ears." This means we don't listen, won't hear, resist change, keep doing things the same old self-defeating way, and aren't receptive to new information. When we have "hard ears," we may try things because others convince us to, but we are not really open to seeing things in a new light. We may close ourselves off from acknowledging pain or hold onto it so tightly there is no room for change. We may dutifully attend treatment and read all the books we can get our hands on, but somehow in the moment of activation lapse unconsciously into familiar patterns of self-pity, self-beratement, striking out, or flustered panic. We may give all the appearance of listening, but we don't allow new ways to touch us where it counts, at the heart of our pain in the moment of activation. For example, we may hear all about the trauma-perpetuating dangers of self-abuse, even take copious notes about it, but slip automatically into calling ourselves stupid, ignore our own needs, or not stand up for ourselves because we indulge in thoughts that we're not worth it. We may beat ourselves up with guilt over the same old things even when we know better. We have to create space for the knowledge in our heads to percolate down to where it really counts and practice, practice, practice. That's why it can be so useful to let trusted others know the practices we are working on, not only for us to declare our commitment but so they can alert us when our patterns come up and help us soften the built-up wax in our hard ears.

Spirit of Mindfulness

Mindfulness, it seems, is being talked about everywhere. It is taught in schools, the military, upper management, hospitals, and community centers. Most people have at least heard of it, but defining it can be more elusive. Although Buddha talked about it 1500 years ago, it was only in the 1980s its value began to be recognized widely in the west. A doctor named Jon Kabat-Zinn had a spiritual practice that embraced mindfulness. He also ran a back-pain clinic and began to wonder what would happen if he taught mindfulness to his patients. He set up an experiment and discovered patients who learned mindfulness were better able to manage pain. He became an advocate for mindfulness and wrote books introducing it to western culture (for example, *Full Catastrophe Living*, 1990/2013). Stephen Levine, a writer and counselor, was another proponent and wrote poetic spiritual explorations of mindfulness (*A Gradual Awakening*, 1989). Both books are still in print and together offer a comprehensive introduction to mindfulness from both medical and spiritual perspectives. Chris Mitchell's little exploration of mindfulness and autism (2013) is an excellent practical guide to how autistic individuals can benefit from taking time to practice the calming, grounding exercise of mindful attention.

Mindfulness will be defined in this book as the *unstrained effort of focusing non-judgmentally on the simple experience of the present moment.* It is important to specify "unstrained" to emphasize how the practice of mindfulness does not involve the pressured exertion of willpower but simply calls for a gentle shift of focus. The simple things we focus on can be bodily sensations (inner ones such as muscle tension or outer ones like the sun on our eyes, the wind on our face, or the feeling of a smooth stone in our hand), a visual point of focus (like a candle burning or a certain spot on the wall), or if we are active, the task before us. What we choose to make our focus can differ, but mindfulness involves attending fully to the experience of it in the present moment. It's not that we only assume this single-pointed focus for the purpose of immersing ourselves in what we're focusing on. Making this effort creates a space of peace and de-escalating stillness in the clarity of which we can perceive the unfolding moment more fully. It's not that we have to shut everything else off. Peripheral awareness remains active and we are better able to respond as an organism to our inner and outer environment because attention is not scattered. It is this grounding effect and how it aims to consciously engage us with the peaceful aliveness of our physical selves that makes mindfulness "the cornerstone of recovery from trauma" (van der Kolk 2014, p.96).

Some people say they can't concentrate on two things at once, mindfulness and what's going on around them. Stepping into a space of mindful awareness makes us more aware of what's going on because it's so anchoring. It clears our mind and de-escalates us. If we work to force distress down rather than accepting it, people sense the tension. We make more of a spectacle trying to force ourselves to be "normal" than we ever would simply allowing ourselves to be imperfect. When we make the shift to mindful acceptance, people don't see the effort of non-effort we are making. They see and feel our greater level of presence. We feel it too.

The part of the task that takes most practice is simply noticing our attention when it drifts away from non-judgmental focus on the present to such complications as worry, regret, analysis, anticipation, alarm, comparison, or judgment. This noticing, followed by the effort of gently shifting attention back to where it is most helpful, is the fundamental practice of mindfulness.

Abundant and growing scientific evidence demonstrates beneficial effects such as relaxation, physiological de-escalation, slower brain waves, more ordered neurological firing, higher levels of mental as well as physical resilience, and measurable performance increases. It is simple, but it takes *practice* to become fluent with the therapeutic shift it calls for. Such effortless effort is sometimes called meditation, but this term has suspicious overtones of cults and religion that may spoil the innocent effort of simply being present for some. The very word imports potentially troublesome complexity that can be avoided by simply talking about mindfulness.

My own introduction to mindfulness was delivered by a spiritual teacher and came with a powerful image that bears repeating. It was a pleasantly warm summer evening in the mid-1980s. I was walking down Toronto's frantic main street with bustling people and honking cars when I noticed a sign on the faded red paint of an unpretentious old doorway. "Free concert—all welcome," it said. I went in assuming I would see a rock band, but there was only a little man in a white tunic sitting cross-legged on the stage playing a flute. There were different musical instruments scattered around the stage, but he was the solitary performer. I was going to leave as a young man whose expectations for adventure had been thwarted, but I was actually captivated by the peacefulness. I took a seat near the back of the shabby auditorium, and before long the man stopped playing and said a few words about inner peace. Someone in the audience immediately shot up their hand and demanded to know how inner peace was possible amid the racing thoughts, anxiety, emotional turmoil, and pressure of modern life. The relaxed, unpretentious little man on the stage, whose face shone with undisturbed tranquility, shifted the energy of the audience with words that still resonate. I continue to share them with clients 30 years later:

> Think of it this way. Think of emotional turmoil as waves crashing on the surface of the ocean. You don't have to be like a cork dashed around by the waves. Bring yourself to the calm inner depths of the ocean. Simply focus on the feeling of your breath going in and out, in and out, and you bring yourself to your calm inner stillness. If everywhere there are still thoughts, think of them as little fish swimming in the ocean. Little fish swimming around don't hurt the ocean. If you try to catch them, they scatter and come back. If you try to get rid of them, they scatter and come back. Just little fish swimming in the ocean. Remember, *you* are the ocean.

His quietly delivered message washed over me, and I felt profoundly moved. I don't remember what else took place that night, don't even remember the man's name. Maybe I never knew. To me he was an anonymous spiritual teacher, and I was honored to stumble upon his message. Much later, I learned that Sri Chinmoy, a spiritual leader who was nominated for the Nobel Peace Prize, used to give peace concerts like this all over the world. Was it him? It doesn't matter. Making therapeutic use of the powerful image the peaceful little man shared that night is the real gift. As an individual managing anxiety and stigma activation, as well as a counselor sharing therapeutic strategies with others, this image powerfully embodies the spirit of mindfulness.

The teacher's reference to seeing thoughts as little fish swimming in the ocean provides a graphic representation of a modern psychological idea known as "cognitive defusion." This is seen as a mechanism through which thoughts are seen simply as thoughts. It involves a shift that allows us to retain healthy emotional distance from the process of thinking rather than becoming attached to and escalated by thoughts as distress-causing realities. Rather than becoming aroused and worried because I start thinking I will look stupid, a common stigma activation mechanism for me, I simply notice that those frequently triggered thoughts are coming up again. This helps me retain my clarity rather than sliding into flustered panic. How to actually make this shift is difficult to articulate, so a graphic image like the one I heard that night is very helpful as a model that makes it real. We cultivate peace by putting attention on a unified focal point in the present moment, noticing thoughts but not giving them importance, making the effort to shift the focus back to the felt experience of the thing we have set ourselves to focus on. If we are not in a moment of deliberate practice attending to something like our breath, this could also be the task we are undertaking in the present moment or simply the path unfolding before us as we move forward.

A spirit of mindfulness must infuse the practices we employ in our escalation toolkit to get the most out of them. Gentle noticing and shifting, noticing and shifting in order to obtain a grounded focus on being alert to ourselves in the present moment is the underlying spirit that brings the following model alive.

NAB it!

When stigma (or any trauma) is activated, we have to *NAB* it in order to maintain self-regulation. We have to *N*otice it happening, or we will just get wrapped up in it and become flustered and overwhelmed. Cultivating a quiet space of watchfulness allows us to notice such escalation happening. We automatically distance ourselves from the reaction. We retain our ability to practice the self-care called for in order to preserve as much wellness as possible during an episode of activation.

The *N* stands for *Notice it*, but to reinforce the power of this noticing *N* also stands for *Name it*. If I am at the drive-through window ordering for a carload of people, I may start getting flustered because I think I'm not going to be good enough to get it right. The weight of all those times people thought I was slow or took over and pushed me aside, got angry, called me a stupid idiot, laughed at me, pitied me, or just gave me *that look* press down on me and stigma is activated. I start feeling flushed, begin tripping over myself, and get even more flustered trying to cover up my loss of functioning. Down the rabbit hole I go, and the best of my ability is diminished in that instant. Rather than compensating for my challenges by mustering attentiveness and clarifying, rather than defusing awkwardness by laughing at myself, rather than preserving the flow of the moment with others by undefensively acknowledging my difficulty, instead I face an overwhelming predicament in which all I can do to is disrupt everything by getting angry or using every ounce of willpower at my disposal just to manage. I can imagine how someone with greater challenges or fewer resources may run away, flap their arms, run in circles, or break down crying. As it is, everyone notices as I desperately attempt to make it look like everything is normal or melt down completely. The nightmare of standing out for not being good enough comes to life once again.

The episode at the take-out window I am describing is an all-too familiar episode of stigma activation. Such episodes are triggered whenever I feel the ghost of rejection, angry judgmental criticism, not being good enough, or feeling "less-than." Either defensive flustering or withdrawal results from such activation. Most of the time my emotional response has little to do with the intentions of the people around me. If I bothered to ask them, they wouldn't know what I was talking about. Yet my behavior, whether it involves escalated defensiveness, aggression and anger, or sudden disengagement, disrupts the flow of relationship in the moment. I draw negative attention to myself and give the message I'm either hard to get along with or unpleasant to be around. People's response in return makes me feel further unwanted. The distance between me and them grows. This is the last thing I want, but is exactly what I create by allowing the activation of invalidation trauma to escalate or deflate me. Most episodes of stigma activation are only momentary, although the effects can linger. The cumulative outcome of repeated stigma activation can seriously undermine self-esteem and damage relationships. When this happens, I need to let the important people in my life know and help them understand my sensitivity, so they can be more conscious of how trauma is activated. I myself need to be more aware of stigma activation so I can manage it better, not allow it to be too disruptive, and not blame others unfairly. Their frustration with repeated episodes of such emotional activation can be mistaken for lack of regard, uncaring moodiness, or plain ornery bad temper.

The impact of stigma is worsened exponentially by developmental trauma involving neglect or abuse. Our parents or caregivers may not have been deliberately abusive, but the rejection of emotionally unavailable parents, repeatedly unpredictable reactions, irritable anger, bearing the brunt of vile moods, and witnessing one of our parents being abused can leave a mark of invalidation that can leave us with easily escalated anxiety, safety distress, and defensiveness the rest of our lives. This is not to create guilt in anyone. We all do the best we can with what we've got from where we are in life. No one is perfect. It simply shows how important it is for parents to do the work of emotional regulation and trauma recovery for themselves (Tsabary 2010, 2016). When we are difficult for our parents to understand because of autisticy, which can involve paradoxical self-isolation and complex needs for belonging, the problem can be exacerbated. The already volatile nature of our more fragile nervous systems may imprint trauma more deeply and add a whole new dimension to potential future escalations. When this kind of trauma is activated it can overwhelm us and trigger a landslide of terror that can go on for days. The importance of trauma activation recovery efforts cannot be over-stated.

Press rewind. The moment the escalation of my stigma activation begins at the take-out window I can *NAB* it by noticing it start to happen. The very noticing allows me to step back from it and stay grounded in myself. I can step back even more by naming it. It doesn't matter what I name it, and I don't have to have a correct theory about why it is happening. Just putting a name to it objectifies it and allows me to function with greater self-control than getting lost in it. The naming itself gives us power, just as the noticing does. Call it an episode of stigma activation, a trauma event, or an emotional hijacking. We can quickly lose our power by going on to deny, dismiss, rationalize, or fight against what is happening. This brings us to the *A* in *NAB* it, which is to practice acceptance. Notice, name, and *accept*. Back at the take-out window, I notice I am becoming escalated rather than going deeper into a flustered state. When I notice, I can reinforce the noticing with some habitual acknowledgment such as saying out loud, "There I go again." Some people put an elastic band on their wrist and pluck it when they notice something amiss to knock the realization into their body. Others snap their fingers or play a drum riff on their stomach. Then, to regain even more control, once I notice the rising escalation I name it for what I think is happening. We are often all too familiar with these episodes. Naming it, calling it for what it is, is easy compared to noticing. We have to work consistently with some kind of mindfulness practice to build our noticing ability. We have to remain alert to ourselves and committed to honest reflection in order to crystallize our noticing. Naming the episode once we notice what is happening further empowers us.

We can still throw all our work so far into the can, though, if rather than accepting our vulnerability at that moment we start making excuses for ourselves, rationalizing our behavior, denying it is a problem, taking our distress out on others, or retreating into some numbing pattern such as substance abuse. By doing this we cancel out our hard-won noticing. Acceptance and humility are the next step. We may be feeling our defensiveness rise, but we defuse this with acceptance for the escalation that is going on at that moment: accepting we are losing our composure, accepting we must take special care of ourselves to remain as present as possible.

To help us remain calm at this point we must remember to *Breathe*, which is the *B* in the first stage of self-recovery when we *NAB* it. Making an effort to control our breathing not only gives us something practical to do, it sends a message to our body that high alert is not necessary. Allowing our breath to get out of control only reinforces and further escalates our growing arousal. Focusing on controlled, full, regular breaths helps keep us calm and puts the brakes on the growing escalation we have noticed starting to happen. The sooner we notice it happening, the more chance we have of taking care of ourselves appropriately so we better manage or keep ourselves from having another embarrassing and disruptive meltdown.

Notice the escalation. *Name* it for what it is. *Accept* we're feeling what we're feeling, even if it is uncomfortable. Remember to *Breathe*. There are plenty of breathing exercises to choose from. Just breathing at a comfortable rate all the way in and all the way out is often a good start to avoid a crisis. *Nabbing* it, which is easier to talk about than put into practice, prepares us to go on with appropriate self-care.

Chapter 9

AFTER CARE: STRATEGIES FOR MOVING FORWARD

Once we *NAB* an episode of escalation, whether it is triggered by stigma, the activation of trauma, anxiety, overwhelming demands, sensory overload, feeling exposed, things not happening the way we think they should, unforeseen changes, or other threatening conditions, it is *N*oticing it start to happen, *N*aming it, *A*ccepting our vulnerability at that moment, and remembering to *B*reathe that we can start to move forward with some measure of self-control. *Nabbing* it puts us in a position to make an effort not to lapse into meltdown, which inevitably makes whatever our situation is worse. Remembering to *B*reathe in a deep, regular, controlled fashion helps defuse the physiological arousal that tips our growing escalation onward. When we recover ourselves quickly, there is minimal damage and things may proceed the way they were with hardly an interruption. When we lose ourselves to a meltdown the situation can be much harder to recover. Sometimes feeling responsible for a "spoiled" moment due to escalation can set us off even more. We want things to be the way they were before the episode, but others aren't as ready to pretend it didn't happen. Even if no one else was there, we may have broken something or lost an opportunity of some kind.

Our behavior during the episode can be disruptive, but *Acceptance* can help us manage things with grace. We carry on forward from wherever we find ourselves when we come back to our senses. We are humble and do what we have to do to get back on track, accepting that we lost ourselves and being prepared to make amends. We may have to be patient with others as they deal with the after-effects of our behavior. We definitely have to be patient with ourselves as we learn from the experience. The key is always this: whatever is happening, as long as we *notice* it we have a choice to perform self-recovery. There is no point beating ourselves up for not catching it sooner, because this further escalates us and make things worse. There is no point wishing it didn't happen, because we can't deal with it if we're wasting our energy wishing it away. *Nabbing* emotional escalation is an art that takes practice. Once we *NAB* it, we are ready to begin *AFTER* care.

Activating Behavior

The *A* in *AFTER* care stands for *Activation*. Once we *NAB* emotional disturbance, the first line of intervention at our disposal is to *activate behavior* in some way to best look after ourselves. You may ask why we need to work at changing anything if we have adopted an attitude of acceptance. Acceptance does not mean resigning ourselves to whatever happens next. It means we accept what is happening in the moment without resistance, denial, or rationalization. This puts us in a position to make our next move with wisdom. It makes self-defeating behavior and passive resignation less likely. As Kabat-Zinn tells us, "To move to greater levels of health and well-being, we have to start from where we actually are today, now, this moment...*now* is the platform for all further possibilities" (Kabat-Zinn and Nhat Hanh 1990/2013, p.357). We may notice and accept that our back is going into spasm, but this does not mean we continue lifting bricks. Accepting the nature of our vulnerability allows us to listen to the message our body is giving us. This means we can take care of ourselves appropriately. For a bad back or sore knee this may mean resting and stretching or taking a muscle relaxant. When we notice stigma activation or other forms of escalation in ourselves, we deploy the strategies in our self-care toolkit to leave the smallest footprint of disruption and recover as quickly as possible. Noticing unfavorable conditions and responding effectively means we get back in a favorable position by deploying pre-determined strategies given the information we have opened ourselves to receiving. Acceptance allows us to direct our behavior wisely, given the conditions.

Behavioral activation is recognized as a powerful intervention for depression. It often takes the form of scheduling activities to get us moving. We may want to lie in bed all day and feel like we don't have the energy for anything. At such times, making the effort to get moving can break the cycle and get us back on the road to recovery.

When things are easy, we take them for granted and do things because we feel like it. At times when wellness is disrupted, we have to accept our vulnerability and make the effort to do things not because we feel like it but with self-care in mind. We have to make the effort to do things that will help us get well, even if most of them are not easy. We have to realize our "feel-like-it" meter is broken and initiate certain behaviors deliberately because they help us recover. This applies equally to anxiety. We may want to avoid certain things or even shy away from life completely because of anxiety. When times are most difficult we may just lie in bed all day. Behavioral activation gives us a tool to break this cycle. It may not even matter what exactly we do, as long as we get ourselves to move. In cases of depression, we may want to move towards things that get our life going again. In cases of anxiety, we may want to move towards the very things we have been avoiding. Any movement at all is preferable to hopeless inaction.

The kind of behavioral activation called for once we *NAB* the emotional escalation of invalidation trauma is equally difficult, just as challenging, and as potentially powerful for recovery. The first thing we need to do is make ourselves feel safe. If we become aware of growing arousal due to sensory overload, we need to gracefully excuse ourselves and get comfortable in a calmer environment. It is not a sign of weakness to respond to our own needs in a timely fashion. If we notice the escalation of stigma or other trauma activation, it helps to relocate in as safe an environment as possible. We should already be deep breathing from when we *nabbed* the escalation, and further grounding ourselves by practicing mindfulness, attending to the simple sensations and demands of the present, rather than worry, panic, and judgment, will help us relax back into a functional state. Whatever we physically do to make ourselves safe is the first line of behavioral activation. This may involve leaving the situation, arranging our workspace to reassure ourselves of safety, calling on someone who helps ground us, or retrieving our handy worry stone and rolling it around. Establishing safety is the first behavior we can respond with to address our growing escalation.

More often than not we are already in a safe environment when shades of Ghost Town come over us. Our escalation may be due to internal triggers that raise our threat level to defensiveness and flustering. We don't always need to remove ourselves to a safe situation but may still feel threatened, unbalanced, and potentially out of control. When we feel like exploding, everything will be pumped out of proportion. We may come across as unruly or even aggressive. Accepting this, rather than feeding our defensiveness, and activating harmless behaviors may sidetrack us from doing damage. For some this will involve hand-flapping, vigorous rocking, moving in circles, running away, yelling, or striking out. Going for a run, chopping wood, or an impromptu exercise session can also defuse excess energy. Laughing or crying is a great way to release. Others who don't understand what we are dealing with may think our behavior is odd, which may increase stigma. Having access to language makes it possible to explain ourselves, which may increase people's awareness if they are compassionate. If we can muster it at the time of escalation, vocalizing our difficulty so people can support us may be even more helpful. If we can get enough distance from our escalation, laughing at ourselves may help us put things in perspective and defuse the tension.

When an episode of stigma activation triggers withdrawal, behavioral activation can help us get back in the game. The man who frequently chooses to work or mow the lawn rather than spend time with family or friends may be dealing with stigma-related withdrawal. Meanwhile, the people in their lives may wonder why we are absent. Autisticy often involves a preference for solitary activity, but if we feel rejected or victimized in our solitary activity, there may be stigma activation involved. Such an episode from years ago stands out in my mind. I lived with socioconventional roommates. We regularly smoked marijuana together which lifted my anxiety and allowed me to laugh heartily at myself. One night I had gone to bed early after working an evening shift. I remember waking up a few hours later and hearing laughter from downstairs. I got up and went to the top of the staircase, pausing there. I desperately wanted to join the fun, but my heart was full of fear. Part of this was familiar social anxiety, but it was intensified by the activation of past stigma. What if I went down to be part of the fun and the gang saw me for who I was, awkward and socially uncomprehending? What if they didn't include me and I had another experience of dismissal and rejection? None of these thoughts were explicit in my mind, but I remember the moment clearly. At the time I could not get a perspective on what was happening. I could not name it for what it was, but only felt lost in the pain of the moment and ended up going back to my room crying. It was my second year of university. If only I could have *nabbed* the moment and activated myself to go downstairs in a courageous act of challenging the anxiety. No such tools were available to me and my memory is rejection, even though I did it to myself.

Depending on what type of person we are and the degree of trauma in our bodies, an episode of stigma activation can cause a cascade of disproportionate escalation. This is the kind of stigma activation I am most familiar with. At such times, making every effort not to make things worse with explosive behavior needs to be our immediate goal. This may be compared to controlling a temper tantrum. Sometimes it is not feasible to stop what we're doing and remove ourselves. Sometimes we have to catch ourselves and redirect the energy of a rogue moment in Ghost Town. Changing thoughts and behavior in midstream is especially difficult for autistic individuals, yet when such escalation hits we need to do something to take care of ourselves to minimize damage. The effort to activate behavior is not the only time recovery calls for doing things we don't feel like or moving towards things we would rather avoid.

Focus

When invalidation trauma stored in the body is triggered, it activates us and presents a challenge. We become escalated and emotionally charged. In this heightened state of arousal we can withdraw or have an explosion. When we *NAB* the moment, we can also do an intervention on ourselves. Our toolkit for doing so consists, first, of mobilizing some kind of therapeutic action. Getting closer to the root of our escalation, we can direct our focus to something more helpful than our pain, how awful things are, or what might happen. We can focus mindful attention on our breath or what we have to do in the situation. I'll always remember the first time I took the train to downtown Toronto. Getting off at Union Station is not like getting off a plane and following the crowd to the luggage carousel. Everyone goes in all directions. I panicked, standing there escalated and feeling stupid. I had a course to attend and knew I'd be late. It was a familiar feeling of paralysis as if my body was a block of toxic waste. Then I pulled myself together, realizing the catastrophic lost feeling and fear of being late would not help me. Instead I deliberately focused on looking for signs telling me which way to go. I managed to get moving and actually made it to my course on time with a success story.

Probably the most troublesome episodes of escalation and stigma activation happen in the course of daily interaction with others. My wife and I may be at home together Sunday afternoon, and she asks me about my messy corner of the basement, or tells me I shrunk another one of her sweaters in the laundry. Perhaps she simply asks me what I want for supper, and I can only put the question back on her because I'm more anxious about getting in trouble for saying the wrong thing than trusting myself to express preferences. A million little things happen that call for a simple honest response, but so often I just get escalated and defensive. Usually this happens when I'm afraid I'm going to be judged, fail to meet expectations, or look stupid. It also happens when I feel wrong or unappreciated, yet I create this myself in advance out of fear and stigma conditioning. It may also happen because I put up resistance to change rather than flowing with the spontaneity of the moment, and this resistance disrupts the happy flow of connection. At such times I feel guilty for wrecking another potentially good day. When escalation takes me out of my clarity, I must be diligent to *NAB* it rather than sliding unconsciously into it. Once that happens, it's usually too late to salvage the moment. It's a loss that happens far too often.

For example, every time I drive through the take-out window with my wife she is horrified by my lack of polite interaction with the clerk. She constantly reminds me to say "Hello" and "How are you doing?" before launching into my order. She urges me to treat the worker like a human being, which is in alignment with my values because I usually try to be a nice guy. She finds being sociable automatic and natural, but for me it is especially challenging. It's not just the effort to remember what is expected but having energy left to be polite. I get anxious about deciding what I want, flustered trying to get my wife's order right, and escalated by the activation of old stigma. Stepping back and taking a more global view of the demands required rather than getting caught up in my own inner challenges is a step in the right direction.

The effort of redirecting our focus from inner processes to the bigger picture of what's going on around us is a key effort we can make in many situations. In moments of escalation, changing our focus becomes more than a practice to avoid awkwardness and takes on the urgency of a crisis intervention technique. If we are triggered, becoming escalated, and falling into whatever Ghost Town looks like for us at that moment, *nabbing* ourselves at that instant and doing an intervention of self-recovery is powerful. Redirecting our focus from panic thoughts and escalation in our body to the demands of the situation is a highly therapeutic self-recovery practice. If my wife mentions a chore she has been asking me to do, I may feel myself escalating because the past stigma of being ineffective triggers an episode of emotional intensity. We may be about to go out and I want to have a nice afternoon together, but if I disrupt the flow of events by getting defensive and moving further into escalation the opportunity may be lost. I have to make an effort to stay focused on my desire to maintain relations rather than escalation. This may involve a huge effort of restraint to resist acting out of the escalation in order not to make things worse until the episode passes. Keeping my focus directed on the desired outcome rather than my inner anxiety and escalation helps. It does not make the awful feeling go away, but it helps me get through the experience with a minimum of damage. Sometimes that's the best thing to shoot for.

Thought Retooling

Ever tried eating soup with a fork? How about steak with a spoon? Hammering a nail with a screwdriver? Sometimes we make things worse if we don't use the right tool, yet we often grab whatever tool is handiest and make do. Making the effort to obtain the right tool is pretty important. We can be lazy, but we should be lazy consciously and take responsibility for the consequences. Thoughts are the most common tool we employ. Using them wisely for our wellbeing is one of the most powerful techniques of invalidation trauma recovery.

Different people often use unique tools because they operate differently or are working with different challenges. My wife is always telling me proper etiquette is a fork, but I use a spoon whenever I can. I only use a fork when food needs to be stabbed, because I tend to poke myself if something's not covering the prongs. Fine eye–hand co-ordination is one of the common challenges of autisticy. We should not make judgments about the tools used by others. They may be compensating for something we don't know or learning lessons their own way. The same thing goes for thoughts as unique tools of wellbeing. By deliberately giving ourselves thoughts we personally find more helpful to focus on we can often de-escalate ourselves and find a way to move forward in difficult situations more gracefully. This technique is evidence-based and equally effective to transform any negativity, self-defeating pattern, or episode where we're about to go down a road we know is not healthy.

Once, for example, I was in the university library. I did not yet have a diagnosis and did not have any other framework for understanding why I seemed so different from everybody else. I had attended the university years before, but no one knew me. It was like having a fresh start. One day I was at the check-out counter to take out some books. The place was really busy. Our class had been doing an assignment together, and a bunch of my classmates were in line behind me. The fluorescent lights hummed and cast a cold academic light over the scene as the librarian told me I had to pay an old fine before I could take books out. I didn't have cash on me, and it was before bank cards. I needed those books to complete my assignment. It didn't seem fair. I had been waiting in line for a while and started getting flustered. I became super-conscious of people pressing in behind me wanting to get moving. I started feeling stupid because I should have paid those fines long ago. I didn't know what to do and started arguing with the librarian, trying to convince her it wasn't fair. She said it was library policy, and I found myself at one of those infuriating bureaucratic dead ends. My escalation rose higher. I became more and more flustered. My head must have been shaking like a bowl of jelly on an unbalanced dryer. I turned to the line of people from my class piled up behind me and looked in the eyes of a girl who appeared to be sorry for me and wondering what was wrong with me at the same time. Old stigma became fully activated. The pressure exploded in my head, and I threw the books down on the counter, yelled, "OK, forget it!" and stomped away. I had a meltdown in front of everybody. As soon as I got out the front door my rage turned to embarrassment. I had blown my cover. Everyone would know how immature and out of control I really was.

Such moments of escalation are not uncommon for those of us who deal with the challenges of autisticy. Despite the growing wisdom of age, increased self-knowledge, and expertise helping people with emotional challenges, I continue to have escalations and meltdowns. I would like to say they are fewer and not as bad, but I'm sure my wife would say this minimizes a troublesome repeating occurrence. It is nothing less than an ongoing effort to counter the automatic thoughts, behaviors, and inner emotional land mines that sabotage us on a daily basis.

If the self I am now could talk to my self at that escalated moment in the library, I would coach him through a strategic thought-targeted self-recovery effort. Call it Operation Whoa-Nelly! First, I would start encouraging him to be mindful and attentive to himself as he walked through the library. I remember him, and although he spent a lot of energy on being self-conscious, it was a frittered away kind of worrying about how he appeared to others and whether he would look stupid. Rather than being self-conscious in this way, I would point him towards being more aware of his body, his breathing, and his thoughts, noticing how he carried himself, his muscle tension, and his posture. At the point where the librarian told him he needed to pay up, I would help him *NAB* his escalation. I would prompt him to notice his growing agitation, accept things weren't going as he expected, and remind him to breathe in a controlled fashion rather than allowing his breaths to get faster and shallower. Then the operation would go into full swing. I would get him to identify the automatic thoughts popping into his head as his discomfort grew. "This isn't fair," he'd say. "I'm going to look stupid in front of everybody." Yes, good noticing, I'd say encouragingly. Now what would be a more helpful thought to focus on in this moment rather than those negative automatic ones? He would pause, step back from his escalation a little more, and come up with something like "I need to cut my losses. I may as well just be courteous and tell her I'll pick up the books tomorrow. They'll still be here. I can keep the peace and let the line keep moving." I would encourage him to practice focusing on this thought, to keep breathing in as regular and controlled a fashion as possible. I would tell him he should be proud that he was taking the high road. "I know it's hard," I'd say, "You're doing great. Stay on course." The jeopardy of the moment would be over as fast as it came, and he would retain his dignity. A successful mission would mean no explosion, no escalating trauma from old stigma getting out of control. There would still be an emotional blip, he might be tired from his effort, but his day would be able to proceed as if it never happened. The others would not have a story to tell their friends about a disruption in the library that day. Mission accomplished! Congratulations!

Don't be fooled. This procedure is not just for isolated episodes of crisis intervention. It can be an ongoing practice. The power is not just the thought retooling itself, but the practice of remaining attentive to ourselves so we can *NAB* such moments. We cannot afford to lapse into automatic pilot if we do not want to slide inexorably back to baseline behaviors that undermine the peace and wellbeing of ourselves and others. This applies not only to stigma activation and meltdown control, but managing anxiety, depression, anger, OCD, addiction, and however Ghost Town tends to sneak up on us.

We may feel victimized by our thoughts, plagued by racing worries, judgments, questions, "what if's," and regrets. One client said, "I'm always trying not to think what I'm thinking but my thoughts just won't stop." That's an important observation about thoughts. You can't stop them. If I tell you to close the book for a moment and not to think about green porcupines, what will happen? Go ahead and put the book down, but whatever happens don't think about green porcupines…

If you are like most people, you probably couldn't stop thinking about green porcupines. Now close the book again. Instead of trying *not* to think of green porcupines, think of flying sailboats…

Was that easier? If we get involved in a power struggle in our brains to stop thinking about something, we escalate ourselves. We actually give an even higher profile to the thoughts we don't want to have. If we try to make ourselves stop thinking about that box of chocolates under the bed when we're driving home, that's probably the first place we'll go when we get back. If we try with all our might to stop thinking about how awful we feel when past stigma is activated, we amplify the activation. It's a much better strategy to simply direct our focus elsewhere. This could be to our breath or the inner stillness within us, but sometimes the thoughts in our head are just too bossy. The answer in such cases is to practice focusing on a thought that will be a more soothing influence and more in line with the way we want to move forward.

The ability to think gives us awesome power, not only for self-recovery but also to stigmatize ourselves. The negative self-judgments that undermine our self-esteem and wellbeing often come upon us like mosquitoes in the woods. If we try to fight them, they lodge themselves with even greater inflammatory horsepower. An alternate strategy is simply *not giving them importance*, defusing their hold on us by turning our attention elsewhere. Turning our intentionality towards action can help. This is not mere distraction, but strategic redirection. The practice of directing our attention to more helpful, inspiring, compassionate, or accepting thoughts can be immensely helpful.

The process technically known as thought restructuring is part of cognitive behavioral therapy (CBT), which is evidence-based and well researched. First developed by Aaron T. Beck (who was recently given a lifetime achievement award for his work in psychology), many versions of the technique identify specific thought distortions such as magical thinking, catastrophic assumptions, or jumping to conclusions. As a crisis worker primarily interested in promoting self-recovery, I find the most important thing is to notice negative feelings, escalation, and self-defeating behaviors. The next step is to identify any unhelpful negative thoughts running through our heads. We then formulate a more helpful thought to practice focusing on and *start working on it.* Just noticing and shifting attention to something more supportive is the helpful core of the strategy. If you have trouble thinking of something positive and helpful, pretend you're supporting someone else. What would you say to your best friend if they were in this situation feeling this way? There is no "right" way as long as our effort helps us feel and function better.

Exposure

The *E* in *AFTER* care is for exposure. A first-line evidence-based treatment for anxiety, it is a relevant self-recovery practice for invalidation trauma because we may find ourselves avoiding life, afraid we will experience more stigma and rejection. No matter what the particulars, it is often a sure sign we need to make an effort to expose ourselves to something if we have been avoiding it. There is a difference between choosing not to subject ourselves to something toxic or disagreeable and avoiding something because it makes us feel anxious. When I was a boy, I remember rocking back and forth on the couch downstairs when it was time to leave for day camp. My mom, who experienced extreme anxiety herself, asked me to consider something. She asked me earnestly if I really didn't want to go or if I was afraid. She knew I loved camp, even though I found social events difficult. I banged back and forth a few more times and thought about it as the springs creaked. "I'm afraid," I admitted. It was a huge conflict and avoidance was winning. In one of those powerful moments of timely parental advice that stay with us forever, Mom said, "Don't let fear stop you, Gordy." I stopped rocking and asked her why not. She said from hard-won experience, "You'll be sorry and miss out on life."

I went and had a great summer of treasured memories. Fifty years later her words come back to me whenever I notice fear coming between me and what I want out of life.

Treatment groups (some prefer to call them classes) provide a wonderful example of exposure. We offer individual counseling as well as groups in our mental health program. Most people say they don't want groups because being in groups makes them anxious. Yet groups can often be more effective, both because skills can be learned more effectively and because peer support can be transformative. It may take a monumental effort of managing anxiety to go to a group, but once behavior is activated and we get there, we're usually better off for it. It's like this with most things. It may take a huge initial effort to get moving but we usually find we benefit just from *showing up*. Maybe we don't turn out liking it, but at least we've seen for ourselves, made an appearance, built our confidence, and taken a bite out of the cycle of anxiety that can diminish our life if we allow it to. It's not the memories of what didn't work out that come back to haunt us later in life so much as the things we didn't even try. There are tools at our disposal to help manage the uncomfortable feelings that come up, such as keeping busy rather than dwelling on the discomfort, being careful what we choose to focus on, and thought retooling. We can expose ourselves to the anxiety-provoking thing in stages, for example having a trusted friend over and then going out with them to meet someone else in a safe public place, going to orient ourselves in the building where a job interview will be, having coffee in the lunch room before returning to work after an absence, or sitting on the front porch if we are afraid to leave the house. This is one of the most crucial self-recovery efforts we can make, and one of the most difficult. Doing it strategically in bits usually works better than all-or-nothing. Any kind of exposure is better than outright avoidance. As always, self-recovery takes courage.

Exposure to build confidence and the ability to function after trauma is very important but complicated by the escalation associated with threat and shame memories in the body. Those who work in the field have found groups to be especially effective in this area because the peer support provides a safe arena to rebuild damaged trust. It is another option of self-recovery to consider, even if it is challenging. Even if the very stigma we are trying to heal from bullies us into not seeking support because we will be seen as "weak" or "one of them," we must try not to sabotage our own best interests or personal growth because of the voice of stigma.

Our inner critic may jump up with an evil gleam in its eye and tell us we're losers because other people would easily be able to do the thing we want to cautiously approach. We can disempower this naysayer by not giving it importance and focusing attention elsewhere. Actors who read bad reviews, salespersons rejected by potential customers, and anyone who's taken a social risk that didn't work out have had to find the resources to do this. We've all done it. When the pesky belittling voice inside us is piping up it can be hard to ignore. If you have ever gone on a camping trip or a walk in the woods and had to deal with bugs, you know how to make a bothersome problem go away by not focusing on it. If we fight the bugs or focus on how much we want them to go away, our time in nature will be miserable. Somehow, we find a way to give them as little importance as possible and focus on enjoying our time in the outdoors. If we can do this, we can defuse our inner critic using the same strategy. Any little step we take to move forward when we feel like giving up is a triumph. Any move towards exposure when we want to avoid something that makes us uncomfortable is an important win. It is meaningless to compare ourselves with others who don't share our challenges. Their own areas of difficulty may not be apparent to us. The only yardstick that matters is our own evolution towards who we want to be and working with whatever challenges we face.

Radical Acceptance

The importance of accepting the challenges we deal with so we can work with them has already been explored. There's no use pretending everything's OK when something uncomfortable, scary, or irritating is creeping up on us. There's no use denying it when Ghost Town is upon us. There's no use wishing it wasn't so or pushing it away when we're confronted with an uncomfortable situation. Radical acceptance means looking at whatever our situation is and assessing it without drama. Like the other self-recovery practices, it's something we can work at if we make the effort. It calls for us to focus on empowering ourselves with open eyes rather than faltering pretend ignorance.

If I have to get back surgery and don't have sick leave, I will reasonably be concerned about the mortgage. I may worry day and night about what will happen. Worry about whether the surgery will make things worse. Worry whether I will be able to go back to work at all. Worry, worry, worry. In a case like this, radical acceptance is a good tool to achieve peace. It means *nabbing* the anxiety, accepting we are reasonably anxious, and remembering to breathe. Rather than fighting it and getting more escalated we empower ourselves by simply noticing our emotional state, stepping back, and suspending the very human tendency to judge. To make the shift to radical acceptance, we open our eyes and take in the situation, considering the possibility that the worst will happen. Maybe we will have to sell the house. Maybe we will have to go on financial assistance for disability. Maybe our whole lives will change. If they do, we will do what we have to do. We don't dwell on negative possibility but assure ourselves we can manage no matter what happens. We will manage, but especially if today is not that day, we can practice focusing on whatever blessings are here and now. If the change is upon us, we can focus on doing what we have to do. Meanwhile we can focus on being thankful for the little blessings we experience right now. The sky. The wind in the trees. The roof over my head. The people I love. Radical acceptance is not depressed resignation, it is emancipating affirmation. It can help us come to terms with our health, our socio-economic status, our isolation, and the losses we have experienced. It can help us seize the blessings of the day whatever they may be.

If we have experienced stigma from the sociodominant world, we may be justifiably angry, worried it will keep happening, and feel like hiding from the world. Radical acceptance in this case involves accepting our difference and our specific challenges without making negative judgments about our value as people. We wouldn't make such a rash judgment about anybody else. We all stumble forward the best we can in the shadow of what we have to work with in life.

The next step of radical acceptance especially regarding invalidation trauma may involve forgiveness. Forgiveness doesn't mean making the offense OK, as if it didn't happen or didn't matter. It doesn't involve condoning or excusing. It doesn't call for reconciliation. Research shows our feelings don't have to involve benevolence towards the perpetrator in order to experience the benefits of moving forward. If "forgiveness" sounds too extreme, think of it as taking power back by plugging the leak in our soul left by the abuser. It means shifting away from hate and revenge as we carefully nurture whatever love and goodness we find in our hearts. It means working through any residue of self-blame in order to promote wellbeing and our own ability to move forward. Focusing on rage or devastation towards the perpetrator's role can become a draining cancer that eats away at us. We practice focusing attention on our wellness in the present and building relationships that nourish us moving forward.

In terms of stigma, we can practice accepting that people are often trapped in the smallness of their familiar little world, do not make allowances for diversity, and tend to strike out unfairly against those who don't fit nicely within the comfortable boundaries of conventional expectation. We can acknowledge the shame this creates and counter our tendency to be hard on ourselves for not meeting such expectations by practicing compassion towards ourselves. We can accept that people can be cruel, either intentionally or unintentionally, and recognize the traumatic potential that accumulates in our bodies after repeated experiences of stigma and abuse. We can recognize how this residue of trauma gets activated in different situations and accept the escalation that happens, even if it doesn't make logical sense or seem justified by the actual threat level at the moment. In the light of this open-eyed acceptance, we are more likely to stop being hard on ourselves about who we are and better able to take appropriate care of ourselves to promote maximum peace and wellness. Forgiveness is a significant resilience factor for abused individuals and forgiveness-based interventions can be more effective than anger management, assertiveness training, drug treatment, or relationship skills training (Miller and Sperry 2014).

The ability to access spiritual intelligence as an inner resource is particularly helpful in applying the self-recovery power of radical acceptance. Those who are safely embraced in the warmth of a faith community don't need to be convinced, but spiritual intelligence does not necessitate selective commitment to a particular belief system or code. Resisting the politics of religion does not need to block us from accessing the healing perspective of spiritual intelligence. Religion is institutionalized, whereas spiritual intelligence is an innate ability to nourish ourselves by tapping into the network of greater complexity all around us. Atheism, or choosing not to believe in God, does not preclude accessing spiritual intelligence.

When my granny died, she did not feel able to embrace any perspective involving awe at the possibilities of the unknown. She was not able to comfort herself by accessing a spiritual sense of the mystery we are all part of or the underlying connectedness of things that typically escapes us. Having rejected religion because of its history of violence, hypocrisy, and injustice she was locked into the mundane details of her concrete existence. She was a person about to leap into one of the greatest mysteries of life who could only wonder why their present circumstances seemed so small and unfulfilling. To access spiritual intelligence we need only open ourselves to multiple possibilities of meaning in the universe around us, realizing we are part of that complexity in ways that can empower us even if we don't understand.

Various practices can provide this greater perspective. Prayer is one, even if our prayers consist of a spirit of gratitude not directed to a specific deity. Meditation, service, yoga, tai chi, getting up early to watch and be altered by the sunrise, and anything that feeds a greater sense of inner spaciousness and connection helps us attend to this dimension of existence. It is an area we can explore in order to cultivate an inner sense of our intertwined connection with the mystery of life, allowing us to transcend our mundane, concrete, limited perspective of life and frequent pettiness. This awareness can bring a sense of wellbeing and provide resilience against many things, including shame. Writer and professor at the University of Houston, Brené Brown, found that spirituality in some form "without exception... always emerged as a component of resilience" in her shame research (Brown 2010, p.64). Again, there are no rules about the content of spiritual intelligence as long as drawing upon it heightens our sense of meaning, expands our perspective, and sensitizes us to compassion for ourselves and other beings. It gives us a channel to rise above our narrow ideas, theories, judgments, and preconceptions in order to draw on the possibilities embraced by a sense of wonder and respect for life and existence. Cultivating the dimension of ourselves characterized by spiritual intelligence can expand the breadth of our engagement with life, deepen the roots of our aliveness, and give us access to more possibilities in life. It connects us with an inner space of openness and potential. It develops our ability to step back and not confine ourselves to the limitations and pressures of how things are or seem to be. If we don't attend to this dimension of awareness, like my granny, we may be kind and accessible to others but feel isolated. We may not even realize it, going dutifully about our daily affairs until something humbles us to a raw vulnerability and our need is great. At that point it may be too late.

We have discussed many good tools of self-recovery in this chapter including activating behavior, being cautious with our focus, thought retooling, exposure, and radical acceptance. Before talking about how teachers, doctors, social workers, and other professionals can be helpful rather than adding to stigma, we will consider another tool the *R* stands for in our arsenal of self-recovery practices.

Chapter 10

SELF-RECOVERY AND EMOTIONAL REIMAGINING

The core of trauma treatment is to imagine new possibilities...so we are not trapped in the identity we have created for ourselves.

Bessell van der Kolk (*Trauma, Memory, and the Restoration of One's Self: When Talk Isn't Enough*, Toronto seminar June 15, 2018)

The therapeutic employment of imagination has long been recognized as a mind–body therapy that promotes relaxation and assists with pain management. Imagery is often used to hone athletic skills. Mental rehearsal can promote physical healing, increase muscle strength, improve co-ordination, and enhance motor performance. Imagery rehearsal is also part of the evidence-based repertoire of CBT. Anxiety is often treated by having clients imagine exposure to feared stimuli. Unwanted behaviors can be diminished by having clients imagine pairing the unwanted behavior with undesirable consequences (covert sensitization). Image rehearsal therapy (IRT) is also used as a nightmare protocol when disturbing dreams, especially after experiences of trauma, cause distress and disrupt sleep. I once found this effective when I woke from a dream in which I saw a polar bear while out jogging. It passed me on the other side of the street but didn't scare me until it turned around and started charging. I froze in terror and awoke with my heart pounding just before being pounced on. I lay in anxious distress before practicing this technique. Rather than pushing the dream away I closed my eyes and allowed the feeling of the attack to flow through me. Instead of remaining frozen and immobile as in the dream, I visualized myself going into action. I ran up the stairs of a nearby house and banged on the door until someone let me in, slammed the door, locked it, and felt safe. When I opened my eyes again the anxiety was almost gone. Reimagining the outcome to one in which I felt safe helped immensely. This technique has been shown to decrease the incidence of nightmares, help with insomnia, and alleviate other symptoms of trauma (Turow 2017).

My personal introduction to calling on imagination for healing came when past experiences of developmental trauma were activated during a trauma course. This activation sensitized me to stigma, and when I overheard one participant say to another, "Asperger's is like schizotypal personality disorder," it really triggered me. The question made me feel exposed, vulnerable, and in danger of being labeled as deficient. The workshop leader referred me to a psychiatrist specializing in trauma. My brief work with this doctor was to give me a powerful self-care tool.

My first session with Dr. Phil Walsh, to whom I pay tribute in the Acknowledgments, was surprisingly painless and over before I knew what hit me. It was like an old band aid covering a forgotten wound getting peeled back. I did not get a chance to worry or protest about how much it would hurt. I did not have to talk at all. Phil, as he invited me to call him, said to close my eyes and allow some disturbing experience from the past to come into my mind. "I have one," I informed him as if I deserved a reward for getting the right answer. I began to speak about the experience but Phil told me gently words didn't matter. He told me to let the image unfold in my mind's eye. In the memory I was four and my mother had accidentally locked us out of our ground floor apartment. She was very upset, almost crying, and panicked. I went to the neighbor's house for help. He got a tool and pried open a basement window, so I could crawl through to let my mom back in the house. After opening the front door and proudly looking to Mom for praise, she only glared at me resentfully. I clearly remembered the hate in her eyes. I shrank back feeling stupid and sorry for taking action. Phil gave me space to let this memory wash over me and asked where I felt the pain. He asked me if I saw any colors or shapes associated with the memory. He encouraged me to sit with the feeling and quietly coached me to stay present. He then calmly suggested I visualize a different outcome. He told me to reimagine the outcome in a way that transformed it into an experience that allowed me to feel safe and comfortable. I visualized myself calmly standing before my mother, asking her with loving concern why she was so upset, confident in my resourcefulness and genuinely curious about her inappropriate response. In my mind, she immediately softened and became apologetically tearful. As I reimagined the moment, she stepped forward to hug me with motherly concern and told me how proud she was. As I sat there in Phil's office my heart grew. The color surrounding the image in my mind turned from black to misty purple. I felt serene, hearing myself sigh with profound relief.

Phil asked how I was feeling. "Are you comfortable?" he inquired.

"Totally comfortable," I replied. He encouraged me to bask in the glow of the moment and take all the time I needed to let it sink in. My heart felt open, my body so relaxed I did not want to snap out of it. Eventually I opened my eyes and came back to the room with a tranquil new sense of power infusing me.

"How do you feel?" he asked again.

"Absolutely amazing," I told him honestly.

"This is the work I love," he said humbly. He called our work *autosomatic training*, because he saw it as more than a time-limited intervention but instruction in an ongoing practice of self-care. Continuing to do it at home was encouraged. Phil believed spirituality and therapy were inseparable. He often quoted a saying of Jesus from the Gospel of Thomas, saying, "If you bring forth what is within you, what you bring forth will save you. If you do not bring forth what is within you, what you do not bring forth will destroy you" (Saying 70). At the time, priding myself on the use of evidence-based techniques as a hospital counselor, I dismissed this spiritual connection. Sometimes we narrow our vision and cut ourselves off from the richness of human experience.

After the initial session, things were not so dramatic. The peace and empowerment I experienced lasted about two weeks. Then I started to go back to my familiar pattern of getting easily defensive, anxious about life, and grumpy. At my next appointment, I told Phil I was frustrated. "Has anything come up?" he asked. I told him I didn't know what to do next. He brought me back to concrete reality by asking me what I did yesterday. I told him I relaxed at home and watched a movie with my wife. He asked how I had felt. I had to think about it but reported I had felt restless. He was curious and wanted to know more. I told him my back had been sore, and I was worried it would go out again. I hadn't brought it up because it didn't seem relevant in a psychotherapy session. "Are you anxious about it?" he asked. I told him I was. "Where do you feel the anxiety?" he inquired. He said to close my eyes and allow myself to go into it. As before, he asked if there were any images coming up. I felt I was doing something wrong because everything was black. He said to sit with the feeling and just be attuned to the blackness. My feeling changed from anxiety to feeling stupid as I sat with nothing but blackness behind my closed eyes. He asked me if there was any movement in the blackness, any variation at all. I told him I felt like I was just drifting. He encouraged me to sit with it and to open my eyes when I felt comfortable. With permission to just sit with the blackness my feeling of stupidity passed and the anxiety melted away. He asked if I was comfortable. I said I was and he told me to enjoy it as long as I wanted and to open my eyes when I was ready.

When I came back to the room, he explained that no image does not mean you're doing something wrong. He said it may mean no trauma is currently activated, we are not ready to experience it, or it is from before the age of three or four. When there is no explicit image, he said it was important to sit with the blackness and be mindful of any sensations in the body. If an explicit image came up, he said to proceed with reimagining it until it came to a comfortable resolution, as I had done in the first session. If it remained black, he said to breathe mindfully and note any bodily sensations until it felt comfortable coming back to the room. He emphasized the importance of regular practice, sitting with whatever comes up and being consciously gentle with the self. In this way, he said, I would remain current and perhaps move closer to any buried trauma which he believed could go as far back as birth itself. He said it was important to be attuned to any feeling of movement in the void. When any uncomfortable feelings had passed, including self-judgment, he said to enjoy the peace until feeling ready to come back. I left the session committed to regular practice. I would be watchful to notice any negativity in my day and practice mindful reimagining as things came up. He suggested carrying a notebook and recording negative experiences.

Despite good intentions I stopped going after a few sessions, but kept up the practice of sitting and reimagining. Nothing more traumatic than the episode in that first session came up. Instead, the images have focused on what I call micro-trauma, or everyday instances of stigma activation, flustering, and anxiety. For example, one day my wife sent me to Tim Horton's for a breakfast treat. I enjoyed my walk to the coffee shop. It was sunny, there was a refreshing breeze, and fluffy white clouds drifted lazily across the blue sky. There was a line-up. When the time came to order, I had my list ready and read the items off to the clerk. I thought I was done, but they didn't have what my wife wanted. I became indecisive and searched my mind for a desirable alternative. I thought I could relax when I came up with something, but the clerk began to bombard me with questions about whether I wanted white or whole wheat, plain this, regular that, or whatever. A familiar feeling of overwhelmed flustering began to take over. My head felt full. Demands came, as Benjamin Ludwig's character Ginny Moon described, "like hands flying up at my face" (2017, p.33). Yet it wasn't the clerk's simple questions that escalated me. Pressure to perform and not stand out like an idiot flooded me. Say the right thing. Respond as expected. Don't make a spectacle of yourself. I know I am capable of answering simple questions, but anxiety amplified by stigma activation was at work. I bumbled through the moment not feeling present or natural, increasingly escalated, and just wanting to get out of there. When I got home and told my wife about it, she smiled as if to say, "That's how you get, isn't it?"

After breakfast I took time for self-recovery practice. I sat with my feelings, allowing the anxiety and residual escalation to arise without trying to push it down, distract myself, or avoid. Sometimes I play soft music in the background, but this time I sat outside feeling the wind on my face and the sun on my eyes. The only effort involved was not a straining effort of willpower but an attentive allowing, accepting the lived moment and noticing feelings. Thoughts came up, but in line with mindfulness I simply noticed when my attention was turning towards thoughts and shifted back to bodily felt sensations. Judgment, catastrophizing anticipation, and should-have blaming faded into the background. This in itself was an unburdening relief that made the practice therapeutic and revitalizing.

Practicing mindful stillness in this gentle, undemanding way is the first step of self-recovery practice. It may sound simple, but for some it is an unfamiliar, alien thing to stop seeking distraction. Some think they have to stop their thoughts, but this is impossible for most of us. Others find themselves in defensive recoil when they experience their own feelings, as if someone was trying to put an unknown object in their mouth. Still others are understandably threatened and easily overwhelmed by their feelings because of the trauma in their bodies.

This is why the practice needs to progress at its own pace like an unfolding process of discovery. It never helps to put demands on the self to "succeed" or "do it right" or "do it all at once." Simply practicing in a spirit of gentle noticing and accepting, in whatever doses are workable for you, is the key thing. The practice itself is what helps, consistent practice, and not avoiding the practice. At the same time, consistent practice does not have to mean regimented time slots and routines, although this is helpful for some. Consistent practice may simply involve making appropriate time as needed in an ongoing manner in response to the needs of the self.

After my Tim Horton's experience, I settled into self-recovery practice in this way. I allowed myself to experience the feelings of anxiety and flustered arousal in my body. At first this was accompanied by a white flashing image. If only vague images accompany the feelings, it is OK. As Levine says of his own Somatic Experiencing approach to trauma work, feeling the sensations in the body is the most important thing. "Body sensations can serve as a guide to reflect where we are experiencing trauma and lead us to our instinctual resources," he says (1997, p.66). He notes that confronting the trauma itself is often too much for us. It may not be the events themselves that most hurt us in the long run, however, but the negative charge of invalidation held in our bodies.

The positive changes brought by this practice are partly due to the grounding influence of mindfulness practice. The reimagining process introduces a healing inner shift addressing the invalidation burned into us by events. There is a transformative effect when we mobilize inner resources even if it is only in the imagination. I have worked with clients who found this helpful, surprising themselves when nothing seemed to be happening in their practice but nevertheless reporting newfound behaviors such as being able to establish healthier boundaries, getting out of activating situations sooner, and staying calm at times when they typically would have been escalated. Polyvagal theory might demystify the process by characterizing it as the deliberate application of internal safety cues that can transform traumatic traces of personal history into calmer physiological states of visceral homeostasis, or calm balance in the body.

The R in our safety distress toolkit, for use AFTER we NAB stigma activation, anxiety, and emotional escalation, stands for Radical acceptance and *R*eimagining. These are among the powerful tools at our disposal to help us break the hold shame has on us in the moment. If we choose to put them into practice, these tools can help us loosen the grip of shame by helping us manage one trauma reaction at a time.

CRITICAL AUTISM

Destigmatizing Autistic Experience

Chapter 11

SOCIOPHENOMENAL DIVERSITY, INTUITION, AND THE POLITICS OF INTERACTION[1]

It's a sad paradox that diversity is so abundant on Earth yet so difficult to embrace by the planet's supposedly most intelligent species. Mother Nature knows diversity is critical for the survival of life—different varieties to fill every nook and cranny of possibility. Yet human beings seem to fear diversity and respond by inflicting pain for non-dominant variation involving things like race, financial status, gender, sexual preference, physical ability, age, and appearance. Stigmatized differences for autism cut across these categories. Certain visible differences may be involved, but the main source of autistic stigma is unfulfilled social expectations in relation to what I call *sociodominance*. Mainstream sociodominant individuals expect others to understand their humor and know when they are being sarcastic. When they use double meanings, they expect other people not only to know what they are saying but appreciate their cleverness. When they use context to stand for unspoken detail, they expect others to think like they do and fill in the blanks. They expect to be looked in the eye for conventional amounts of time but not too intensely. They seem to need others to engage in conversation according to unspoken rules shared by other sociodominants and tend to devalue those not comfortable with ways of relating that come naturally to them.

Sociodominants observe rituals designed according to their own logic. For example, when they ask "how are you?" and don't mean

---

1   This chapter is based on earlier essays published in the peer-reviewed online journals *Autism's Own* (2016) and *Autonomy: The Critical Journal of Online Studies* 1 (5) July 10, 2017.

it everyone is supposed to understand their lack of sincerity. Such individuals expect others to give the same priority to social interaction they have come to expect from the majority. They expect people to speak when they think it's appropriate and remain silent for periods they deem correct. They frown on the expression of impulses they don't understand and often get angry with frequent requests for clarification about things they take for granted. They can get upset when things are not carried out in ways they determine most efficient and abusive about subtle things like unconventional facial expressions and eye movements. Anything can happen when they receive social responses that don't conform to their comfort zone of familiarity. They may make accusations of rudeness, treat ASHFA like they were uncaring idiots, or expect an apology. Of course, we may not see it that way. We may not have meant anything by it. We may have "innocently" said what we were thinking and believe we just have to explain what we meant so the person will no longer be offended. Our explanations often make things worse, so we ask them to help us understand why they are so upset. All this logic can make us seem even less sensitive. There is a fundamental stand-off involving seemingly irreconcilable perspectives and communication styles. Negotiating the stand-off calls for undefensive flexibility on both sides. There are many kinds of diversity, but I am most familiar with this particular kind because I have suffered from the stigma associated with it all my life. I and others like me experience chronic marginalization due to lack of tolerance for *sociophenomenal* diversity.

At least for those of us who do not have intellectual impairment or significant physical challenges, it is sociophenomenal diversity that is most related to our difficulty fitting in and the stigma we experience. Although stigma can arise from other sources, it is accumulated invalidation trauma related to constant reactions of frustration, anger, and dismissiveness due to unfulfilled social expectation that leads ASHFA to their often desperate need for a validating discourse to make sense of the stigma and marginalization they experience. A validating discourse says, "There's nothing fundamentally wrong with *me*— I'm just different in a coherently valid human way." Neurodiversity is another framework for understanding the differences involved. Advocates maintain that conditions like autism and ADHD are not best seen as disorders or disabilities but as different ways of being human to be celebrated. This is fundamentally opposed to the impairment-based medical model that revolves around pathology. Neurodiversity advocates tell us these individuals should be proud of who they are rather than focused on pathology labels. This is an exciting way to see people who are different from the mainstream. It is anti-oppressive, strengths-based, and instills people with pride rather than shame. However, there is a contradiction at the heart of neurodiversity that undermines its emancipating core philosophy. By adopting a neurological orientation, neurodiversity bases itself on medical assessment to determine physiological disorder. This presupposes the very model of impairment neurodiversity proponents are rejecting. Despite the exciting social implications of diversity philosophy, neurodiverse identities become associated with a form of validation that is fundamentally inconsistent with the values of personhood at the heart of the community.

This contradiction underlying the neurodiversity movement was identified as a paradox at the heart of my research on stigma. Participants preferred to see their autism as part of who they were rather than impairment, yet medical diagnosis was seen to provide validation for their difference from the dominant mainstream. In accepting diagnosis as a framework of legitimation, participants did not see they were unwittingly endorsing the impairment-based philosophy they rejected. In the autistic population, this not only leads to an inner contradiction but creates fertile ground for the controversial practice of self-diagnosis, which can be seen to constitute an effort to take power back from the medical profession and escape the dehumanization of "biocertification" (Sarrett 2016, p.24). The effort is futile as long as diagnosis is the validating discourse of difference. Autistic individuals and autistic cousins will rest their identity on an inherently disempowering social framework unless diagnosis is uncoupled from membership in their communities of difference.

There is nothing inherently wrong with obtaining a diagnosis. Yet diagnosis is only meant to identify pathology and not to define us or validate the fundamental differences between us. People who have been living with the stigma associated with autism without an explanation for their marginalization often find diagnosis transformative. I felt this way when I was diagnosed. Finally, an explanation for my difference! Sociophenomenal diversity, as a lived range of natural human being that involves differences of social intuition and behavior, offers a different validating perspective that does not reduce personhood to impairment or certain neurological profiles. The core issues of stigma and marginalization related to ASHFA are more poignantly associated with sociophenomenal than neurological diversity. Much of the stigma autistic people face has more to do with sociophenomenal diversity and the way they communicate, relate to others, and present in the eyes of sociodominant others.

For ASHFA, it is not as simple as learning a bunch of social rules to fit in more effectively. Even if it were that simple, autistic writer Damien Milton (2014) points out that by addressing their challenges of co-existence with social skills training autistic people have their "fragmented social perceptions reinforced" (p.798). Porges (2017) maintains that social behaviors are "more an emergent property of our biological state than they are 'skills' in social learning" (p.233).

Social Intuition

The negatively perceived differences of social intuition associated with autism are seldom studied. This is largely because the very idea of intuition is often seen as vague, flawed, and unscientific in our objectivistic evidence-based culture. Various attempts have been made to name and describe the ability of humans to experience each other socially as unique beings. One of the earliest and most established is "theory of mind." ASFHA often hate this term, as if we couldn't have a solid theory of just about anything. The terms "metacognition" and "mentalization" are sometimes used, but these also focus narrowly on the cognitive aspect of sociality. Although the ability to appreciate the unique experience of others has been said to lie "at the very core of our humanity" (Bateman and Fonagy 2011, p.xv), most of the terms used to operationalize this idea tend to valorize the role of thinking and not capture the living process of encounter.

A narrow focus on cognition in relationship prioritizes the politicized aspect of interaction deliberately concocted to present the self in a desired manner to achieve certain ends. Social behavior is put under strict executive control. Social justice is undermined because intellectually challenged individuals may be seen as somehow less human in their ability to experience others. This puts their moral status in jeopardy. The experience of encounter in everyday life goes far beyond the intellectual. *Social intuition* is a precognitive experience and lies at the core of interaction between people. This definition is consistent with polyvagal theory's socio-organic perspective because this implicit knowledge comes from the physiological bedrock underlying conscious personality. Our experience of each other arises from deep within us and the way we impact each other generates a response long before thought has a chance to intervene.

As early as 1929 Wolfgang Köhler noted how people seem to respond in an immediate way to each other's feelings, thoughts, and intentions (Hacking 2009a, 2009b). Building an early case for social intuition, Köhler described the sense in which people's "inner situations are directly obvious" (1947, p.137). It is interesting that Köhler published a book on the behavior of apes early in his career, especially in light of autistic author Dawn Eddings Prince's powerful description of how she began her journey from being homeless and profoundly marginalized to being a professor of anthropology and critical autism writer by quietly observing apes and experiencing belonging in their presence (Prince 2013). The organic agency of social responsiveness may be better described in terms of a felt inner sense than any inferential process. Philosophical exploration about how people apprehend each other's intentionality through the flesh of encounter can be found in various philosophers, including Merleau-Ponty (1945/2006) and Wittgenstein (1980). Smith (2010) provides a good overview of this issue and articulates the sense in which he feels he can "know my baby daughter is miserable simply by looking" (p.748).

As the telegraphic sense behind human social plasticity, social intuition cannot be sufficiently operationalized with checkboxes. The participants in my study talked about an inarticulate feeling they couldn't put into words when they knew something had gone wrong with interpersonal interaction. I described this as the *telegraphic* stigma of inadvertent social code violation, a painful experience of social intuition that makes us acutely aware of stigma. No one talked about it in the study, but this made me reflect on my access to forms of intuition that tell me when making a certain statement or behaving in a certain way (or not) is going to cause a potential relationship disturbance. The faint voice of this inner alert system may be based on past experience, implicit logic, or some oft-ignored inner sense, but speaking for myself it can help me function socially if I hearken to it. Listening to social intuition can help us address the challenges of autisticy and work with sociophenomenal diversity.

We have to cultivate a certain amount of inner stillness to hear that voice and nothing compels us to listen but the strength of our higher values. It's next to impossible to nourish the required inner stillness when we're escalated. That's why breathing and mindfulness are so important. Finding the motivation to focus on higher values can be especially difficult when feeding easily enacted natural impulses. It may be really hard not to listen to rationalizations, but it can be done. It's like fine tuning our radar of encounter to pull in a weaker frequency that has a better program. It demands extra effort, but it's humanly possible.

Politics of Social Interaction

The way ASHFA relate to others involves a different quality of social intuition. Our politics of interaction are not the same. An interesting example of this came up just the other morning while I was waiting for my car at the garage. Flipping randomly through the pages of a local newspaper, I found myself reading an etiquette column about the interpersonal complexities of gift giving. A woman had written in wondering if it was appropriate to give an expensive present to a man she had just started dating. The columnist told her it was a risk that could lead to awkwardness if her effort wasn't reciprocated. She advised her to drop hints about her gift-giving intentions, so if he did not reciprocate the woman would supposedly know the guy was "a cheapskate, or an emotional trifler, or a clueless clod who can't take a hint" (Vanstone 2016, p.11). The columnist advised this because such behavior is considered politically correct in socioconventional circles. However, the idea that a person is a "clueless clod" if they don't recognize hint dropping (and other sometimes unspoken political strategies in relationship) reveals unintentional prejudice towards those who do not operate this way. It brings stigma on those who do not fit with mainstream assumptions and ways of operating. The person may not be in a financial position for such gift giving or may not value the giving of gifts. More fundamentally, stigma is generated towards ASHFA as a group of people who do not appreciate this politicized kind of social behavior and prefer direct, explicit communication. Negative judgments based on sociophenomenal difference can sting. I know all too well what it's like to be considered a "clueless clod" because of sociophenomenal difference.

Frith, Happé, and Siddons (1994) distinguished appropriate social responses rooted in true "theory of mind" from behavior the authors refer to as "hacking," or constructing responses using rational deduction geared towards desired outcomes (p.110). The authors felt such deliberate efforts camouflaged the "impairment" they were seeking to demonstrate. They theorized such behavior would not generalize from controlled research contexts to complex life situations. In reality, ASHFA frequently resort to deductive processes to engage with socioconventional others when intuitive responses lead to social code violations and stigma. Channon and colleagues (2014) believe such social disconnects are evidence ASHFA have impairments of mentalization. Maybe, however, we are just different and our difference is not sufficiently negotiated.

Intuition, Safety Distress, and Impairment

Sociophenomenal differences can make Autistic people seem like "perfect victims" (Klin *et al.* 2000, p.56). An overwhelming and frustrated desire to fit in, sometimes leading to indiscriminate people pleasing, helping, and over-accommodation, can be one factor related to this vulnerability. Those autistics who take the opposite route, angry disdain for socioconventionals, may not be so susceptible. Difficulty making out the underlying social intentions beneath dissembling others is common to both types. The fact that ASHFA can become police officers (NPAA 2016) reminds us this "impairment" can be overcome with practice. Generally, people who live with autisticy are more vulnerable to what Courtois calls "traumas of betrayal" (2014, p.9). The invalidation trauma experienced by Autistic individuals often results in a strong inner need to bolster their devalued humanity. This vulnerability exposes them to seemingly friendly people all too willing to provide the validation they need who may have hidden agendas of their own. Protective boundaries seem to fall apart. Polyvagal theory points to the importance of subtle cues deeply rooted in physiologically connected social behavior such as muscle tension, facial expression, and eye movement. Autistic cues can trigger safety distress in socioconventionals when they don't conform to familiar expectation, and this leads to inadvertent stigma. Some people learn to read these cues to identify vulnerable others for their own advantage. Exploring the conditions that make safety distress over-reactive as well as the vulnerabilities that short-circuit this inner warning system is a form of human maintenance allowing us to calibrate and correct safety scanning for maximum ethical encounter and best overall self-protection.

Safety distress plays a role in the social drama of stigma that goes far beyond subtle interactions leading to exploitation and marginalization. Police officers, for example, may find themselves in life-or-death situations with the power to cause harm. Safety distress triggered by unfamiliar or stereotyped others can impair responsiveness leading to disproportionate damage inflicted on stigmatized populations despite good intentions. Addressing this phenomenon adds a new dimension to racism- and stigma-countering efforts. Police, with their pressurized work in complex social environments, provide a highly visible model for processes we all experience. To take another example, we can learn valuable lessons from research on the inadvertent stigma inflicted on victims of sexual assault through unspoken cues of blame and judgment by police (Greeson, Campbell, and Fehler-Cabral 2016). Combating autistic stigma is not just a matter of better understanding an "impairment" but means appreciating the kind of safety distress, associated social cues, and the forms of social intuition at work.

Active Response Emerging from Encounter

The two roommates in my study responded to each other with care and foresight. Terms like "theory of mind" and "metacognition" do not do justice to the phenomenon of attentive, bodily felt social intuition demonstrated by these individuals regarding each other. Far beyond any calculation of mental states, the bodily felt encounter demonstrated by these roommates is the same kind of intuitive responsiveness that allows a performer to "feel the room" and sense how long to hold a silence or allow a laugh. It is how a counselor senses when to introduce an appropriately challenging new perspective in line with the client's tolerance for change; how acquaintances, friends, and lovers seem to know when to release a hug, how job applicants sense how long to hold a handshake with potential new employers to make a good impression, and how individuals sharing guilty knowledge sense how long to hold a knowing look without drawing attention to themselves. The participants all described experiencing such situations. They also described how the organic sense emerging from encounter is often supplemented with various degrees of explicit cognitive calculation, although this diminishes spontaneity and makes social interaction more dependent on executive functioning.

It is possible to exert deliberate cognitive control to override social intuition for socioconventional and autistic people, for example when lying, manipulating, trying to fit in, or practicing diplomacy. Did you ever hear the one about autistic people not being capable of deception? This is not accurate. It's just that autistic folks are more likely to act from the impulsivity flowing from their natural social intuition. If we want something, we can be as manipulative as socioconventional others selfishly trying to get what they want. The efforts people with autism sometimes make to avoid stigma by deliberately faking responses to look "normal" is also an indication of their ability to exert cognitive control in relationship. Generally, it is not theoretically determined mental states we respond to in others. We respond to the bodily felt call and response of social encounter itself. This, at least, is when we experience the kind of interpersonal flow and belonging the ASHFA roommates in my study demonstrated as opposed to the strain of constituted performance. This may be part of the reason people with autism, even more than mainstream others, flourish when they live in communities where there is a supportive fabric of relationships. It is not primarily due to impairment that needs to be accommodated, but because it is more easily possible to be ourselves and flow with the uniqueness of our differently activated social intuition with less judgment.

Modernity, Authentic Presence, and Autistic Deliberation

Merleau-Ponty describes how modern western culture is "obsessed with objective thought" (1945/2006, p.393). For him, the way modernity tends to "idolize objectivity" leads to lack of authenticity (1948/1991, p.91). This can be seen in the all too common sociocon-ventional politics of interaction like our gift-giving example above. The social world becomes what Merleau-Ponty describes as an "objective setting" or "task zone" of interpersonal calculus based on a manipulative politics of exchange. This can be found most clearly in bureaucratic organizations where the ability to facilitate humanly nourishing relationship has been lost. The way ASHFA use cognitively constructed strategic behavior to fit in can be seen as another form of what philosopher Jean-Paul Sartre might call "bad faith." Modernity's dominant paradigm of objective relationship is reflected in ASHFA's tendency to navigate the social world of dominant conventional others with objective calculation. For autistics, it is out of necessity to defend against stigma. For socioconventionals, this deliberately concocted sociophenomenal orientation is a habitually chosen facade that devalues social intuition and considers honest spontaneity undesirable.

McDonagh (2007) wonders why autism was not noticed until the 1940s and points out that those professionals who worked with disturbed children before that could only seem to discern variations of "imbecility." He points to the cultural trauma of World War II, the "intense subjectivism" of the late modern period, and relates modern western culture's fascination with autism to "something we [all] carry within ourselves" (p.115). This "something" is estrangement. Around the time of World War II this isolation from each other took on an urgency in which autism emerged as a profound living example. Autistics, with their "naive" impulsive responsiveness grounded in unpolitical self-absorption, represent nostalgia for a natural connection with ourselves that is overshadowed by complex social posturing. At the same time, their perceived isolation from others came to be seen as a defining factor of their "disability." Autistic isolation became a poignant model of the pervasive alienation that characterizes modernity. The tension between expressive spontaneity and cognitively controlled instrumental repression may be at the heart of this estrangement.

The most rigorous and elegant exploration of this can be found in Merleau-Ponty as he explores authentic and constituted human presence in the world. His work, which also emerged in the shadow of World War II, describes a natural spontaneity that involves the "fusion of soul and body in the act" (1945/2006, p.84). He articulates the way we project ourselves into the world by simply responding to the needs of the moment with others and characterizes authentic presence as the experience of being in "spontaneous accord with the intentions of the moment" (1945/2006, p.25). Authentic interaction proceeds "without any calculation on my part" (1945/2006, p.122). He compares this to the experience of a musician who "is no longer producing or reproducing the sonata...the sonata sings through him or cries out so suddenly that he must 'dash on his bow' to follow it" (1968, p.151). Köhler describes a pianist who "lives in a current of dynamic events which are clearly organized" (1947, p.130). Leonard Angel describes this kind of spontaneity as "the infusion of grace in agency" (1987, p.60). Oliver Sacks, in a posthumously published essay, associates the power of authentic presence with the fundamental creativity of aliveness and describes the experience fondly, saying it "represents the best part of me" (2017, p.147).

The language of sociophenomenal diversity, social intuition, and authentic presence provides an empowering framework of diversity. Different sociophenomenal orientations can be identified along this spectrum that emerge from a normalized range of cultural and individual human variation all can relate to. We go back and forth on this behaviorally and psychologically complex spectrum. Socioconventionals often prioritize a deliberately manipulative form of objective interaction as if social intuition was less sophisticated. Autistics often lose touch with social intuition by prioritizing impulsive self-absorbed reactivity. This range of sociophenomenal diversity is a tension we all carry within us. Seeking to enact a quality of relationship characterized by curiosity and flexible receptivity aligned with our highest values of ethical encounter calls for therapeutic efforts we can all benefit from. If we are mindful and see any indication that we are putting expectations, assumptions, conventions, theories, agendas, self-absorbed interests, or dogmatic systems of belief ahead of authentic encounter, these can be taken as red flags that the focus of our attention needs to be brought back in alignment with relationship, the wellbeing of people, respect for human diversity, and mutual survival.

Chapter 12

AUTISM, AUTHENTIC EXPRESSION, AND SUPPORT

Donvan and Zucker (2016) provide an excellent history of autism that makes me proud to be autistic, almost like pride in my bit of Scottish ancestry when I hear bagpipes or watch the Highland Games. However comprehensive and sensitive their reporting, however, the authors do not include the voices of autistic people who communicate with typing. Such individuals are in a pivotal position to report personal experiences that can guide, challenge, and provoke new insight into what it means to be CLAWHS. Donvan and Zucker report that when Douglas Biklen claimed taking their reports into account could "revolutionize our view of autism," it apparently caused an uproar because he was not seen as qualified to make such a statement (p.360). He was not expressing this sentiment to make a claim of expertise. He was recognizing the revolutionary implication of first-hand accounts. These before-now silent individuals suddenly communicating for themselves create the possibility that traditionally accepted notions of autism uninformed by first-hand accounts will be challenged. Many of the reports these individuals make call commonly accepted assumptions into question, for example that individuals who can't communicate or express themselves in recognizable ways must be intellectually impaired (Delahooke 2015). Whenever conventional beliefs are challenged there is resistance from society, especially by authoritative "experts" whose opinions are based on established convention. Many CLAWHS are mistrustful of so-called experts, who they feel are "locking their ranks against us" (Freeman 2016).

Jason Travers, assistant professor and behavior analyst in the Department of Special Education at the University of Kansas, is such an "expert." He and a colleague seem to blatantly marginalize and dismiss the authenticity of one CLAWHS voice because the person communicates with the assistance of facilitated communication (FC). Biklen wrote a paper about inclusive education with Jaime Burke (2006), a young man diagnosed with "classic" autism who he had known since childhood. Travers and Ayres (2015) charge that Biklen must have exploited Burke, who they conclude could not have been speaking for himself. They also imply that Burke's chapter in Biklen's 2005 qualitative study exploring the experience of CLAWHS who type to speak was also an example of exploitation:

> FC has never been demonstrated to be valid and, given the extensive investigation afforded FC, we must conclude that words attributed to Burke are not reflective of his own true thoughts, opinions, or experiences; they instead represent the subconscious thoughts of his facilitator(s). Unfortunately, this is not the only exploitation of Burke. (2015, p.273)

The authors' point to how the content of messages conveyed using facilitated communication have been shown under test conditions to contain facilitator influence and they conclude that his contribution to these projects cannot be his own. This is extremely stigmatizing and not only dismisses his contribution in the name of logic but invalidates the voice of all the study participants. It marginalizes people who type to speak, at least those who require this level of support in order to do so.

When I asked Amy Sequenzia, a disability advocate who started to communicate with supported typing at the age of eight, she typed, "I think what this Jason Travers says is so ridiculous…his pathetic assertion is pure crap." When I found a way to contact him, Jamie Burke said he wanted to reply to this comment after he attended an upcoming wedding. I did not hear from him in time for publication but look forward to hearing his perspective.

The technique of facilitated communication or supported typing often employed by these individuals is indeed controversial. Reports of sexual abuse have been made in the course of facilitated typing sessions that have damaged families and been deemed false after investigation. Seldom do we hear about such allegations that are proven true, which is odd because such vulnerable individuals are at higher risk of abuse (Sevlever, Roth, and Gillis 2013). False allegations continue to make the news, for example in a Prince Edward Island group home (McDonald 2016). Donvan and Zucker go so far as to call any hope CLAWHS will learn to communicate a "dream" (2016, p.369). Critics maintain facilitated communication has been thoroughly debunked, never results in independent communication, and should be abandoned entirely even though many individuals say they would have impoverished lives without it. Critical disability scholars tell us a common oppressive strategy of the status quo to silence first-hand reports questioning convention is to perpetuate beliefs and assumptions about the marginalized population that deny the legitimacy of their voice (Liegghio 2013). This is what seems to be taking place with Autistics and others who type to speak who require the support of facilitated communication. Their writing and even their participation in research is devalued and dismissed.

Research can be found on both sides of the supported typing question. Interestingly most qualitative studies find FC to be effective and useful to at least some vulnerable people while all the quantitative studies I am aware of have found clear evidence of facilitator influence. This issue polarizes quantitative and qualitative research. Neither proponents nor advocates seem to recognize any middle ground. Those who will not consider anything unless it can be demonstrated concretely with solid evidence reject facilitated communication on the basis of significant results that leave no doubt of facilitator influence. Those who appreciate the empowering influence it has with vulnerable people accept it. Critics wonder how supporters could hold illogical beliefs in the face of contrary evidence. Proponents wonder how dismissive critics could hold such cold beliefs in the face of its benefit for many vulnerable individuals.

In the name of responding to the needs of vulnerable individuals and what works for them to have higher quality of life, one would think qualitative researchers would design experiments based on naturalistic environments that could provide their quantitative colleagues with something like the kind of validation of authentic communication they seek. At the same time, if quantitative researchers could design studies imaginatively evaluating this authenticity without relying on intimidating question-and-answer trials they might get better results. Demanding such proof only of a targeted population is a hurtful, unfair form of sociophenomenal profiling, and part of the problem is that the people being tested may freeze under the objective scrutiny of judgment. This possibility is jeered at by "experts" who say this is "obviously ridiculous" (Travers, Tincani, and Lang 2014, p.197). Autistic people have a tendency to get flustered under pressure and also have difficulty regulating their emotions. These responses, like the "impairments" they are supposed to be based on, can be context-specific. When the invalidation trauma such individuals have experienced is taken into account, their anxiety and emotional paralysis under such fundamentally challenging conditions is understandable. As Heisenberg found when he revolutionized physics, sometimes researchers affect their results with the techniques they are using. It is worth having a compassionate appreciation of how intimidating formal evaluations might overwhelm an autistic person, especially when communication is one of their most precarious functions. Michael Monje types that he would even "go non-verbal in job interviews *because I had to prove I could do it*" (Sequenzia and Grace 2015, p.89). Imagine being told your communication would no longer be valued as your own if you failed a test under threatening judgmental conditions. Then imagine you are already vulnerable, feeling rejected by society, and tend to lose your ability to communicate under stressful conditions. Researchers should be able to find better ways to assess authentic expression than such invalidating formal examinations. You'd think we'd all work together, quantitatively and qualitatively, to maximize this population's language experience and honor their humanity without further stigmatizing them. So far this doesn't seem to be happening.

"Experts" say qualitative research "cannot prove the authenticity of FC" (Travers *et al.* 2016, p.93). Yet observation-based study in the context of real life could provide confirmation from triangulated sources. Ido Kedar's parents, for example, sought to prove the legitimacy of his communication when he first started typing. He would shut down when he sensed this happening, not only making verification difficult but hurting his feelings. What convinced them was a time he told his mother about something that happened on the school bus that day. His mother talked to the driver and the information was confirmed. This kind of verification could be designed into quite sophisticated variations that could provide reasonable assurance of authentic communication in lived conditions. Admittedly this does not provide the certainty of randomized trials in a carefully controlled setting, but not everything lends itself to this kind of study. Authentic or genuine human expression is a complex behavior that allows us to access our creativity and discover things we didn't even know were in us. Such expression comes from deep within the self and often provides information that could not come from any other source. The ability to do this cannot be tested and confirmed the way we test the effectiveness, for example, of a new medication. There are too many variables and too many things we don't understand. It's like demanding proof that someone's love is real. At least currently, science cannot sufficiently grasp the depth of this all too human phenomenon. If we were tested based on accuracy and correct reporting, how many of us would have our love deemed inauthentic? Human authenticity in its various dimensions is not so straightforward.

Originality reflecting a person's experience and character makes communication authentic. Even in emails, one gets a sense they are *talking to a person* expressing who they are and striking the same familiar range of character over time. Even though they may have different facilitators and be in different moods at different times, you get a sense about the kind of responses to expect, learn how to engage with them as the unique people they are, and feel you get to know them. You *encounter* a person through communication. This cannot be reduced to a matter of simple accuracy. It cannot be tested in a lab under controlled conditions. It is the felt agency animating interaction and can only be "validated" by the experience of it. As unscientific as that sounds, this is the kind of authentic communication supported typing makes available to those who can't access it any other way. "To type my real thinking I need a trusted person to encourage me through the reaching out of my words," says Philip Rays, "my true self is revealed in my typed words" (Sequenzia and Grace 2015, p.115).

There are other, more evidence-based methods of communication training. PECS, or the picture exchange system, is designed for object identification and the communication of basic needs. The pointing board can be used to communicate anything, but it is slow and laborious and makes inventive genuine expression difficult to attain. It too has to be facilitated at times due to movement difficulties, although it does not involve the same level of motor control as typing. All these methods call for extreme effort to overcome a variety of challenges, not only with movement but also with a sometimes precarious grasp of speech formulation. Many people who type to speak, as well as autistics generally, report that this ability is subject to stress, anxiety, energy level, and many other personal factors. ASHFA Mandy Klein says she has to write things down right away or the "words disappear" (Sequenzia and Grace 2015, p.75).

Cvitkovic (1997) did field research into facilitated communication in his Master's thesis at the University of Toronto. His review of research found seven indicators suggesting evidence of genuine communication using facilitated communication. These include consistent style, speed, and accuracy of typing across facilitators, typographical errors unique to the communicator across facilitators, phonetic or invented spellings consistent across facilitators, content not characteristic of facilitators, and content not known to facilitators. The study involved three autistic students being observed in the classroom and school grounds. His overall conclusion was that supported typing provided an important source of communication enrichment for some autistic people, although he acknowledged his study did not conclusively prove anything. To further research this, he suggested that future "validation studies should include communications that are more personally meaningful to clients, such as needs and desires" (p.31). The only admissible evidence to this day, however, is direct black and white objective answers to neutral content strictly controlled by the examiners. An effort must be made by researchers to correct for this. In his discussion of research results 20 years ago, Cvitkovic thought it unfortunate that facilitated communication was "quickly being abandoned as a communication technique with autistic individuals" (p.31). He may have been correct about organizations using the process less frequently, but he would have been happy to see the technique continue to be used extensively by autistic people whose voices are becoming more and more prominent. An anthology of such voices published by editors who also type to speak (Sequenzia and Grace 2015) contains biographies of each writer who responded to a public call for contributions. Their words are quoted generously in this chapter.

Developing our knowledge of autism by listening to the people who actually live with these conditions is not to be guilty of an "authority fallacy" (Travers and Ayres 2015, p.374). Appealing to supposed expertise rather than actual evidence happens when we listen blindly to dominant authority figures whose status is sanctioned by the power structures of society. Listening to the voices of autistic people about autism is not like that. To confuse these things only shows how the language of expertise has gotten out of hand. Everybody wants to be an "expert." Listening to the voices of those who actually experience the condition we are interested in is not appealing to expertise or authority. It is wisely taking an important kind of evidence into account and learning from an insider perspective.

If there is something of the influence of the facilitator in supported communications, it may be due to the same unconscious ideomotor muscle movement that made the Ouija board popular, especially when a pointing board rather than a typewriter is employed. It may also be due to the currently unmeasurable shared emotional connection between facilitator and typist. There is something of the influence of others in all human communication. That is how communication helps humanity evolve. Still, facilitated communication advocates must do better at correcting for this factor so the baby is not thrown out with the bathwater when potentially damaging errors occur, such as false sexual allegations. Ideally, facilitators should be well trained and adhere to best practices. The incident that took place in Prince Edward Island was facilitated by a group home worker who may not have had sufficient training. On the other hand, having a family member or friend provide supported typing support can make it more accessible and less threatening. Having a combination of professional and informal facilitators is a good solution. Not allowing this method of communication cuts people off from an important avenue of authentic expression.

The facilitated communication issue is one of the most controversial in autism. Debate often rages in disability organizations between those who think it should be accepted as valid and those who think it "unscientific" and unendorsable. Many come out with a "no" position based on the apparent weight of objective evidence. Listening dutifully to the "experts," groups that would be unlikely to adopt such a marginalizing position denounce the very process that allows a growing number of increasingly (so to speak) vocal individuals to rise above the limitations that greatly exacerbate their social isolation. Supported typing provides many with a connection to the rest of humanity they would not otherwise experience.

Conventional ideas about autism include assumptions about lack of intelligence when people can't communicate. One "expert" concluded "it is untenable to claim that a subject has a high level of intelligence or literacy just because very abstract concepts or sophisticated statements seem to be produced when someone uses FC with the subject" (Kezuka 1997, p.592). The implication that there could be an intelligent agent within a severely autistic body not able to communicate lacks acceptable evidence for these "experts," who ridicule the idea that people with severe autism are "trapped minds needing to be liberated" (Travers and Ayres 2015, p.376) or that there are "intellectually intact individuals trapped in broken bodies" (p.384). Those who have had this experience specifically report that before supported typing gave them access to communication they were "smart, intact people trapped in a non-responsive body" (Kedar 2012, p.96). Roy Bedward types that he felt like "nothing more than an animal in the zoo" (Sequenzia and Grace 2015, p.119). Emma Struder says, "I became me" when she experienced the "pure joy" of communication that supported typing made possible for her (p.33). Sagarika Vaydia, another individual who communicates using this method, believes from first-hand experience that supported typing "saves trapped souls and helps them bloom and grow" (Sequenzia and Grace 2015, p.40). I was very disturbed learning about the stigma and oppression CLAWHS experience. At one point I appealed for a reality check and sent an email to Amy Sequenzia. I exclaimed, "if there is even one person out there trapped inside not being able to communicate and not receiving appropriate support because of skepticism, I feel compelled to do whatever I can to address this terrible situation. Do you think I'm being over-dramatic?"

She wrote back, "Not over dramatic. Reality."

The confusion around intellectual impairment and autism raises pressing ethical issues. Kedar calls it a "crime against humanity" when an intelligent person who is unable to communicate does not receive support to express complex ideas and tap into their creative intelligence with authentic language (2012, p.56). How many CLAWHS are assumed to have intellectual impairment because they have not yet found a way to communicate in a recognizable way? No one knows. If we can invent cars that respond to thoughts and electric wheelchairs that respond to brainwaves and emotions, one would think science could make an application capable of measuring neural activity that could provide evidence of active intelligence in people who cannot communicate. This would provide a positive way of identifying such individuals so appropriate strategies to help them could be deployed.

Facilitated communication is a passionate issue for many people. It culminated in a jail term for Anna Stubblefield, who had sexual relations with a disabled man she claimed gave consent using facilitated communication supported by her. This was a conflict of interest to say the least. The most disturbing thing about the case from an advocacy position was not that supported typing was ruled inadmissible in court. It was that the disabled man was pointed to as a helpless victim in a show of sanctioned exploitation by the prosecution. It is highly offensive to many that he was treated this way. No attempt was made to give him any kind of voice (Sequenzia 2015). It is tragically ironic that as a philosophy professor Stubblefield wrote powerfully on the oppression of vulnerable individuals caused by continued dismissiveness towards facilitated communication. She wrote that inflexible anti-supported typing rhetoric "functions as hate speech" (2011). It's amazing what trouble we get ourselves into when we are moved by unconstrained passion and caught up in the one-sided view of an issue at the expense of fully evaluating the complex predicaments we and other people find ourselves in. Stubblefield believed so vehemently she did not explore all aspects of the situation to find a workable solution. We should be careful not to make the same mistake no matter what side of an issue we are on.

Movement and Silence

Right after sarcastically mentioning "supernatural autistic telepathy" and "divine inspiration" as possible explanations for facilitated communi-cation, Travers and colleagues tell us, "advocates continue to suggest that people with ASD have difficulty making their bodies move in ways that correspond to mental intention" (not even acknowledging that many Autistic individuals themselves report this). They then claim, "there remains no creditable empirical evidence" for this (Travers *et al.* 2016, p.99). Reflecting the diagnostic conventions of the DSM, they say autism "is not a motor disorder" (p.98). This is meant to further discredit the philosophy of supported typing insofar as CLAWHS seemingly unable to communicate are seen as possibly able mentally but prevented by physical limitations. Despite skepticism in this regard, textbooks on the neurophysiology of autism (e.g. Konopka 2013) describe specifically impaired mechanisms of movement associated with autism. A growing number of CLAWHS who have learned to communicate with supported typing describe how their proprioception and capabilities of movement are hampered (Biklen 2005; Higashida 2007; Kedar 2012). To dismiss such reports is unethical. The hospital where I work is an environment solidly based on science and scientific evidence. If any patient in the hospital tells any doctor, from the greenest intern to the greatest surgeon, that his leg hurts, no doctor will say, "Sorry, I can't accept your report due to lack of objective evidence about your communicative competence." Yet this is what happens when "experts" do not accept autistic self-reports of movement difficulty.

Conventional medical approaches may not recognize physical impairment as part of autism, but many professionals believe our understanding of autism should be restructured to reflect the experience of the individuals who live with the condition (Donnellan, Hill, and Leary 2013). Difficulties with movement can be explained by a disturbance of corollary signals. As discussed in the section on autism and schizophrenia, corollary (or efferent) discharges are copies of originary brain impulses sent to other areas of the brain to provide real-time feedback enabling motor control and movement prediction. It is the process that gives rise to proprioception, the inner sense letting us know the location of our body parts. If a person's intention to scratch an itch does not result in both a motor signal directed to the arm *and* a corollary discharge, or this impulse gets disrupted, it becomes difficult to manage the muscle control necessary to complete movements. Such simple things as changing the body's position in desired ways, pointing, stepping, reaching, and targeting a typewriter key can become monumental challenges. Current DSM definitions of autism do not account for such research.

Presumed Competence

Part of the philosophy of facilitated communication, assuming an attitude of *presumed competence* can minimize the number of individuals left to languish in stigma and exclusion because of undetermined communication abilities. Andrew Bloomfield, in a personal email communication, says he will only allow people into his life if he feels they believe he is "smart like anyone." This means they must value his communication. For those who have not found a way to communicate, it means people must assume an attitude of genuine presumed competence. Professionals in the area of disability support write that adopting this attitude helps them attain required levels of "effort and attention" to be of service even when they lack evidence of a person's intelligence or have not yet been able to connect emotionally with them (Hussman 2017). Individuals with autism have repeatedly stated that this orientation helps them feel respected and included (Soraya 2014). A closed Facebook group of non-speaking Autistic people (*Autism: Presumed Competence*) purports to have 469 members endorsing an Autistic blog that advocates for and reports the value of presumed competence for this population (Sequenzia 2011). "Experts" may think presumed competence is nothing more than an unproven educational technique, ignoring those such as Henry Frost who tell us "not presuming my competence hurts" (Sequenzia and Grace 2015, p.58). Presumed competence does not mean we make performance demands on a person they may be unable to satisfy. It means we speak to them in the same tone of voice, in the same natural way, with the same respect and assumption of understanding we adopt with others their age.

Counselors often advise people who are in the room with a loved one who is in an unresponsive state to adopt the same attitude. We encourage them to maintain a calm, respectful demeanor and talk to their loved one normally, not because of an unjustified assumption about their ability but so they promote the vulnerable person's chances of wellness in every possible way. This is not a knowledge claim but a caring ethical stance similar to what is meant by presumed competence. It is an attitude not only thoroughly consistent with but demanded by the rigorously articulated framework of ethical encounter developed by Levinas (1961/1969). It is a special case of ethical encounter calling on us to interact with unfamiliar others in our own fullness even as we retain open receptivity to the potential of their personhood when the call and response of conventional mutuality is absent or not apparent.

Travers asks us repeatedly to withhold and suspend judgment until we have evidence. One problem with this is that the kind of evidence we think we need may not currently be available. Should we take a chance on demeaning vulnerable individuals until we satisfy our need for proof? The real problem is we don't naturally withhold judgment at all. We have to make a special effort not to patronize, resort to stereotypes, and impose potentially damaging limitations. In an ideal world non-judgmental interaction would be our natural response. Presumed competence is a special case of ethical encounter that allows us to correct for our stigmatizing tendencies when another person cannot convey what they are capable of. Education professionals developing learning strategies might retain a certain "agnosticism of ability" (Travers and Ayres 2015, p.377), but this term implies detached skepticism. Presumed competence demands full-bodied respect grounded in a practical ethics of encounter towards people we don't understand. Educators must balance the use of what might be unreasonably demanding material for an individual whose intelligence is undetermined with exposure to material that can challenge any undemonstrated but not conclusively established intellectual ability. As fellow human beings, ethical encounter demands we relate to such individuals as equals who are as capable as others in their age group so we don't further traumatize them with patronizing invalidation based on an assumption of intellectual impairment. This is not to say anything demeaning about those who do have intellectual impairment, only to point to the invalidating frustration of being identified as such a person and being treated like one when it isn't the case. The stigmatizing experiences CLAWHS report alert us to the fact that intellectually impaired people themselves are habitually treated in a harmfully dismissive manner. This is something we all have to be more mindful of. It shouldn't be necessary as a deterrent, but it may help to remember that increasing technology allows more people to have eyes on our behavior and gives more of them a voice to report with.

If it wasn't just a few "experts" taking their own narrow commitment to what they believe are the highest standards of science too far, we might take away their vote, strip them of their high school and post-secondary diplomas, order teachers to stop giving them grades based on their communication, and charge people who use supported typing for plagiarism since they may be passing other people's thoughts off as their own. No one suggests any of this. Maybe if the "experts" had their way, we would. It's the logical outcome of the position they are holding so fast to.

Non-verbal individuals who communicate using assistive technology report being called "retard," treated as if they were "stupid," and often exposed to minimally challenging educational content (Bloomfield 2011; Kedar 2012). Higashida (2007) wrote, "I used to wonder why the Non-Speaking Me had ever been born" (Q 10). Carly Fleischmann typed to her father, "You know how people talk behind people's back? With me, they talk in front of my back" (Fleischmann and Fleischmann 2012, p.125). Feeling the sting of people's derision and lack of respect played out before me as if I was invisible and not being able to say anything is the most stigmatizing experience I can imagine. Being "locked within my shell, and too often a shell that seems empty to the outside world," is how Christy Oslund describes this experience (Sequenzia and Grace 2015, p.46).

ASHFA who do not identify as disabled maintain that the picture of a whole person trapped inside an autistic body is stigmatizing because for them autism is inherently part of who they are. Autistics who identify as disabled endorse this image whole-heartedly. Who should we believe? Both are true from their own perspective. Rather than picking and choosing what's true from a safe distance, we must adopt an ethics of encounter that allows us to let the personhood of individual people educate us. Theories, conventions, and assumptions are not the bottom line. People are. Anything less is a stigmatizing violation of social justice and ethical encounter.

Bridges-Over-Barriers

Bridges-Over-Barriers was started by a small group of men who type to speak and have been meeting in Guelph, Ontario since 2004. After trying unsuccessfully for almost a year to find a local group of CLAWHS who type to speak, I only stumbled upon their existence when I sent a letter to an organization called Mamre thinking they were an autism service provider close to my home town. The organization turned out to be in Australia, but they were kind enough to refer me to Bridges. That's how I came to correspond with Andrew Bloomfield, who has been very helpful educating me about this population's challenges. The group has posted several YouTube videos and published a film and book (*Bridges-Over-Barriers: In Our Own Words*, 2010). Andrew published his memoir in 2011 (*Bridges Over Barriers in My Life with Autism*). *Holding in the Storm*, a film produced by Christine Zorn and inspired by Bridges, premiered on World Autism Day 2014 and won several film festival awards.

Andrew is keen to educate people about his condition. He answered all my questions, sometimes having to take time between emails because he wasn't feeling well. For example, he experiences what he calls "grey mode" when he can't focus, think clearly, or sleep. Other times he said he had to wait until he could work with a facilitator who could best encourage and help him express more complex thoughts.

In a double supported typing session with Ken Moon of Bridges in which they both answered questions reviewed by Amy Sequenzia, he said, "sometimes my body does not listen to my head." Ken agreed with this, and wished he had learned to express himself using facilitated communication as a child rather than an adult. Both he and Andrew had been taught to communicate using pictures and sign language but neither found these allowed them to tap sufficiently into their lively intelligence. Amy Sequenzia, in separate correspondence, said the same was true for her.

Another member of Bridges-Over-Barriers said that before he learned to communicate with supported typing, "people treated me like I had no feelings or intelligence. My life was hell. Being able to communicate frees me to feel like a human being." Andrew said before he discovered facilitated communication he felt "trapped." Ken typed, "I felt like a handicapped person. Now I am a real man because I can talk with facilitated communication and people understand me." He added, "I don't like being an autistic man." He said, "people don't like me using FC because they think I am not doing the talking. They don't want to believe in FC. They don't want to listen to me. They think I should be hidden away and I should not speak because I am a handicapped man." Andrew, who said, "I think autism makes me a better person," responded with touching emotional support. He empathized, saying, "I feel so sad for you I want you to know you are a real man do not let others stop you from being the great person you are. We love you."

When asked if they would want a cure for autism, Ken said, "Yes I would." Another member of the group said, "I would be frightened to lose some of my special abilities like understanding others through their auras and seeing the world in numbers and symbols. I'm not sure I would understand a different kind of world." Andrew, with the positive energy I've learned is characteristic of him in our short acquaintance, said simply, "I am not sure I need a cure. I like who I am." Ken told Andrew enthusiastically that he wanted his full name to appear in the book because he was proud of his contribution and wanted everyone to know how unhappy he was that facilitated communication was not allowed in his group home. He said he hoped this access to complex communication and authentic expression would be reintroduced.

The thing that strikes me most about Andrew is how happy and safe he repeatedly says he is. He does not talk about any bothersome residue of trauma or invalidation, unpleasant escalation, or interpersonal conflict. He just keeps saying how happy, loved, and thankful he is. I wish I could report the same about my overly self-complicated, often defensive, and frequently triggered life. When I asked what he would do to decrease the stigma autistic people experience, he said, "*please listen*." Another member of the group, who sent his answers to Andrew separately, said, "See through my behaviors to the person I really am." He added that people should "listen with their hearts."

Of course, these words were typed with the help of a supported typing facilitator. Should this invalidate their communication? Many of the "experts" would say so, apparently not conscious of the stigma they are directing at other human beings. Kimberly Dixon types, "people need to become friends with us who cannot speak so they can understand our struggles as well as our joys" (Sequenzia and Grace 2015, p.65). In alignment with this powerfully destigmatizing sentiment, I count myself lucky to be getting to know such an interesting, eager to help, curious-to-learn person as Andrew John Bloomfield the Third. Familiarity is the best antidote for stigma in the presence of decent human goodness.

The Demands of Hospitality

As one of the giants of contemporary philosophy, Jacques Derrida never addressed the situation of people who type to speak but he provides a therapeutic way of regarding stigma in general. This appeal to Derrida's work may be based less on textual expertise than the manner in which his lively and exquisitely written discussions inspired me as a philosophy student years ago. I could not even articulate the full nature of this inspiration. His words can be moving in an almost unspecifiable way and are more than a sum of logical formulations.

Derrida's work underscores the "ethical significance" of moving towards a model of genuine acknowledgement in relationship that does not involve a strict determination of accuracy under controlled conditions attempting to expose some kind of objective underlying certainty. He is critical of the over-simplified quaintness of advocating a return to "the *neighborliness* in the small communities *where everyone knows everyone else*" (1967/1997, p.137; italics added), but he urges upon us a spirit of relationship consistent with the ongoing theme of hospitality that runs through his work and which his friend Michael Nass explores in detail (2005). This spirit of ethical encounter demands a reception of "unconditional welcome" towards others (Derrida 2000, p.77). Practical considerations such as legality and safety often call for protective boundaries, but there is no necessary constraint that forces us to compromise the principle of "unlimited hospitality" by stigmatizing others and making them feel their humanity, their value as unique individuals, or the contribution of their expression is in question.

Philosopher Mark Westmoreland says, "we must embrace hospitality as an interruption—an interruption of the self" (2008, p.9). When it comes to ethical encounter, this must not be taken as a *rude* interruption as if we were set upon and bothered but rather a *transformative* interruption in which we make ourselves receptive in order to be expanded by the other person's presence and perspective. We set aside our own agenda in order to take on a spirit of welcoming. We are challenged by the other person to step back from ourselves in order to create space for them. I'm sure this can be challenging for anyone. For ASHFA, at least for me, the often sudden change of orientation involved can be grueling. It takes years of practice to accomplish gracefully and never gets easy. Autistics of various shades are notorious for having difficulty with this shift. If we can work on it, so can others.

All of us tend, sometimes cruelly and often carelessly, to disrespect and undermine people for lack of effort to appreciate their personhood. We don't bother to understand their perspective, listen to what they have to say, or open ourselves to them sufficiently. What prompts us to compromise the ethical principle of pure hospitality in this way? Sometimes just because we think we can get away with it and not get called out on our bad manners. Sometimes we do it out of regressive childish coping. It may have something to do with the way our fear of the unfamiliar is often handled with defensive projection and cynicism. A stigmatizing attitude can be related to a myriad of factors including anger, ungrateful privilege, unresolved grief, early trauma, and our own internalized oppression. This can all be challenging to step back from and reconfigure in line with greater insight and wider values, especially if the need for healing is unrecognized. Luckily the *NAB* it framework can provide a strategy of ethical crisis intervention, helping us notice when we're "transgressing" what Derrida calls "*the law of hospitality*" due to internal escalation and emotional disturbance (2000, p.77).

We can also find ourselves marginalizing and hurting others when we are too narrowly focused on agendas that don't make room for the feelings of other people or consideration for their wellbeing. Autistics, at least ASHFA, can be like this all too easily. So can science in its driest "value-free" forms, and hospitality is compromised unnecessarily for no good reason because of inflexibility.

What if we don't realize we're causing injury? Defending ourselves as "innocent" never helps. Instead we can evaluate our behavior against the golden ideal of pure hospitality and be honest with ourselves about our performance. As parents the balance between necessary constraints to hospitality and often unintentionally erosive assaults on personhood can be especially delicate. Children are very vulnerable and may not have the higher-order thinking or social experience necessary to know when they should take another person's behavior with a grain of salt. They depend on caregivers to provide the hospitality needed for creating an environment of safety that allows them to grow in their own way and feel worthy in order to blossom. The parenting role demands awareness, purposefulness, and insight into the significant influence adults have on the developing identities of children. If not, the resulting trauma can create distress cycles of self-hatred, shame, aggression, isolation, and dissociation. This does not mean everything has to be perfect and pleasant all the time. Hardship is also crucial for growth, but a bedrock of caring hospitality must be in place or things go awry for socially complex human organisms. Furthermore, this need for well-rooted hospitality never goes away, even though people become "harder-shelled" as they go through life (Peterson 2018, rule 1, p.15). People with ongoing vulnerability because of differences from the mainstream, people who to various degrees do not fit in with the dominant population, call on us to be particularly mindful of our hospitality. This is not only because their difference in itself can trigger stigma when we react to our own discomfort with it, but because it is easy to join the pack of disrespectfulness towards them when they are outnumbered.

Another protective mechanism against stigma and abusive viola-tions of ethical hospitality involves applying the "Golden Rule." This appears in various forms across different cultures and, as we all know and often clean forget, involves treating others the way we would *like* to be treated ourselves (Neusner and Chilton 2009). No matter how oppressed and unworthy we may feel or how poorly we expect to be treated, we would almost all like to be treated in fundamentally the same way: with dignity, respect, and kindness. We must always remember that the Golden Rule applies equally and sometimes with more urgency to ourselves. It is often extremely difficult to treat ourselves with compassionate kindness, especially when traumas of invalidation are burned into us. When we are targeting ourselves with shaming thoughts and self-destructive behaviors this can cue us to make an extra-special effort to show ourselves decent hospitality. When we become arrogant, it underscores the importance of making extra efforts to apply the Golden Rule with intelligent consistency towards others.

We can also stay on track with ethical encounter by obtaining feedback, whether by explicitly asking about a person's response to the way we are acting, making an effort to observe the effects of our behavior, or carefully considering the input of third parties who are intimately acquainted with the one(s) we are having an impact on. This is not to say we should rely on the advice of "experts" or other authorities, but carefully heed the feedback of those who have lived caring involvement with the people it is appropriate for us to be monitoring our level of hospitality with. All these ethical safety techniques call on us to acknowledge the importance of attending to the perspective of others, which especially as an Autistic I must admit can be bothersome at times and often a show-stopping challenge.

Human relationship for Derrida has no place for the kind of stigma that results when speech is seen as somehow superior to writing, whatever level of support is required to access complex expression. In a spirit of subverting convention and upholding the promise of humanity, we should not frame this kind of ethical interaction in the nostalgic form of a romantic past ideal, but in terms that don't back away from the messy complexity of living flesh-and-blood diversity as people struggle to make multiple meanings in the world together. Small towns and even families where "everyone knows everyone else" can be hotbeds of judgment, rejection, and demands for conformity. We can never take the demand for hospitality lightly or for granted. The model of relationship Derrida outlines does not broach exclusion on the basis of difference or the expectation of others, although it is always wary about the possibility of oppression.

There is no substitute for the kind of openness that leads to familiarity, and the ethics of encounter found in Levinas can be a powerful tool to help us approach dignity-preserving hospitality better than the judgments, prejudices, assumptions, detached proclamations, unimaginatively imposed scientific conventions, paternal "I-know-what's best" convictions, power-hoarding, lazy complacency, and various defensive reactions we sometimes seem to value more than people. This book has cited various research demonstrating the kind of neurological and other physiological damage done by socially oriented abuse and invalidation, not to mention the untold amounts of personal suffering and social disruption that striving for ethical encounter can help avoid.

Autism and the ethics of encounter both came into being in the shadow of World War II. They belong together and together provide powerful lessons about stigma and the *use-of-self* called for to remove our social blinders. There is no better medicine for social harmony and healthy relationship than ethically grounded encounter, whether it is online or face to face, in families, at work, the boardrooms of commerce and politics, the pursuit of science, or everyday interactions on the street with all varieties of sociophenomenal and other kinds of diversity.

Final Words

Adopting an ethics of encounter like I did in my study to protect vulnerable individuals from potential harm due to my diagnosis can help mainstream sociodominant others from marginalizing autistic individuals. It also provides an important safeguard against stigma, oppression, and runaway theory because it puts the receptivity of genuine encounter before assumptions, agendas, theories, beliefs, and defensive patterns. Sometimes self-protection is a necessary factor deferring such openness, but a conscious ethics of encounter combined with the *NAB* it and *AFTER* care framework allows us to manage our own disruptive influence and recognize when we are imposing personal defensive habits, expectations, and ideas on others. It allows us to "listen with our hearts" whenever possible, notice when we're not, and practice strategies to counter our automatic responses.

As a social worker in Ontario, I do not discuss diagnosis with clients. If a potential diagnosis is prominent, I may refer a client to some book or discussion forum to explore it for themselves, so they can intelligently discuss it further with their doctor. I find with many clients discussing the challenges of autisticy and how the role of trauma can make them worse provides a helpful framework to understand their experience. Discussing patterns of escalated safety distress and exploring self-recovery practices frequently provides a way to move forward rather than waiting for a diagnosis to "see what's wrong."

The model often proves useful to normalize behavior patterns that fall between the cracks of diagnosis but which people find painful and confusing. They may have been told, "Nothing's wrong with you." It allows them, like an undiagnosed autistic, to account for the stigma and frustigma they have been experiencing without beating themselves up and feeling like they are weak, bad, or "less-than." Most importantly, it gives them a recovery framework they can start practicing that provides traction for recovery without a waiting list.

Life can be hard. As a child I used to rock and chant "I love my ghosts" to help me through the hard times. As an adult I say a prayer to help me to keep going when I find myself in turmoil. I quietly say to myself:

> May I have the courage to move forward on the path life is unfolding before me.

By "prayer" I only mean to say "brave words of empowerment." We pray to whatever source of strength greater than our isolated personal self in this great universe we feel we might be able to draw strength from, even if this remains a mystery. During difficult periods we may not feel grateful for living, but it is still important to practice gratitude. We can find it in ourselves to acknowledge the miracle of life even when it's easy to take for granted or we don't feel part of it. Sometimes it would be easier to shrivel up and hide. We all have times when it is necessary to forge ahead like pioneers until we see the light.

It's hard but we can do it. We can help others do it.

We can do it together.

References

Many general interest references are accompanied by a brief annotation.

Adewunmi, B. (October 4, 2011). Racism and skin colour: The many shades of prejudice. *The Guardian*. Retrieved from www.theguardian.com/world/2011/oct/04/racism-skin-colour-shades-prejudice.

Alda, A. (2017). *If I understood you, would I have this look on my face? My adventures in the art and science of relating and communicating*. New York: Random House.

American Psychiatric Association (2013). *Diagnostic and statistical manual of mental disorders (5th edition)*. Arlington: American Psychiatric Association.

Angel, L. (1987). *The spiritual foundations of philosophy*. Vancouver: Aleph House.

AnxiousAdvocate (2015). Why I left ABA [Web blog]. Socially Anxious Advocate. Retrieved from https://sociallyanxiousadvocate.wordpress.com.

Aston, M. (2003). *Aspergers in love: Couple relationships and family affairs*. London: Jessica Kingsley Publishers.

Attwood, T. (2007). *The complete guide to Asperger's Syndrome*. London: Jessica Kingsley Publishers.

Autistic Self Advocacy Network (2012). *Loud hands: Autistic people, speaking*. Washington: Autistic Press.

Bandstra, C., Camfield, C., and Camfield, P. (2008). Stigma of Epilepsy. *Canadian Journal of Neurological Science* 35, 436–440.

Barnbaum, D. (2008). *Ethics of autism: Among them but not of them*. Bloomington: Indiana University Press.

Bateman, A. and Fonagy, P. (eds) (2011). *Handbook of mentalizing in mental health practice*. Arlington: American Psychiatric Publishing.

Bellamy, L. (2013). *Field notes from an Aspie's wife: Is this neurotypical or Asperger's syndrome?* n.p.

Bennet, M. (2016). The importance of interviewing adults on the autism spectrum about their depression and suicidal ideation experiences. *Journal of Autism and Developmental Disorders* 46 (4), 1492–1493.

Berg-Dallara, A. (2014). *The dark side of autism: Struggling to find peace and understanding when life's not full of rainbows, unicorns, and blessings*. New York: Morgan James.

Bettelheim, B. (1967). *The empty fortress: Infantile autism and the birth of the self*. New York: The Free Press.

Biklen, D. (2005). *Autism and the myth of the person alone*. New York: New York University Press.

Biklen, D. and Burke, J. (2006). Presuming competence. *Equality and Excellence in Education*, 39, 166–175.

Bloomfield, A. (2011). *Bridges over barriers in my life with autism*. Guelph: Friends of Andrew Bloomfield and Guelph Services for the Autistic.

Bluesky (October 21, 2010). Re: Alcoholism Drug Addiction Help and Information: Asperger's Syndrome [Online forum comment]. Retrieved from www.soberrecovery.com/forums/mental-health/143188-aspergers-syndrome.html.

Bradshaw, J. (1988/2005). *Healing the shame the binds you*. Deerfield: Health Communications.

Brown, B. (2015). *Rising strong: The reckoning. The rumble. The revolution*. New York: Random House.

Brown, B. (2010*). The gifts of imperfection: Let go of who you think you're supposed to be and embrace who you are*. Minnesota: Hazelden.

Brown-Lavoie, S., Viecili, M. and Weiss, J. (2014). Sexual knowledge and victimization in adults with autism spectrum disorders. *Journal of Autism and Developmental Disorders* 44 (9), 2185–2196. Online version retrieved from www.ncbi.nlm.nih.gov/pmc/articles/PMC4131130/pdf/10803_2014_Article_2093.pdf.

Buckholtz, M. (2017). Autistic, gifted, and Black: An interview with Mike Buckholtz. *Thinking Person's Guide to Autism: Autism, News and Resources: From Autistic People, Professionals, and Parents.* Retrieved from www.thinkingautismguide.com/2017/09/autistic-gifted-and-black-interview.html.

Buckholtz, M. (March 28, 2012). The invisibles: Autistic adults [Web blog]. *CNN ireport.* Retrieved from http://ireport.cnn.com/docs/DOC-768049.

Butler, R. and Gillis, J. (2011). The impact of labels and behaviours on the stigmatization of adults with Asperger's disorder. *Journal of Autism and Developmental Disorders* 41, 741–749.

Butts, H. (2002). The black mask of humanity: Racial/ethnic discrimination and post-traumatic stress disorder. *Journal of the American Academy of Psychiatry and the Law* 30, 336–339. Retrieved from https://pdfs.semanticscholar.org/bc2a/4b95735581805a89b629952d1d83f7384a6c.pdf.

Capriola, N., Maddox, B., and White, S. (2017). No offense intended: Fear of negative evaluation in adolescents and adults with autism spectrum disorder. *Journal of Autism and Developmental Disorders* 47 (12), 3803–3813.

Channon, S., Crawford, S., Orlowska, D., Parikh, N., and Thoma, P. (2014). Mentalising and social problem solving in adults with Asperger's syndrome. *Cognitive Neuropsychiatry* 19 (2), 149–163.

Ciaramidaro, A., Bolt, S., Schlitt, S., Hainz, D., Poustka, A., Weber, B., Bara, G., Freitag, C., and Walter, H. (2015). Schizophrenia and autism as contrasting minds: Neural evidence for the hypo-hyper-intentionality thesis. *Schizophrenia Bulletin* 42 (1), 171–179.

Countryboy (June 23, 2010). Re: Asperger's and Substance Abuse [Online forum comment]. Retrieved from www.bluelight.org/vb/threads/470621-Aspergers-and-substance-abuse.

Courtois, C. (2014). *It's not you, it's what happened to you: Complex trauma and treatment.* Dublin, OH: Telemachus Press.

Crespi, B. and Badcock, C. (2008). Psychosis and autism as diametrical disorders of the social brain. *Behavioral and Brain Sciences* 31, 241–320. Retrieved from https://pdfs.semanticscholar.org/f069/df78727581b3732a75ca5c9f38b9b40a11c5.pdf.

Critchfield, T., Doepke, K., Epting, K., Becirevic, A., Reed, D., Fienup, D., Kremsreiter, J., and Ecott, C. (2017). Normative emotional responses to behaviour analysis jargon or how not to win friends and influence people. *Behaviour Analysis Practice* 10, 97–106.

Cvitkovic, L. (1997). A study of the usefulness of facilitated communication with autistic individuals [Master's thesis]. University of Toronto. Retrieved from https://tspace.library.utoronto.ca/handle/1807/11510.

Delahooke, M. (2015). Being "non-verbal" doesn't mean I can't think [Web blog]. Mona's Blog. Retrieved from www.monadelahooke.com/being-nonverbal-doesnt-mean-i-cant-think.

Derrida, J. (1967/1997). *Of grammatology* (Gayatri Chakravorty Spivak, trans.). Baltimore: Johns Hopkins University Press.

Derrida, J. (1999). *Adieu to Immanuel Levinas.* Stanford: Stanford University Press.

Derrida, J. (2000). *Of hospitality* (R. Bowlby, trans.). Stanford: Stanford University Press.

Dolmage, J. (2017). *Academic ableism: Disability and higher education.* Ann Arbor: University of Michigan Press.

Donnellan, A., Hill, D., and Leary, M. (2013). Rethinking autism: Implications of sensory and movement differences for understanding and support. *Frontiers in Integrative Neuroscience* 6 (124), 1–11. Retrieved from www.frontiersin.org/articles/10.3389/fnint.2012.00124/full.

Donvan, J. and Zucker, C. (2016). *In a different key: The story of autism.* New York: Crown Publishers.

Dubin, N. (2009). *Asperger's syndrome and anxiety: A guide to successful stress management.* London: Jessica Kingsley Publishers.
  An Autistic psychologist provides helpful anxiety management strategies.

Ducharme, R. and Gullota, T. (eds) (2013). *Asperger Syndrome: A guide for professionals and Families.* New York: Heidelberg Dordrecht.

Faherty, C. (2016). Asperger's syndrome in women: A different set of challenges. In *Asperger's and Girls: World renowned experts join those with Asperger's syndrome to resolve issues that girls and woman face every day!* (pp.9–14). Arlington: Future Horizons.

Feinberg, I. (1978). Efference copy and corollary discharge: Implications for thinking and its disorders. *Schizophrenia Bulletin* 4 (4), 636–640.

Fleischmann, A. and Fleischmann, C. (2012). *Carly's voice: Breaking through autism.* Toronto: Simon & Schuster.

Fonagy, P., Luyten, P., and Strathearn, L. (2011). Borderline personality disorder, mentalization, and the neurobiology of attachment. *Infant Mental Health Journal* 32 (1), 47–69.

Ford, J. and Mathalon, D. (2004). Electrophysiological evidence of corollary discharge dysfunction in schizophrenia during talking and thinking. *Journal of Psychiatric Research* 39 (1), 37–46.

Foucault, M. (1963/1998). Preface to transgression. In J. Faubion (ed.), *Aesthetics, Methods, and Epistemology: The Essential Works of Michael Foucault 1954–1984*, vol. 2 (pp.69–87). New York: New Press.

Foucault, M. (1975/1995). *Discipline and punish: The birth of the prison* (2nd edition). New York: Vintage Books.

Foucault, M. (1976/1994). Truth and power. In J. Faubian (ed.), *Power: The Essential Works of Michael Foucault 1954–1984*, vol. 3 (pp.326–348). New York: New York Press.

Foucault, M. (1982/1994). The subject and power. In J. Faubian (ed.), *Power: The Essential Works of Michael Foucault 1954–1984*, vol. 3 (pp.111–133). New York: New York Press.

Francis, A. (2013). *Saving normal: An insider's revolt against out of control psychiatric diagnosis, DSM-5, big pharma, and the medicalization of ordinary life*. New York: William Morrow.

Freeman, B. (July 9, 2016). Reply to Amy Sequenzia's blog post *Communication and autism specialists*. Ollibean. Retrieved from https://ollibean.com/autism-specialists.

Frith, C. (2016). *Discovering the mind: Selected works of Christopher D. Frith*. New York: Psychology Press.

Frith, U., Happé, F., and Siddons, F. (1994). Autism and theory of mind in everyday life. *Social Development* 3 (2), 108–124.

Gates, G. (2014) Cognitive difference in a postmodern world: Asperger's, autism, stigma, and diagnosis [Master's thesis]. Victoria: University of Victoria. Retrieved from http://voyager.library.uvic.ca/vwebv/holdingsInfo?bibId=3171439.

Giles, D. (2014). "DSM-V is taking away our identity": The reaction of the online community to the proposed changes in the diagnosis of Asperger's Disorder. *Health* 18 (2), 179–195.

Goffman, E. (1967). *Interaction ritual: Essays on face to face behavior*. New York: Pantheon.

Goffman, E. (1966). *Behaviour in public places: Notes of the social organization of gatherings*. New York: Free Press.

Goffman, E. (1963). *Stigma: Notes on the management of spoiled identity*. New York: Simon & Schuster.

Goffman, E. (1956). *The presentation of the self in everyday life*. Edinburgh: University of Edinburgh Social Sciences Research Center. Retrieved from https://monoskop.org/images/1/19/Goffman_Erving_The_Presentation_of_Self_in_Everyday_Life.pdf.

Goleman, D. (1996). *Emotional intelligence: Why it can matter more than IQ*. London: Bloomsbury Publishing.

grassroots (March 14, 2016). The Word "Cousin" [Online forum thread]. Retrieved from www.aspiescentral.com/threads/the-word-cousin.15680.

Greeson, M., Campbell, R., and Fehler-Cabral, G. (2016). "Nobody deserves this": Adolescent sexual assault victims' perceptions of disbelief and victim blame from police. *Journal of Community Psychology* 44 (1), 90–110.

Gunderson, J. (2010). Revising the borderline diagnosis for DSM-5: An alternative proposal. *Journal of Personality Disorder* 24 (6), 694–708.

Hacking, I. (2009a). Autistic autobiography. *Philosophical Transactions of the Royal Society B* 364 (1522), 1467–1473.

Hacking, I. (2009b). Humans, aliens, and autism. *Daedalus* 138 (3), 44–59.

Hartmann, K., Urbano, M., Manser, K., and Okwara, L. (2012). Modified dialectical behavior therapy to improve emotional regulation in autism spectrum disorders. In E. Chaz and R. Wood (eds), *Autism Spectrum Disorders* (pp.41–72). New York: Nova Science Publishers.

Herbert, M. and Weintraub, K. (2012) *The autism revolution: Whole body strategies for making life all it can be*. New York: Harvard Health Publications.

Herek, G. (1996). Why tell if you're not asked? Self-disclosure, intergroup contact, and heterosexuals' attitudes toward lesbians and gay men. In G. Herek, B. Job, and R. Carney (eds), *Out in force: Sexual orientation in the military* (pp.197–225). Chicago: University of Chicago Press.

Herman, J. (1992/2015). *Trauma and recovery: The aftermath of violence from domestic abuse to political terror*. New York: Basic Books.

Herman, J. (March 10, 2007). *Shattered shame states and their repair* [John Bowlby Memorial Lecture]. Retrieved from www.challiance.org/Resource.ashx?sn=VOVShattered20ShameJHerman.

Higashida, N. (2007). *The reason I jump: One boy's voice from the silence of autism*. New York: Random House.

Hoffer, A. (2004). *Healing schizophrenia: Complementary vitamin and drug treatments*. Toronto: CCNM Press.

Hoover, D. (2015). The effects of psychological trauma on children with autism spectrum disorders: A research review. *Review Journal of Autism and Developmental Disorders* 2 (3), 287–299.

Howard, A. (November 7, 2014). Jerry Seinfeld believes he has autism: I think I'm on the spectrum. *MSNBC*. Retrieved from www.msnbc.com/msnbc/jerry-seinfeld-believes-he-has-autism-i-think-im-the-spectrum.

Hussman, J. (2017). Presume competence: Autism support 1.0. Catonsville: Hussman Institute for Autism. Retrieved from http://www.hussmanautism.org/wp-content/uploads/pdf/PresumeCompetence_HussmanInstitute.pdf.
A guide to successful, evidence-based principles for supporting and engaging individuals with autism.

Iland, L. (2016). Girl to girl: Advice on friendship, bullying, and fitting in. In *Asperger's and Girls: World renowned experts join those with Asperger's syndrome to resolve issues that girls and women face every day!* (pp.33–63). Arlington: Future Horizons.

Institute for Attachment and Child Development (February 2017). Why kids don't "outgrow" reactive attachment disorder (and what happens when they grow up without help). Retrieved from http://instituteforattachment.org/why-kids-dont-outgrow-reactive-attachment-disorder-and-what-happens-when-they-grow-up-without-help.

Iyengar, R. (November 20, 2014). Jerry Seinfeld says he's not on the spectrum after all. *Time*. Retrieved from http://time.com/3596612/jerry-seinfeld-autism-spectrum-aspergers-syndrome-neurotypical.

Johnston, K. and Iarocci, G. (2017). Are generalized anxiety and depression symptoms associated with social competence in children with and without autism spectrum disorder? *Journal of Autism and Developmental Disorders* 47 (12), 3778–3788.

Jones, E., Farina, A., Hastorf, A., Markus, H., Miller, D., and Scott, R. (1984). *Social stigma: The psychology of marked relationships.* New York: W.H. Freeman.

Kabat-Zinn, J. and Nhat Hanh, T. (1990/2013). *Full catastrophe living: Using the wisdom of your body and mind to face stress, pain, and illness.* New York: Bantam.

Kedar, I. (2016). Spectrum or Different? [Web blog]. Ido in Autismland. Retrieved from http://idoinautismland.com/?cat=74.

Kedar, I. (2012). *Ido in autismland: Climbing out of autism's silent prison.* United States: Sharon Kedar.

Kelly, K. and Ramundo, P. (1995). *You mean I'm not lazy, stupid, or crazy?!: A self-help book for adults with attention deficit disorder.* New York: Scribner.

Kerns, C., Newschaffer, C., and Berkowitz, S. (2015). Traumatic childhood events and autism spectrum disorder. *Journal of Autism and Developmental Disorders* 45 (11), 3475–3486.

Kezuka, E. (1997). The role of touch in facilitated communication. *Journal of Autism and Developmental Disorders* 27 (5), 571–593.

Kirkham, P. (2017). The line between intervention and abuse: Autism and applied behavioural analysis. *History of the Human Sciences* 30 (2), 107–126. Retrieved from http://journals.sagepub.com.ezproxy.library.uvic.ca/doi/full/10.1177/0952695117702571.

Kleijnen, J. and Knipschild, P. (1991). Niacin and vitamin B6 in mental functioning: A review of controlled clinical trials. *Biological Psychiatry* 29 (9), 931–941.

Klin, A., Volkmar, F., and Sparrow, S. (eds) (2000). *Asperger Syndrome.* New York: Guilford Press.

Köhler, W. (1947). *Gestalt psychology: An introduction to new concepts in modern psychology.* Scarborough: New American Library.

Konopka, G (ed.) (2013). *Neurobiology of autism.* Cambridge: Academic Press.

Krisnamurti, J. (1972). *You are the world: Talks and discussions at American universities* [Pdf version]. Retrieved from www.basharantoon.com/ebooks/You_are_the_World.pdf.
Famous Eastern philosopher who renounced the role others expected of him and spent his life travelling and speaking, often to university students.

Laucius, J. (June 2, 2013). Women with Asperger's help each other through the social minefields of life [Newspaper article related to "Asperfemme" conference in Ottawa]. Ottawa Citizen. Retrieved through *Special Needs Digest*, May 23, 2014 from www.specialneedsdigest.com/2013/06/from-ottawa-citizen-by-joanne-laucius.html.

Lester, J. and Paulus, T. (2012). Performative acts of autism. *Discourse Society* 23, 259–273.

Levinas, E. (1961/1969). *Totality and infinity: An essay on exteriority* (Alphonso Lingis, trans.). Pittsburg: Duquesne University Press.

Levine, P. (1997). *Waking the tiger: Healing trauma.* Berkeley: North Atlantic Books.

Levine, S. (1989). *A gradual awakening.* Woodson: Anchor Books.

Lewis, L. (2017). A mixed methods study of barriers to formal diagnosis of autism spectrum disorder in adults. *Journal of Autism and Developmental Disorders* 47 (8), 2410–2424.

Liegghio, M. (2013). A denial of being: Psychiatrization as epistemic violence. In B. LeFrancois, R. Menzies, and G. Rheaume (eds), *Mad Matters: A Critical Reader in Canadian Mad Studies*. Toronto: Canadian Scholar's Press.

Lindblom, A. (2014). Under-detection of autism among First Nations children in British Columbia, Canada. *Disability and Society* 29 (9), 1248–1259.

Linehan, M. (1993). *Cognitive behavioural treatment of borderline personality disorder*. New York: Guilford Press.

Ludwig, B. (2017). *Ginny Moon*. Toronto: Park Row Books.

Mandell, D. (2013). Adults with autism: A new minority. *Journal of General Internal Medicine* 28 (6), 751–752.

Mandy, W., Wang, A., and Lee, I. (2017). Evaluating social (pragmatic) communication disorder. *Journal of Child Psychology and Psychiatry* 58 (10), 1166–1175.

Martin, A. and Vahabzadeh, A. (November, 2014). Children of color and autism: Too little, too late [Web blog]. *HuffPost*. Retrieved from www.huffingtonpost.com/areva-martin/children-of-color-and-aut_b_6133354.html.

Martin, I. and McDonald, S. (2003). Weak coherence, no theory of mind, or executive dysfunction? Solving the problem of pragmatic language disorders. *Brain and Language* 85, 451–466.

Martin, S. (2011). *Born standing up*. New York: Scribner.

Maté, G. (1999). *Scattered minds: The origins and healing of attention deficit disorder*. Toronto: Vintage Canada.

Matson, J. and Kozlowski, A. (2011). The increasing prevalence of autism spectrum disorders. *Research in Autism Spectrum Disorders* 5, 418–425.

McDonagh, P. (2007). Autism and modernism: A genealogical exploration. In M. Osteen (ed.), *Autism and representation* (pp.99–116). London: Routledge.

McDonald, M. (June 30, 2016). "Facilitated communication" and a PEI family's nightmare. CTV News. Retrieved from www.ctvnews.ca/canada/facilitated-communication-and-a-p-e-i-family-s-nightmare-1.2968186.

Mehtar, M. and Mukaddes, N. (2011). Posttraumatic stress disorder in individuals with diagnosis of autistic spectrum disorders. *Research in Autism Spectrum Disorders* 5, 539–546.

Merleau-Ponty, M. (1945/2006). *The phenomenology of perception* (Colin Smith, trans.). London: Routledge and Kegan Paul.

Merleau-Ponty, M. (1948/1991). *Sense and nonsense* (Herbert and Patricia Dreyfus, trans.). Evanston: Northwestern University Press.

Merleau-Ponty, M. (1964). *Signs* [translated by Richard McCleary]. Evanston: Northwestern University Press.

Merleau-Ponty, M. (1968). *The visible and the invisible* (Alphonso Lingis, trans.). Evanston: Northwestern University Press.

Miles, J., Takahashi, N., Haber, A., and Hadden, L. (2003). Autism families with a high incidence of autism. *Journal of Autism and Developmental Disorders* 33 (4), 403–415.

Miller, L. and Sperry, L. (2014). A forgiveness intervention for women with fibromyalgia who were abused in childhood: A pilot study. *Spirituality in Clinical Practice* 1 (3), 203–217.

Milton, D. (2014). Autistic expertise: A critical reflection on the production of knowledge in autism studies. *Autism* 18 (7), 794–802.

Mitchell, C. (2013). *Mindful living with Asperger's Syndrome: Everyday mindfulness practices to help you tune into the present moment*. London: Jessica Kingsley Publishers.

Mohamed, G., El-Serafi, D., Sabray, W., Eirasheed, A., Abdel, R., Ghada, S., Soliman, A., and Armar, W. (2016). Executive dysfunctions in borderline personality disorder: Correlation with suicidality and impulsivity. *Middle East Current Psychiatry* 23 (2), 85–92.

Murray, S. (2012). *Autism*. New York: Routledge.

Nadesan, M. (2013). Autism and genetics: Profit, risk, and bare life. In J. Davidson and M. Orsini (eds), *Worlds of Autism* (pp.117–142). Minneapolis: University of Minnesota Press.

Naeem, F., Gul, M., and Aub, M. (2015). Brief culturally adapted CBT for psychosis (CaCBT-p): A randomized clinical control trial from a low-income country. *Schizophrenia Research* 164 (2–3), 143–148.

Nass, M. (2005). "Alors, Qui etes-vous?" Jacques Derrida and the question of hospitality. *SubStance* 34 (1), 6–17.

Neusner, J. and Chilton, B. (eds.). (2009). *The Golden Rule: The ethics of reciprocity in world religions*. London: Bloomsbury Academic.
    Explores how the rule to treat others as you would like to be treated yourself appears in religions across the world.

NPAA (2016). National Police Autism Association [Website]. Retrieved from www.npaa.org.uk.

Oxford Dictionaries ("stigma" definition 1) (2018). Retrieved from https://en.oxforddictionaries.com/definition/stigma.

Paris, J. (2013). *The intelligent clinician's guide to the DSM-5.* Oxford: Oxford University Press.

Peterson, J. (2018). *12 Rules for life: An antidote to chaos.* Toronto: Random House.
Resonates with current demand for renewed attention to ethics and moral growth as it explores powerful rules for living well.

Porges, S. (2017). *The pocket guide to Polyvagal Theory: The transformative power of feeling safe.* New York: W.W. Norton & Company.
A distinguished researcher presents a groundbreaking theory about trauma and social life, describing how safety is a crucial factor in human wellness.

Porges, S. (2011). *The polyvagal theory: Neurophysiological foundations of emotions, attachment, communication, and self-regulation.* New York: W.W. Norton & Company.

Porges, S. and Dana, D. (eds) (2018). *Clinical applications of the polyvagal theory: The emergence of polyvagal-informed therapies.* New York: W.W. Norton & Company.

Porter, T. (January 28, 2018). Parents are making their children drink bleach to cure them of autism. Newsweek. Retrieved from www.newsweek.com/parents-are-making-their-children-drink-bleach-cure-them-autism-793197.

Prince, D. (2013). All the things I have ever been: Reflections on academic writing and autism. In J. Davidson and M. Orsini (eds), *Worlds of Autism* (pp.319–330). Minneapolis: University of Minnesota Press.

Prizant, B. (2016). *Uniquely human: A different way of seeing autism.* New York: Simon & Schuster.

Purdie-Vaughns, V. and Eibach, R. (2008). Intersectional invisibility: The distinctive advantages and disadvantages of multiple subordinate group identities. *Sex Roles* 59, 337–391.

Quinn, D. and Chaudoir, S. (2009). Living with a concealable stigmatized identity: The impact of anticipated stigma, centrality, salience, and cultural stigma on psychological distress and health. *Journal of Personality and Social Psychology* 97 (4), 634–651.

Rahim, M. (2014). Developmental trauma disorder: An attachment-based perspective. *Clinical Child Psychology and Psychiatry* 19 (4), 548–560.

Reisz, S., Duschinsky, R., and Siegel, D. (2018). Disorganized attachment and defense: Exploring John Bowlby's unpublished reflections. *Attachment and Human Development* 20 (2), 107–134.

Rigles, B. (2017). The relationship between adverse childhood events, resiliency and health among children with autism. *Journal of Autism and Developmental Disorders* 47 (1), 187–202.

Rimland, B. (1964/2015). *Infantile autism: The syndrome and its implications for a neural theory of behaviour* [Edited by S. Edelson]. London: Jessica Kingsley Publishers.
Fiftieth anniversary edition contains interesting commentary that helps us understand the insightful contributions of this towering autism researcher.

Robertson, K. (2017). For thy child. *New Human City.* Retrieved from http://newhumancity.com/2017/04/17/healing.

Robison, J.E. (2007). *Look me in the eye: My life with Asperger's.* New York: Broadway Books.
Early and still popular autobiographical account of life as ASHFA.

Rosqvist, H. (2012). Normal for an Asperger: Notions of the meanings of diagnosis among adults with Asperger's Syndrome. *Intellectual and Developmental Disabilities* 50 (2), 120–128.

Rossiter, A. (2011). Unsettled social work: The challenge of Levinas's ethics. *British Journal of Social Work* 41 (5), 980–995.

Roy, M. and Balaratnasingam, S. (2010). Missed diagnosis of autism in an Australian Indigenous psychiatric population. *Australasian Psychiatry* 18 (6), 534–537.

Ruzzano, L., Borsboom, D., and Geurts, H. (2015). Repetitive behaviours in autism and obsessive-compulsive disorder: New perspectives from a network analysis. *Journal of Autism and Developmental Disorders* 45 (1), 192–202.

Sacks, O. (2017). *The river of consciousness.* New York: Alfred A. Knopf.

Sacks, O. (1995). *An anthropologist on Mars: Seven paradoxical tales.* New York: Vintage Books.

Sarrett, J. (2016). Biocertification and neurodiversity: The role and implications of self-diagnosis in autistic communities. *Neuroethics* 9 (1). Retrieved from www.researchgate.net/publication/291949788_Biocertification_and_Neurodiversity_the_Role_and_Implications_of_Self-Diagnosis_in_Autistic_Communities.

Sasamoto, A., Miyata, J., Hirao, K., Fujiwara, H., Kawada, R., Fujimoto, S., *et al.* (2011). Social impairment in schizophrenia revealed by autism spectrum quotient correlated with gray matter reduction. *Social Neuroscience* 6 (5–6), 548–558.

Schmidt, G. (2007). Remapping the border: Experiences of being diagnosed with borderline personality disorder [Master's thesis]. Victoria: University of Victoria. Retrieved from https://dspace.library.uvic.ca//handle/1828/1281.

Schultz, K. (2017). An Open Letter to The Mighty on Their Continued Support of the Hate Group Autism Speaks [Web blog]. Medium. Retrieved from https://medium.com/@KirstenSchultz/an-open-letter-to-the-mighty-on-their-continued-support-of-the-hate-group-autism-speaks-20cceb8b485.

Scott, J. (1992). Experience. In J. Butler and J. Scott (eds), *Feminists theorize the political* (pp.22–40). New York: Routledge.

Sequenzia, A. (2016). Autistic conversion therapy. Autistic Women's Network [Blog post]. Retrieved from https://autismwomensnetwork.org/autistic-conversion-therapy.

Sequenzia, A. (2015). Disabled lives and respect [Web blog]. Ollibean. Retrieved from https://ollibean.com/disabled-lives-and-respect.

Sequenzia, A. (2014). Is Autism Speaks a Hate Group? [Web blog]. Autism Women & Nonbinary Network. Retrieved from https://autismwomensnetwork.org/is-autism-speaks-a-hate-group.

Sequenzia, A. (2011). My Parents Presumed Competence [Web blog]. Ollibean. Retrieved from https://ollibean.com/presuming-competence.

Sequenzia, A. and Grace, E. (2015). *Typed word, loud voices.* Fort Worth: Autonomous Press.

Sevlever, M., Roth, M., and Gillis, J. (2013). Sexual abuse and offending in autism spectrum disorders. *Sexuality and Disability* 31 (2), 189–200.

Shtayermman, O. (2009). An exploratory study of the stigma associated with a diagnosis of Asperger's: The mental health impact on young adults diagnosed with a disability with a social nature. *Journal of Human Behaviour in the Social Environment* 19 (3), 298–313.

Silverstein, S., Del Pozzo, J., Roché, M., Boyle, D., and Miskimen, T. (2015). Schizophrenia and violence: Realities and recommendations. *Crime Psychology Review* 1 (1), 21–42.

Simeon, D. and Abugel, J. (2006). *Feeling unreal: Depersonalization and the loss of the self.* Oxford: Oxford University Press.

Sinclair, J. (2005). *Autism Network International: The development of a community and its culture.* Retrieved from www.autismnetworkinternational.org/History_of_ANI.html.

Singer, J. (1998/2016). *Neurodiversity: The birth of an idea.* n.p.

Sivec, H., Montesano, V., Skubby, D., Knepp, K., and Munetz, M. (2017). Cognitive behavioural therapy for psychosis (CBT-p) delivered in a community mental health setting: A case comparison of clients receiving CBT informed strategies by case managers prior to therapy. *Community Mental Health Journal* 53 (2), 134–142.

Sizoo, B. and Kuiper, E. (2017). Cognitive behavioural therapy and mindfulness based stress reduction may be equally effective in reducing anxiety and depression in adults with autism spectrum disorders. *Research in Developmental Disabilities* 64, 47–55.

Sizoo, B., van den Brink, O., Koeter, M., van Eenige, M., van Wijngaarden-Cremmers, P., and van der Gaag, R. (2009a). Using the Autism Spectrum Quotient to discriminate autism spectrum disorder in adult patients with and without comorbid substance abuse disorder. *Journal of Autism and Developmental Disorders* 39, 1291–1297.

Sizoo, B., van den Brink, O., van Eenige, M., and van der Gaag, R. (2009b). Personality characteristics of adults with autism spectrum disorders or attention deficit hyperactivity disorder with and without substance abuse disorders. *Journal of Nervous and Mental Disease* 197, 450–454.

Sizoo, B., van den Brink, O., van Eenige, M., Koeter, M., van Wijngaarden-Cremmers, P., and van der Gaag, R. (2010). Treatment seeking adults with autism or ADHD and comorbid substance abuse disorder: Prevalence, risk factors, and functional disability. *Drug and Alcohol Dependence* 107 (1), 44–50.

Skinner, B.F. (1971). *Beyond freedom and dignity.* Indianapolis: Hacket Publishing.

Smith, A. (2005). *Conquest: Sexual violence and American Indian genocide.* New York: South End Press.

Smith, J. (2010). Seeing other people. *Philosophy and Phenomenological Research* 81 (3), 732–748.

smoothroundstone (undated). Cousins, ACs, autistics and cousins, autistic cousins, etc. [Web blog]. As Small as a World and as Large as Alone. Retrieved July 11, 2017 from http://withasmoothroundstone.tumblr.com/post/88305423555/cousins-acs-autistics-and-cousins-autistic.

Soraya, L. (January 31, 2014). Acceptance, empathy, and presuming competence: Some attitudes make big differences in the life of a child. *Psychology Today* (Asperger's Diary). Retrieved from www.psychologytoday.com/intl/blog/aspergers-diary/201401/acceptance-empathy-and-presuming-competence.

Spacetraveller (January 17, 2014). DSM 5 and the elimination of AS, and severity levels [Online forum comment]. Message posted to www.wrongplanet.net/postxf249890-0-15.html.

Sterzing, P., Shattuck, P., Narandorf, S., Wagner, M., and Cooper, B. (2012). Bullying involvement and autism spectrum disorders: Prevalence and correlates of bullying involvement among adolescents with an autism spectrum disorder. *Archives of Pediatric Adolescent Medicine* 166 (11), 1058–1064.

Stoddart, K., Burke, L., and King, R. (2012). *Asperger Syndrome in adulthood: A comprehensive guide for clinicians.* New York: W.W. Norton & Company.

Stubblefield, A. (2011). Sound and fury: When opposition to facilitated communication functions as hate speech. *Disability Studies Quarterly* 31 (4). Retrieved from http://dsq-sds.org/article/view/1729/1777.

Takahashi, J., Tamaki, K., and Yamawaki, N. (2013). Autism spectrum, attachment styles, and social skills in university students. *Creative Education* 4 (8), 514–520. Retrieved from https://file.scirp.org/pdf/CE_2013080613391794.pdf.

Takenaback (June 5, 2016). What do I think of self-diagnosis? I think it's the height of arrogance [Online forum comment]. *Wrongplanet.* Retrieved from http://wrongplanet.net/forums/viewtopic.php?t=320116.

Talaga, T. (2017). Seven fallen feathers: Racism, death, and hard truths in a northern city. Toronto: House of Anansi.
Chilling journalistic account of the social injustice in Ontario First Nation reserves, how residential school trauma continues, and the mysterious death of seven Aboriginal students in Thunder Bay.

Tammet, D. (2017). *Every word is a bird we teach to sing: Encounters with the mysteries and meanings of language.* New York: Little, Brown and Company.

Tashiro, T. (2017). *Awkward: The science of why we're socially awkward and why it's awesome.* New York: William Morrow and Company.

TheCaffeinatedAutistic (2013). Why I am against Autism Speaks (and you should be, too) [Web blog]. TheCaffeinatedAutistic. Retrieved from https://thecaffeinatedautistic.wordpress.com/2013/03/05/why-i-am-against-autism-speaks-and-you-should-be-too-2.

Travers, J. and Ayres, K. (2015). A critique of presuming competence of learners with autism or other developmental disabilities. *Education and Training in Autism and Developmental Disabilities* 50 (4), 371–387.

Travers, J. and Krezmien, M. (in press). Racial disparities in autism identification in the United States during 2014. *Exceptional Children.*

Travers, J., Tincani, M., and Lang, R. (2014). Facilitated communication denies people with disabilities their voice. *Research and Practice for Persons with Severe Disabilities* 39 (3), 195–202. Retrieved from http://rps.sagepub.com/content/39/3/195.full.pdf+html.

Travers, J., Tincani, M., Thompson, J., and Simpson, R. (2016). Picture exchange communication system and facilitated communication: Contrasting an evidence-based practice method with a discredited method. In B. Cook and M. Tankersley (eds) *Instructional practices with and without empirical validity* (Advances in learning and behavioural disabilities, vol. 29) (pp.85–110). Bingley: Emerald Publishing.

Tremain, S. (2005). *Foucault and the government of disability.* Ann Arbor: University of Michigan Press.

Tsbary, S. (2010). *The conscious parent: Transforming ourselves, empowering our children.* Vancouver: Namaste.
Compassionate book of parenting helps us work to avoid passing trauma and self-defeating behaviours on to our children. Foreword by the Dalai Lama himself.

Tsbary, S. (2016). *The awakened family: How to raise empowered, resilient, and conscious children.* New York: Penguin.

Tsai, L. (2013). Asperger's disorder will be back. *Journal of Autism and Developmental Disorders* 43 (12), 2914–2942.

Turow, R. (2017). *Mindfulness skills for trauma and PTSD: Practices for recovery and resilience.* New York: W.W. Norton & Company. Mindfulness-based book of practical exercises for trauma recovery.

van der Kolk, B. (2018). Foreword. In S. Fischer, *Neurofeedback in the treatment of developmental trauma.* New York: W.W. Norton & Company.

van der Kolk, B. (2014). *The body keeps the score: Brain, mind, and body in the healing of trauma*. New York: Viking Penguin.
   A must-read for anyone interested in better understanding both the physical and psychological effects of trauma, the insidious manner in which it occurs, the far-reaching devastation it can cause, and the latest approaches to recovery.

van der Kolk, B., Herron, N., and Hostetler, A. (1994). The history of trauma in psychiatry. *Psychiatric Clinics of North America* 17, (3), 583–600.

van der Kolk, B., Perry, J., and Herman, J. (1991). Childhood origins of self-destructive behaviour. *American Journal of Psychiatry* 148 (12), 1665–1671.

van der Kolk, B., Spinazzolla, J., Blaustein, M., Hopper, J., Hopper, E., Korn, D., and Simpson, W. (2007). A randomized clinical trial of eye movement desensitization, fluoxetine, and pill placebo in the treatment of posttraumatic stress disorder: Treatment effects and long-term maintenance. *Journal of Clinical Psychiatry* 68 (1), 37–46.

Van Steensel, F., Bogels, S., and Perrin, S. (2011). Anxiety disorders in children and adolescents with autism spectrum disorders. *Child and Family Psychology Review* 14 (3), 302–317.

Vaughan, K. and McConaghy, N. (1999). Megavitamin and dietary treatment in schizophrenia: A randomized, controlled trial. *Australian and New Zealand Journal of Psychiatry* 33 (1), 84–88.

Wakabayashi, A., Baron-Cohen, S., and Ashwin, C. (2012). Do the traits of autism-spectrum overlap with those of schizophrenia or obsessive-compulsive disorder in the general population? *Research in Autism Spectrum Disorders* 6 (2), 717–725.

Walker, P. (2013). *Complex PTSD: From surviving to thriving (A guide and map for recovering from childhood trauma)*. Lafayette: Azure Coyote Publishing.
   Individual with developmental trauma as well as 20 years' counselling experience shares his perspective on recovering from this kind of distress.

Wallace, B. (May 12, 2014). Autism spectrum: Are you on it? *New York News and Politics*. Retrieved from http://nymag.com/news/features/autism-spectrum-2012-11.

Wang, H., Jeffries, J., and Wang, T. (2016). Genetic and developmental perspective of language abnormality in autism and schizophrenia: One disease occurring at different ages in humans? *The Neuroscientist* 22 (2), 119–131.

Watt, M. and Wagner, S. (2013). Parenting a child with autism spectrum disorder: Parental work context. *Community, Work, and Family* 16 (1), 20–38.

Weinstein, Y., Levav, I., Gelkopf, M., Roe, D., Yoffe, R., Pugachova, I., and Levine, S. (in press). Association of maternal exposure to terror attacks during pregnancy and the risk of schizophrenia in the offspring: A population-based study. *Schizophrenia Research: The Official Journal of the Schizophrenia International Research Society*.

Westmorland, M. (2008). Interruptions: Derrida and hospitality. *Kritike* 2 (1), 1–9.

Wharton, S., James, I., and Turkington, D. (2006). Befriending vs CBT for schizophrenia: A convergent and divergent reality check. *Behavioural and Brain Sciences* 34 (1), 25–30.

Willey, L. (2012). *Safety skills for Asperger women: How to save a perfectly good female life*. London: Jessica Kingsley Publishers.
   After describing the experience of being different both first-hand and from a mother's perspective, the author goes on to address how to manage the unique safety and other challenges of female ASHFA.

Willey, L. (1999). *Pretending to be normal: Living with Asperger's*. London: Jessica Kingsley Publishers.

Wing, L. (1981). Asperger's syndrome: A clinical account. *Psychological Medicine* 11 (1), 115–129.

Winkler, I. and Czigler, I. (2012). Evidence from auditory and visual event-related potential (ERP) studies of deviance detection (MMN and vMMN) linking predictive coding theories and perceptual object representations. *International Journal of Psychophysiology* 83 (2), 132–143.

Wiseman, R. (2016) *Queen bees and wannabes: Helping your daughter survive cliques, gossip, boys, and the new realities of girl world* (3rd edition). New York: Harmony.

Wiseman, R. (2013). *Masterminds and wingmen: Helping our boys cope with schoolyard power, locker-room tests, girlfriends, and the new rules of boyhood*. New York: Harmony.

Wittgenstein, L. (1980). *Remarks on the philosophy of psychology*, vol. 2. Chicago: University of Chicago Press.

Wylie, M.S. (April 2, 2014). The great DSM-5 debate: An interview with Allen Francis. *Psychotherapy Networker*. Retrieved from www.psychotherapynetworker.org/blog/details/192/the-great-dsm-5-debate.

Zorn, C. (producer/director) (2014). *Holding in the storm: My life with autism* [DVD]. Kitchener: Waterloo Region Family Network.
   About the autistic life of Andrew Bloomfield.

Subject Index

Author Index